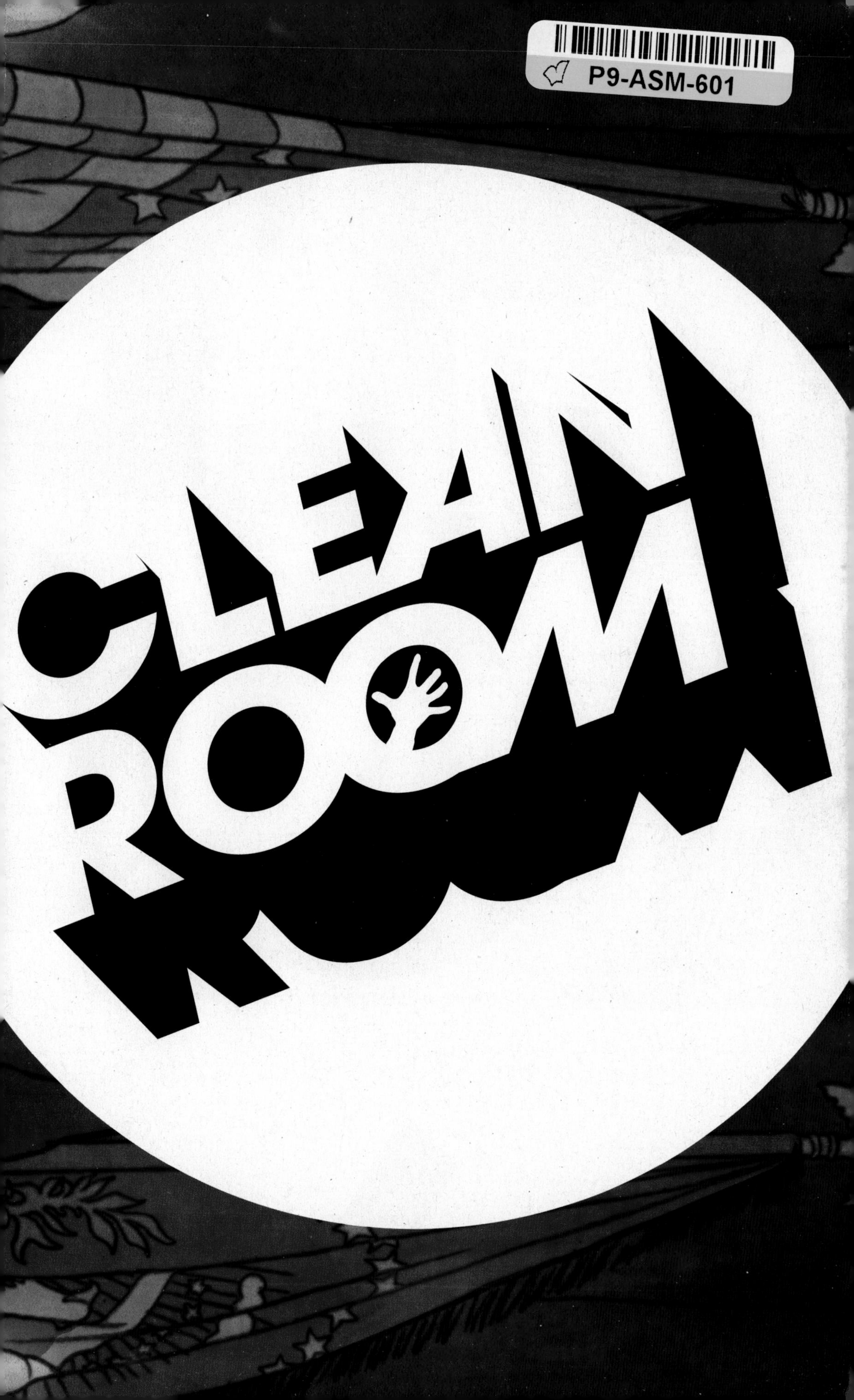
CLEAN
ROOM

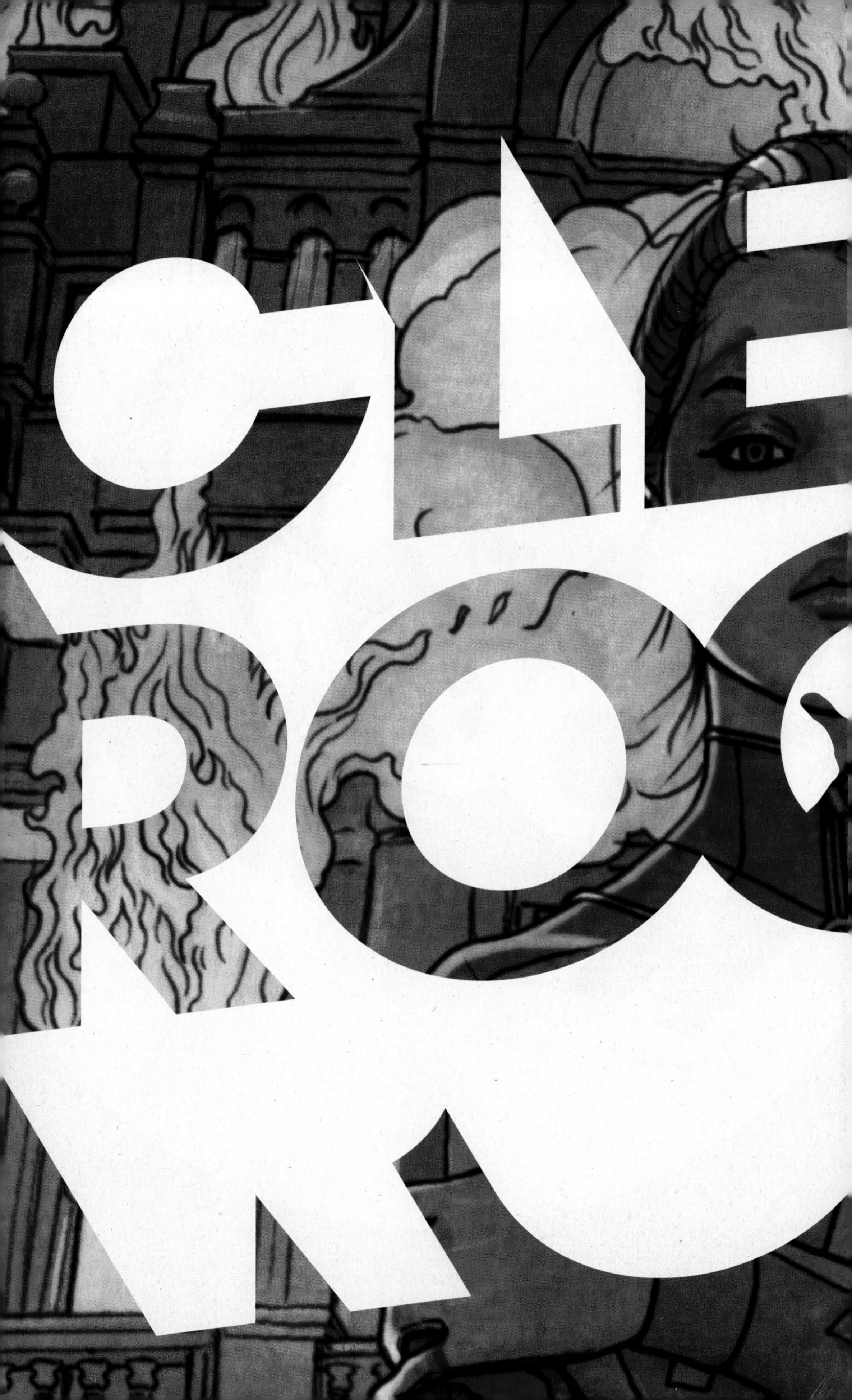

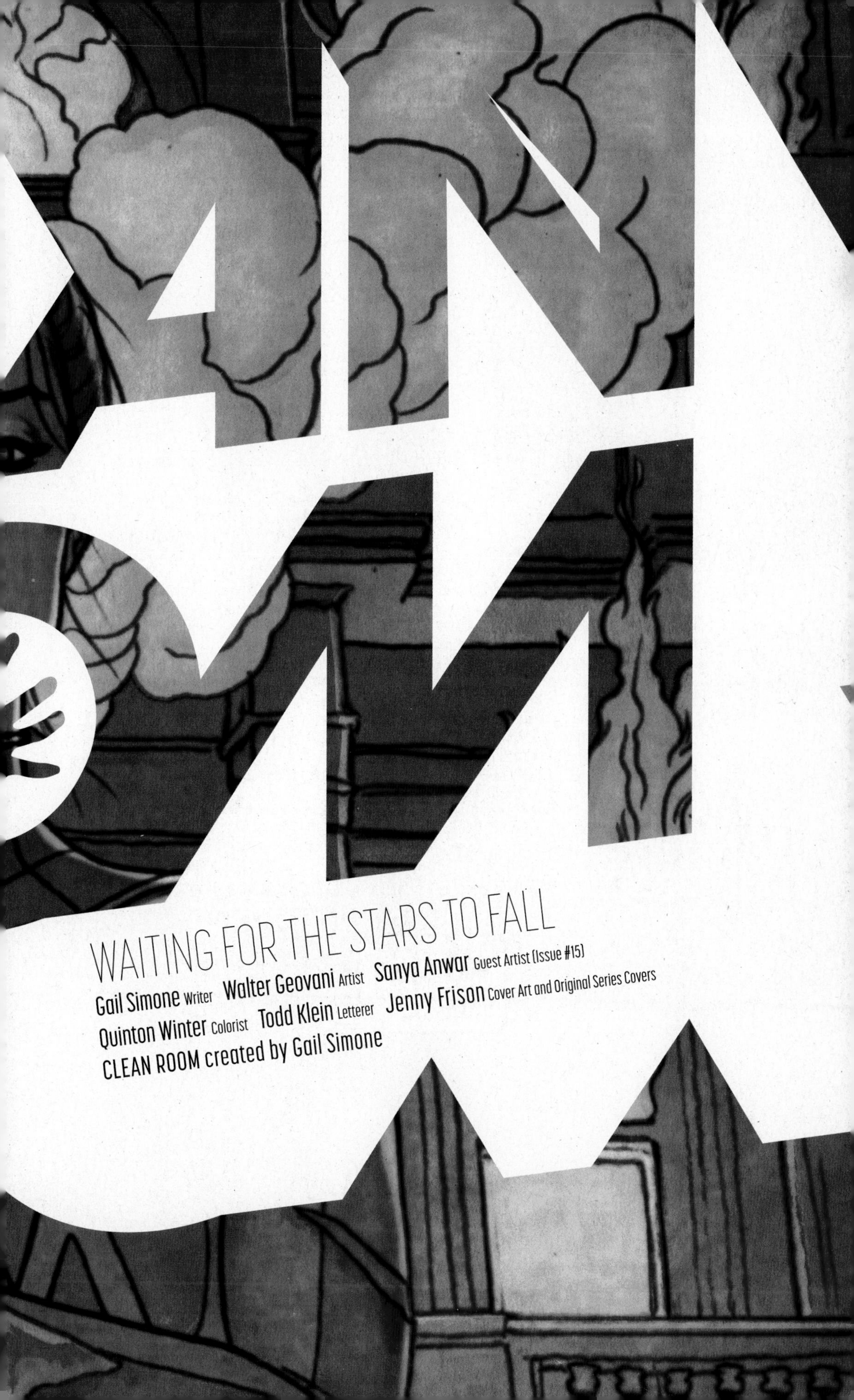

WAITING FOR THE STARS TO FALL

Gail Simone Writer **Walter Geovani** Artist **Sanya Anwar** Guest Artist (Issue #15)
Quinton Winter Colorist **Todd Klein** Letterer **Jenny Frison** Cover Art and Original Series Covers
CLEAN ROOM created by Gail Simone

MOLLY MAHAN Editor – Original Series
MAGGIE HOWELL Assistant Editor – Original Series
JAMIE S. RICH Group Editor – Vertigo Comics
JEB WOODARD Group Editor – Collected Editions
SCOTT NYBAKKEN Editor – Collected Edition
STEVE COOK Design Director – Books
LOUIS PRANDI Publication Design

DIANE NELSON President
DAN DiDIO Publisher
JIM LEE Publisher
GEOFF JOHNS President & Chief Creative Officer
AMIT DESAI Executive VP – Business & Marketing Strategy,
Direct to Consumer & Global Franchise Management
SAM ADES Senior VP – Direct to Consumer
BOBBIE CHASE VP – Talent Development
MARK CHIARELLO Senior VP – Art, Design & Collected Editions
JOHN CUNNINGHAM Senior VP – Sales & Trade Marketing
ANNE DePIES Senior VP – Business Strategy, Finance & Administration
DON FALLETTI VP – Manufacturing Operations
LAWRENCE GANEM VP – Editorial Administration & Talent Relations
ALISON GILL Senior VP – Manufacturing & Operations
HANK KANALZ Senior VP – Editorial Strategy & Administration
JAY KOGAN VP – Legal Affairs
THOMAS LOFTUS VP – Business Affairs
JACK MAHAN VP – Business Affairs
NICK J. NAPOLITANO VP – Manufacturing Administration
EDDIE SCANNELL VP – Consumer Marketing
COURTNEY SIMMONS Senior VP – Publicity & Communications
JIM (SKI) SOKOLOWSKI VP – Comic Book Specialty Sales & Trade Marketing
NANCY SPEARS VP – Mass, Book, Digital Sales & Trade Marketing

CLEAN ROOM: WAITING FOR THE STARS TO FALL

DC Comics
2900 West Alameda Avenue
Burbank, CA 91505
Printed in Canada. First Printing.
ISBN: 978-1-4012-7109-1

Logo design by STEVE COOK

Library of Congress Cataloging-in-Publication
Data is available.

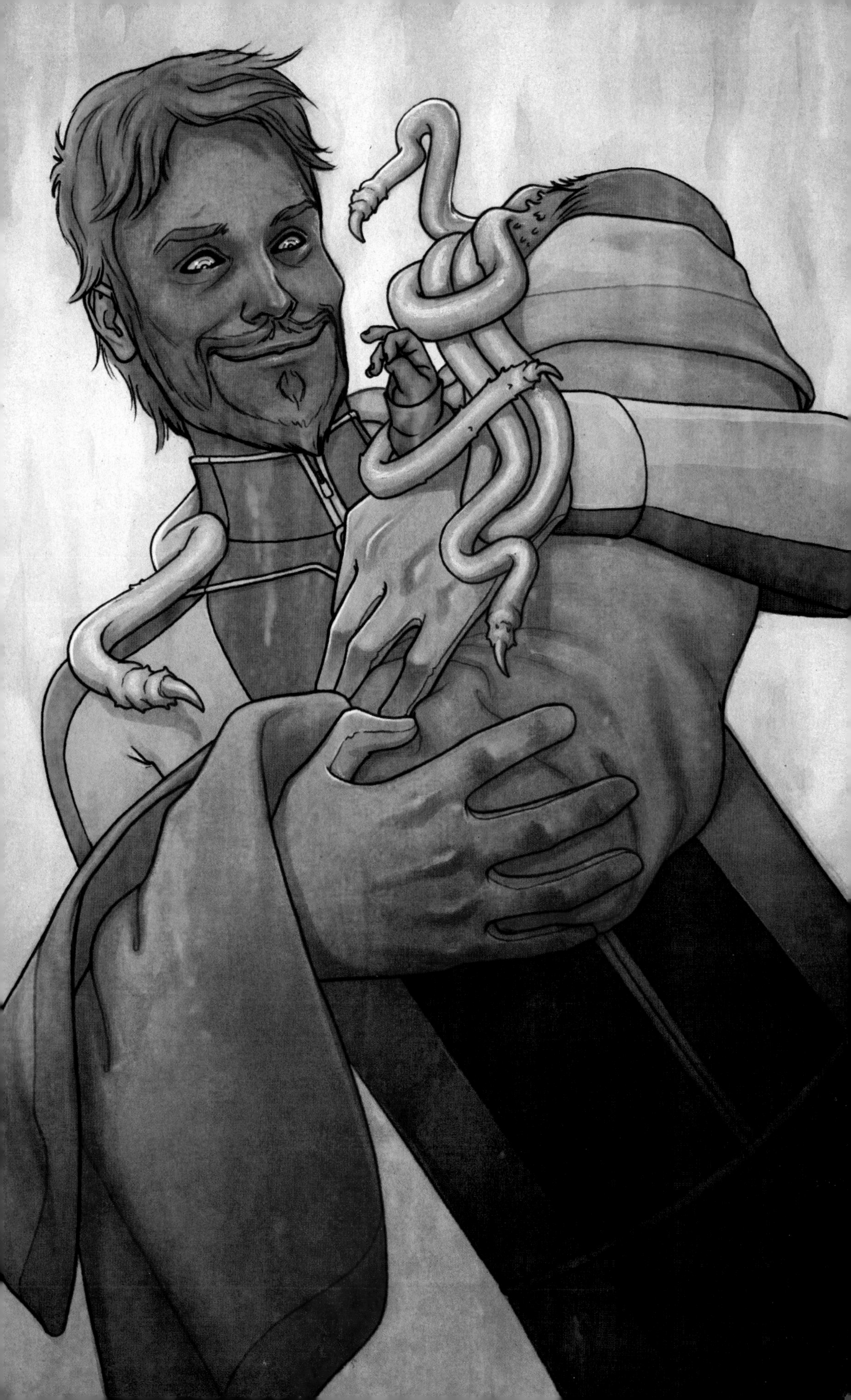

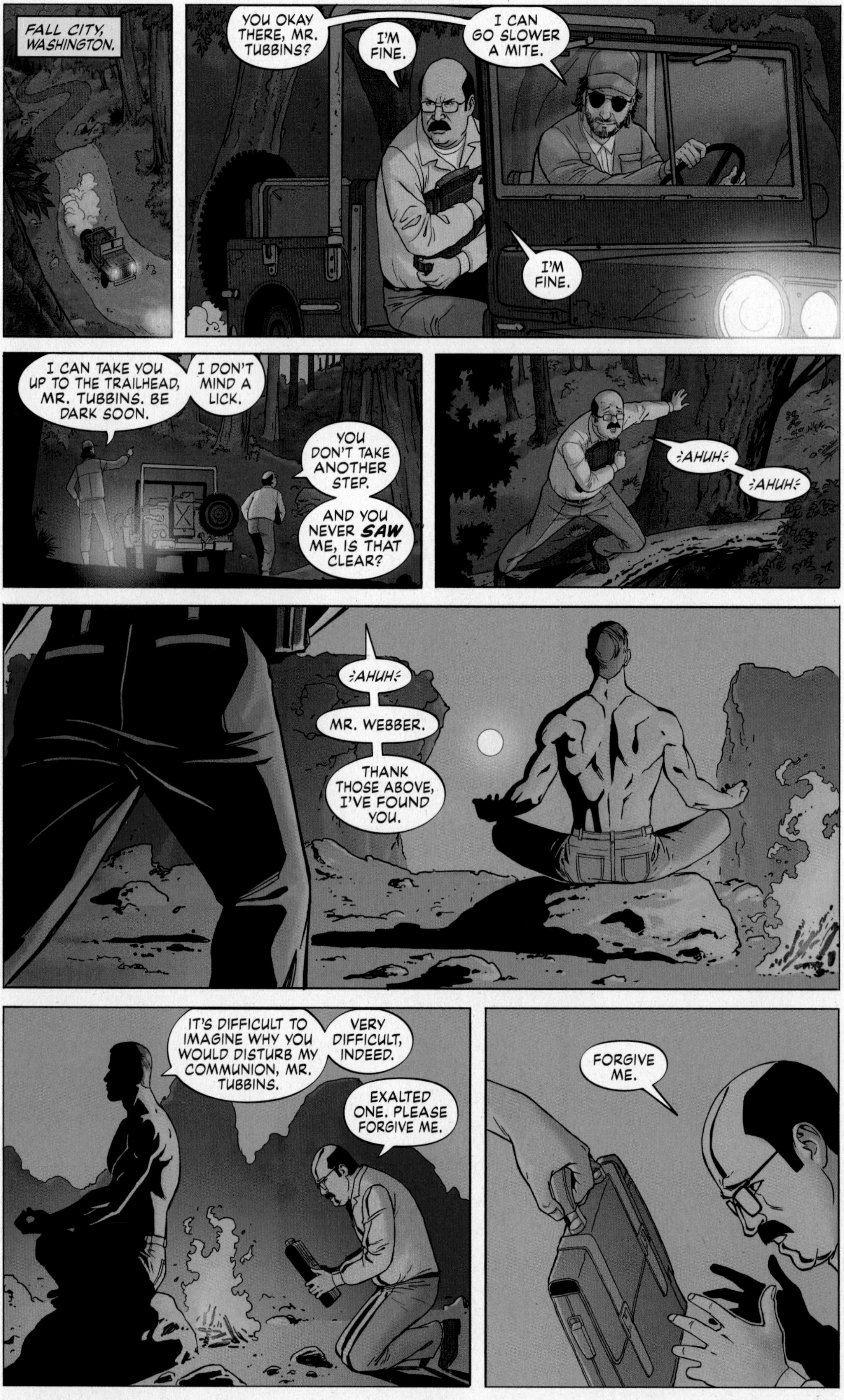
FALL CITY, WASHINGTON.
YOU OKAY THERE, MR. TUBBINS?
I'M FINE.
I CAN GO SLOWER A MITE.
I'M FINE.
I CAN TAKE YOU UP TO THE TRAILHEAD, MR. TUBBINS. BE DARK SOON.
I DON'T MIND A LICK.
YOU DON'T TAKE ANOTHER STEP.
AND YOU NEVER **SAW** ME, IS THAT CLEAR?
AHUH
AHUH
AHUH
MR. WEBBER.
THANK THOSE ABOVE, I'VE FOUND YOU.
IT'S DIFFICULT TO IMAGINE WHY YOU WOULD DISTURB MY COMMUNION, MR. TUBBINS.
VERY DIFFICULT, INDEED.
EXALTED ONE. PLEASE FORGIVE ME.
FORGIVE ME.

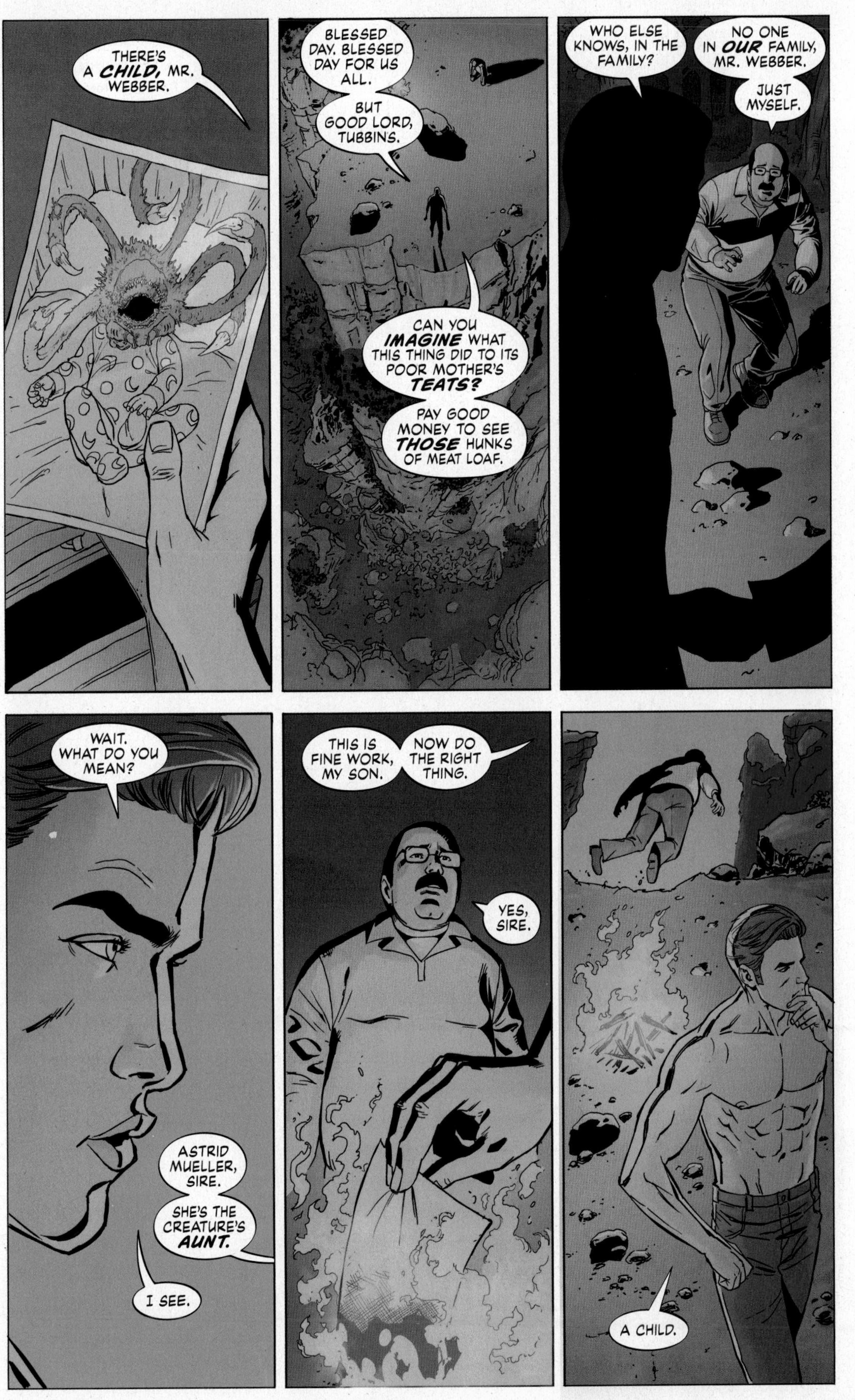
THERE'S A CHILD, MR. WEBBER.
BLESSED DAY. BLESSED DAY FOR US ALL.
BUT GOOD LORD, TUBBINS.
CAN YOU IMAGINE WHAT THIS THING DID TO ITS POOR MOTHER'S TEATS?
PAY GOOD MONEY TO SEE THOSE HUNKS OF MEAT LOAF.
WHO ELSE KNOWS, IN THE FAMILY?
NO ONE IN OUR FAMILY, MR. WEBBER.
JUST MYSELF.
WAIT. WHAT DO YOU MEAN?
ASTRID MUELLER, SIRE.
SHE'S THE CREATURE'S AUNT.
I SEE.
THIS IS FINE WORK, MY SON.
NOW DO THE RIGHT THING.
YES, SIRE.
A CHILD.

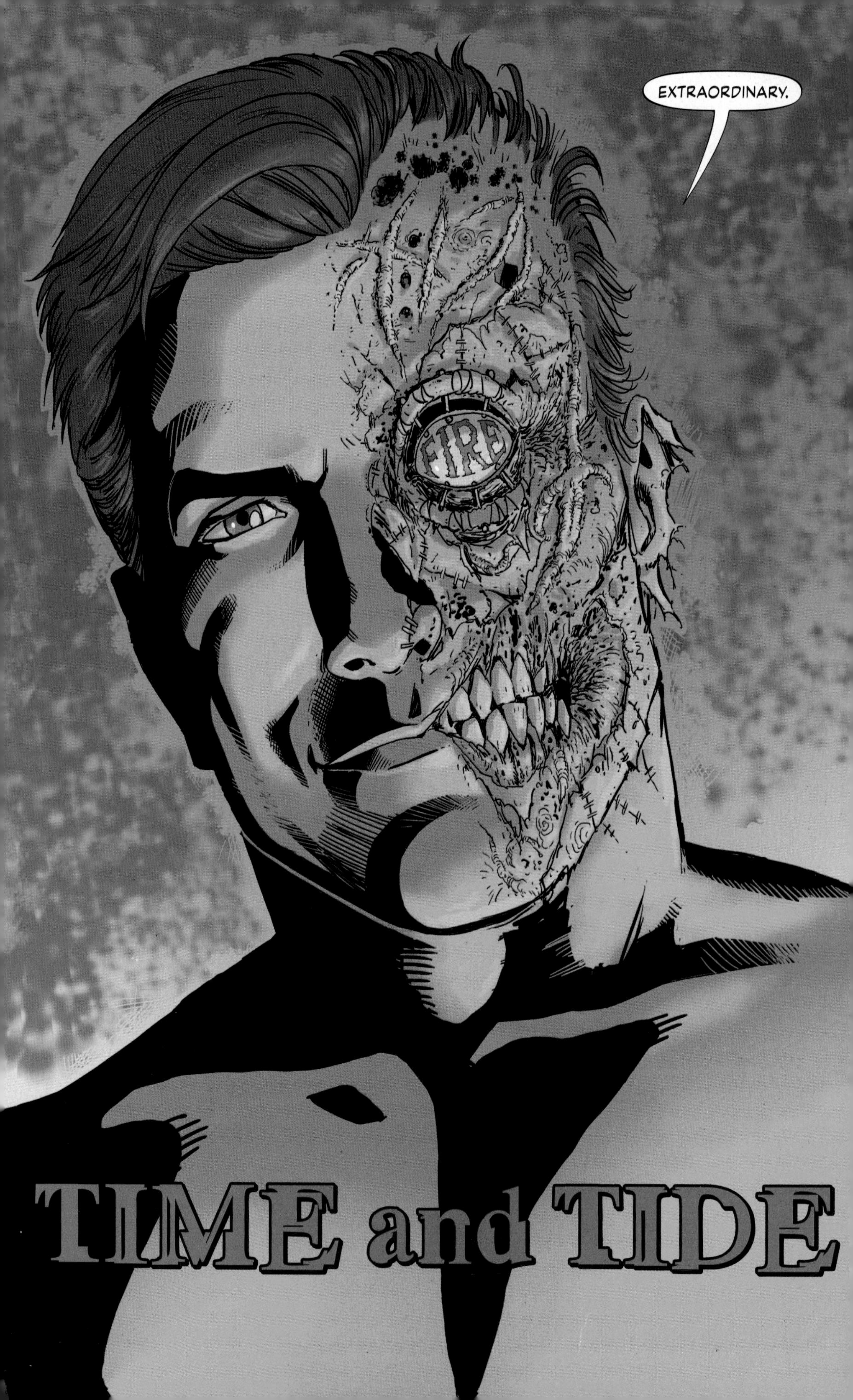
EXTRAORDINARY.
FIRE
TIME and TIDE

THE HONEST WORLD FOUNDATION, CHICAGO.

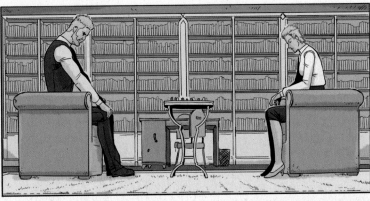

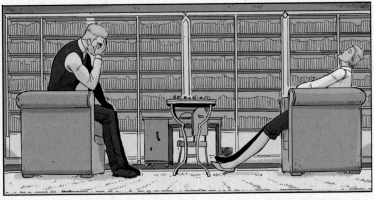

SO, YOU OKAY?

YOUR HAND LOOKS GOOD.

YEAH, FINE.

FINE.

MS. MUELLER'S READY TO SEE YOU BOTH.

NOT IN HER OFFICE.

IN THE *ROOM*.

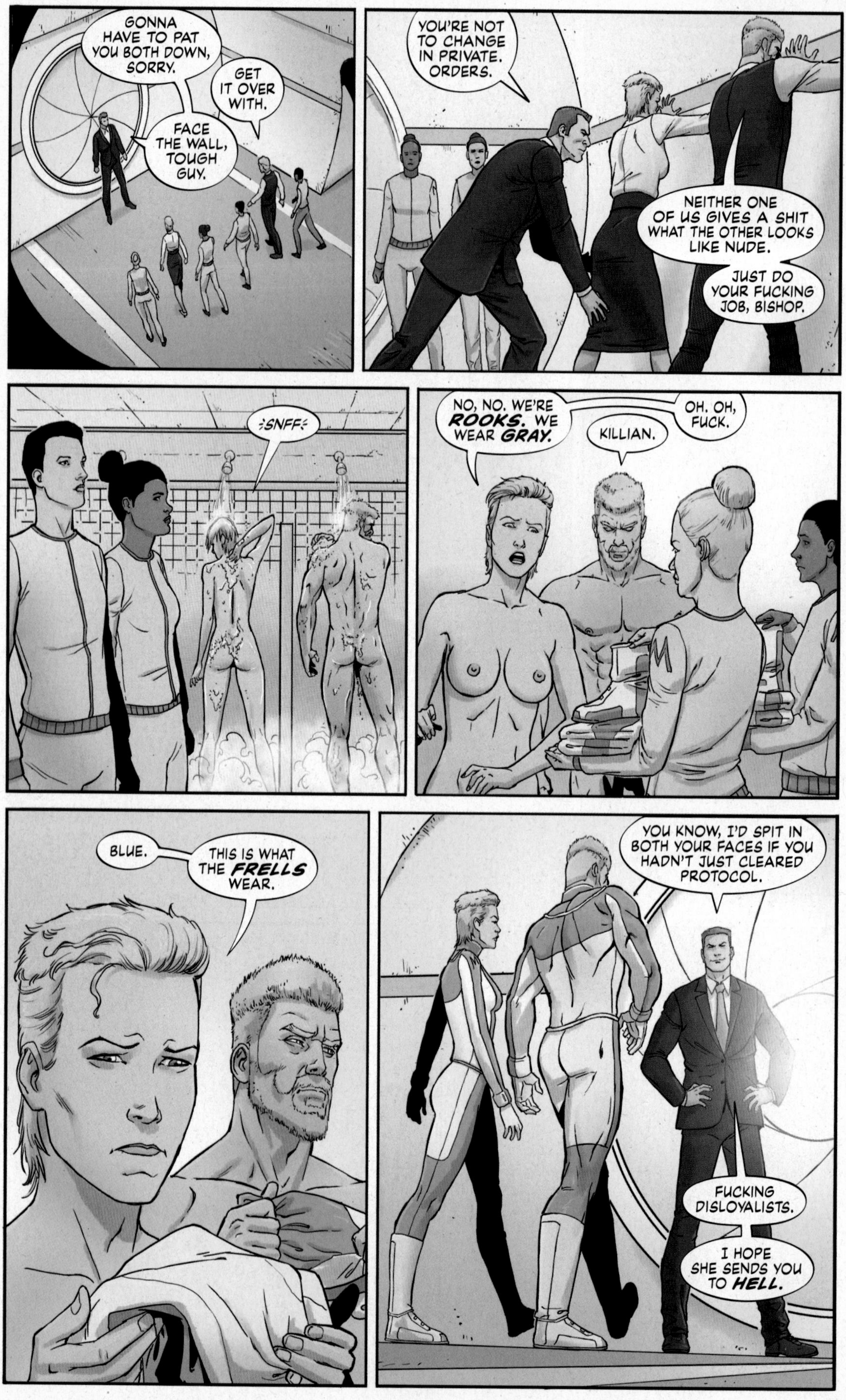
GONNA HAVE TO PAT YOU BOTH DOWN, SORRY.
GET IT OVER WITH.
FACE THE WALL, TOUGH GUY.
YOU'RE NOT TO CHANGE IN PRIVATE. ORDERS.
NEITHER ONE OF US GIVES A SHIT WHAT THE OTHER LOOKS LIKE NUDE.
JUST DO YOUR FUCKING JOB, BISHOP.
SNFF
NO, NO. WE'RE ROOKS. WE WEAR GRAY.
KILLIAN.
OH. OH, FUCK.
BLUE.
THIS IS WHAT THE FRELLS WEAR.
YOU KNOW, I'D SPIT IN BOTH YOUR FACES IF YOU HADN'T JUST CLEARED PROTOCOL.
FUCKING DISLOYALISTS.
I HOPE SHE SENDS YOU TO HELL.

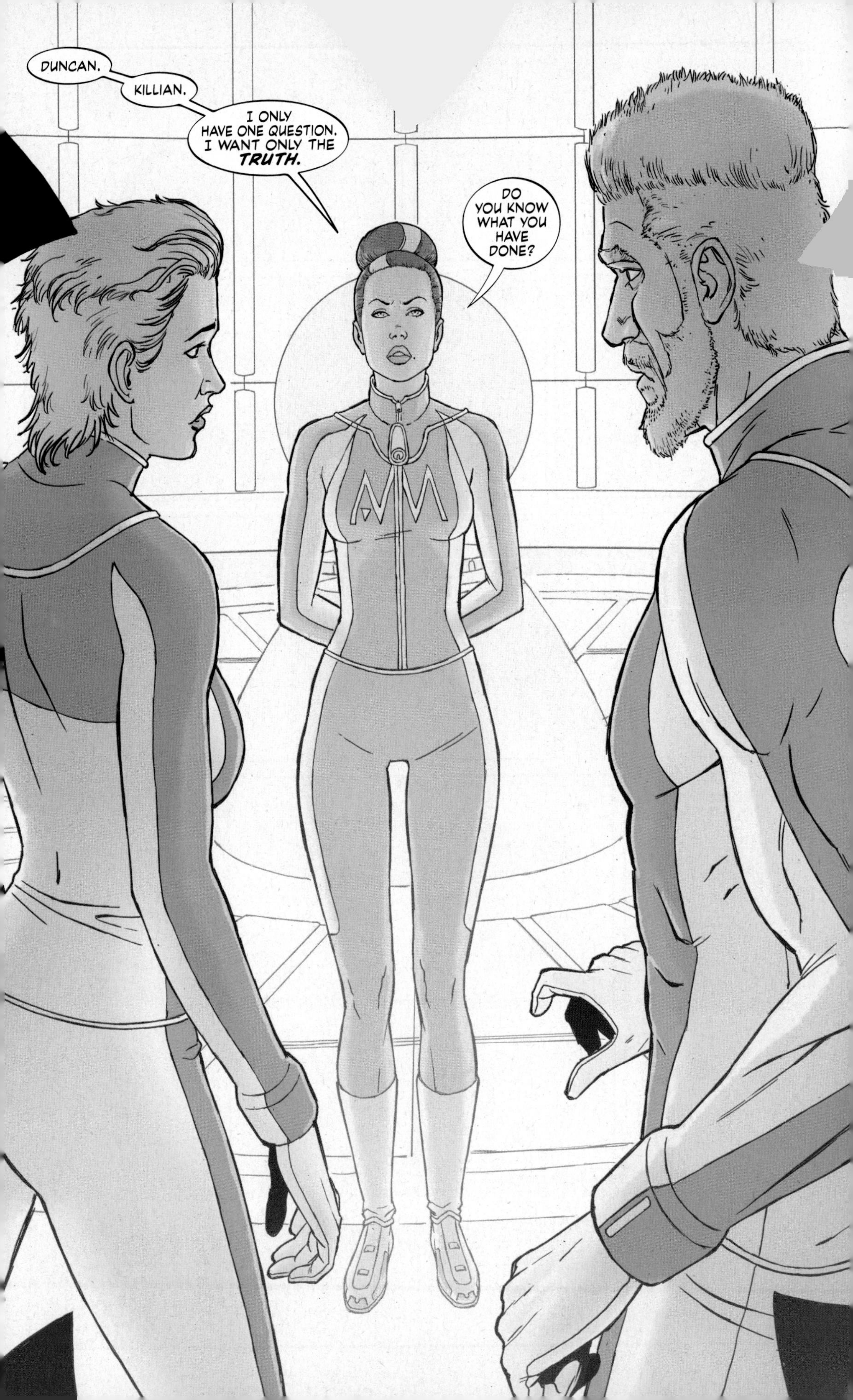
DUNCAN.
KILLIAN.
I ONLY HAVE ONE QUESTION. I WANT ONLY THE **TRUTH.**
DO YOU KNOW WHAT YOU HAVE DONE?

ASTRID, WE--

DON'T *TOUCH* ME!

AND DON'T YOU *DARE* CALL ME THAT NAME.

FRIENDS CALL ME THAT. *ROOKS* CALL ME THAT.

HOW COULD I HAVE TRUSTED THE TWO OF--

≶GKK≶

≶HUKK≶

≶KKKC≶

≶SNNF≶

GET ON YOUR *KNEES*, PLEASE.

FOR MY OWN SAFETY.

I'LL ASK *AGAIN.* FOR THE FINAL TIME.

DO YOU KNOW WHAT *YOU HAVE DONE?*

I TRIED TO SAVE MY BOYFRIEND FROM UNIMAGINABLE TORTURE.

WE LET THE ENTITY GO *FREE.* HE SAVED US.

WE RISKED THE WORLD. DOOMED IT, MAYBE.

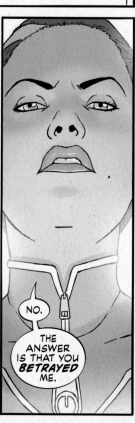
NO.

THE ANSWER IS THAT YOU *BETRAYED* ME.

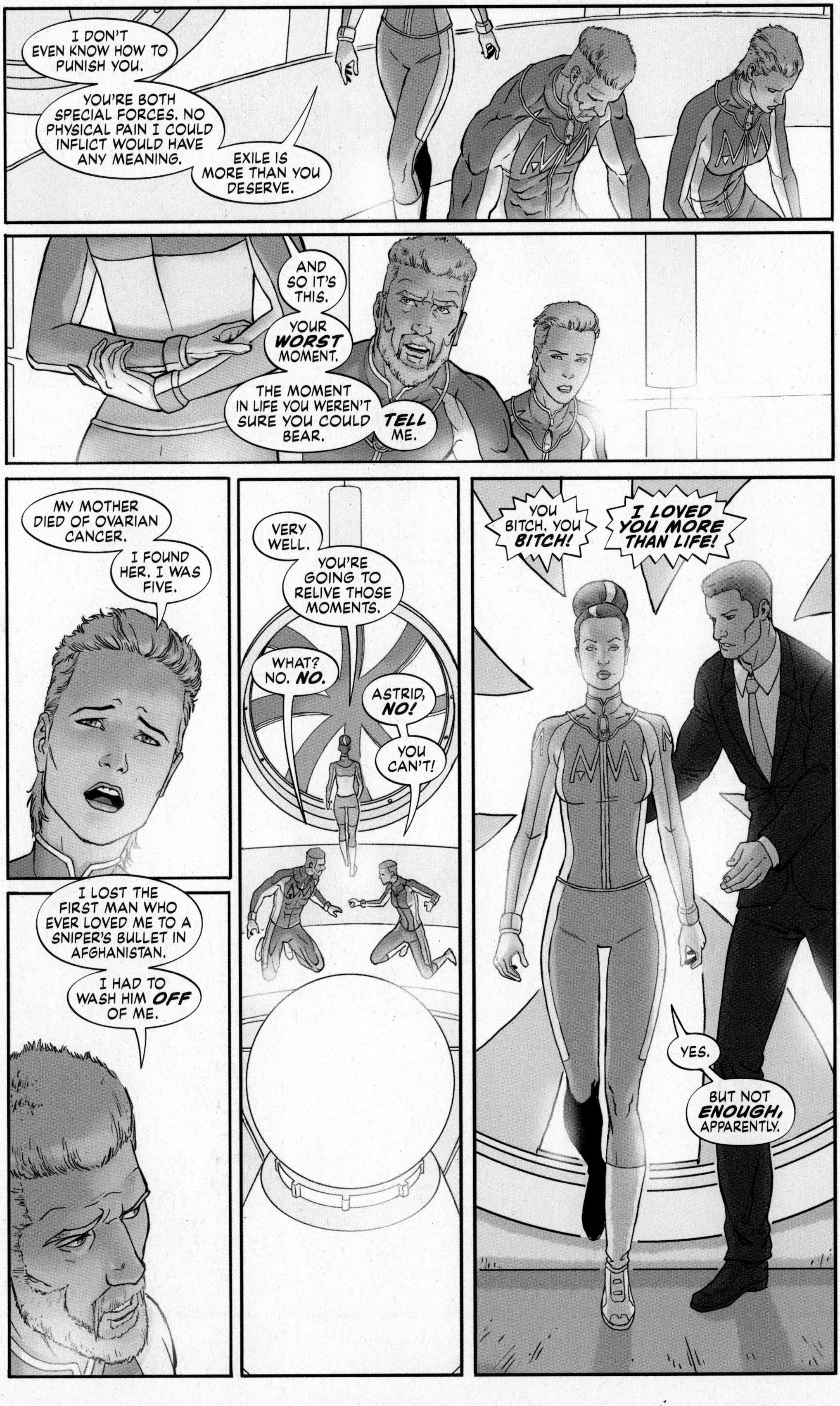
I DON'T EVEN KNOW HOW TO PUNISH YOU.
YOU'RE BOTH SPECIAL FORCES. NO PHYSICAL PAIN I COULD INFLICT WOULD HAVE ANY MEANING.
EXILE IS MORE THAN YOU DESERVE.
AND SO IT'S THIS.
YOUR **WORST** MOMENT.
THE MOMENT IN LIFE YOU WEREN'T SURE YOU COULD BEAR.
TELL ME.
MY MOTHER DIED OF OVARIAN CANCER.
I FOUND HER. I WAS FIVE.
I LOST THE FIRST MAN WHO EVER LOVED ME TO A SNIPER'S BULLET IN AFGHANISTAN.
I HAD TO WASH HIM **OFF** OF ME.
VERY WELL.
YOU'RE GOING TO RELIVE THOSE MOMENTS.
WHAT? NO. **NO.**
ASTRID, **NO!**
YOU CAN'T!
YOU BITCH. YOU **BITCH!**
I LOVED YOU MORE THAN LIFE!
YES.
BUT NOT **ENOUGH,** APPARENTLY.

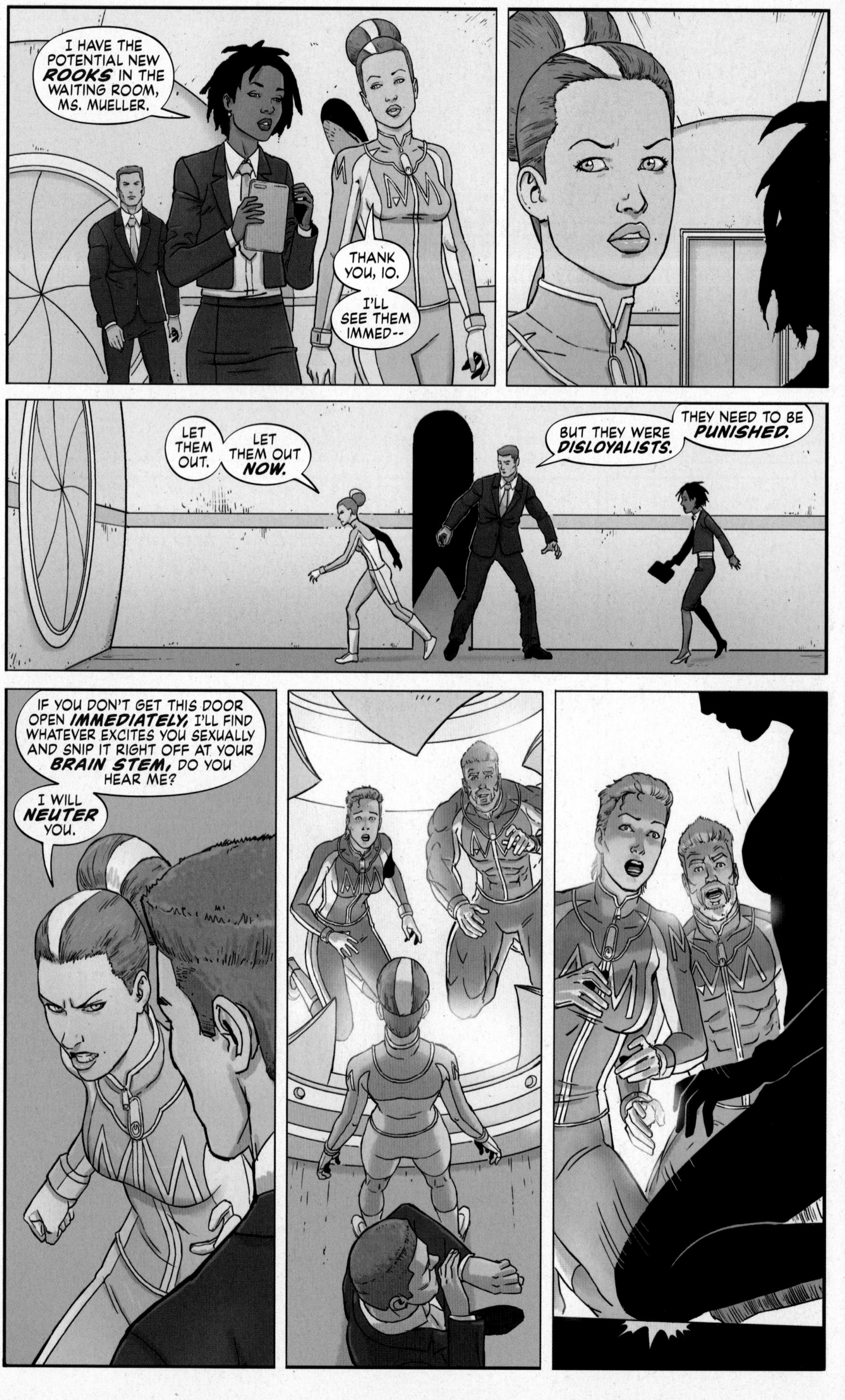
I HAVE THE POTENTIAL NEW ROOKS IN THE WAITING ROOM, MS. MUELLER.
THANK YOU, IO.
I'LL SEE THEM IMMED--
LET THEM OUT.
LET THEM OUT NOW.
BUT THEY WERE DISLOYALISTS.
THEY NEED TO BE PUNISHED.
IF YOU DON'T GET THIS DOOR OPEN IMMEDIATELY, I'LL FIND WHATEVER EXCITES YOU SEXUALLY AND SNIP IT RIGHT OFF AT YOUR BRAIN STEM, DO YOU HEAR ME?
I WILL NEUTER YOU.

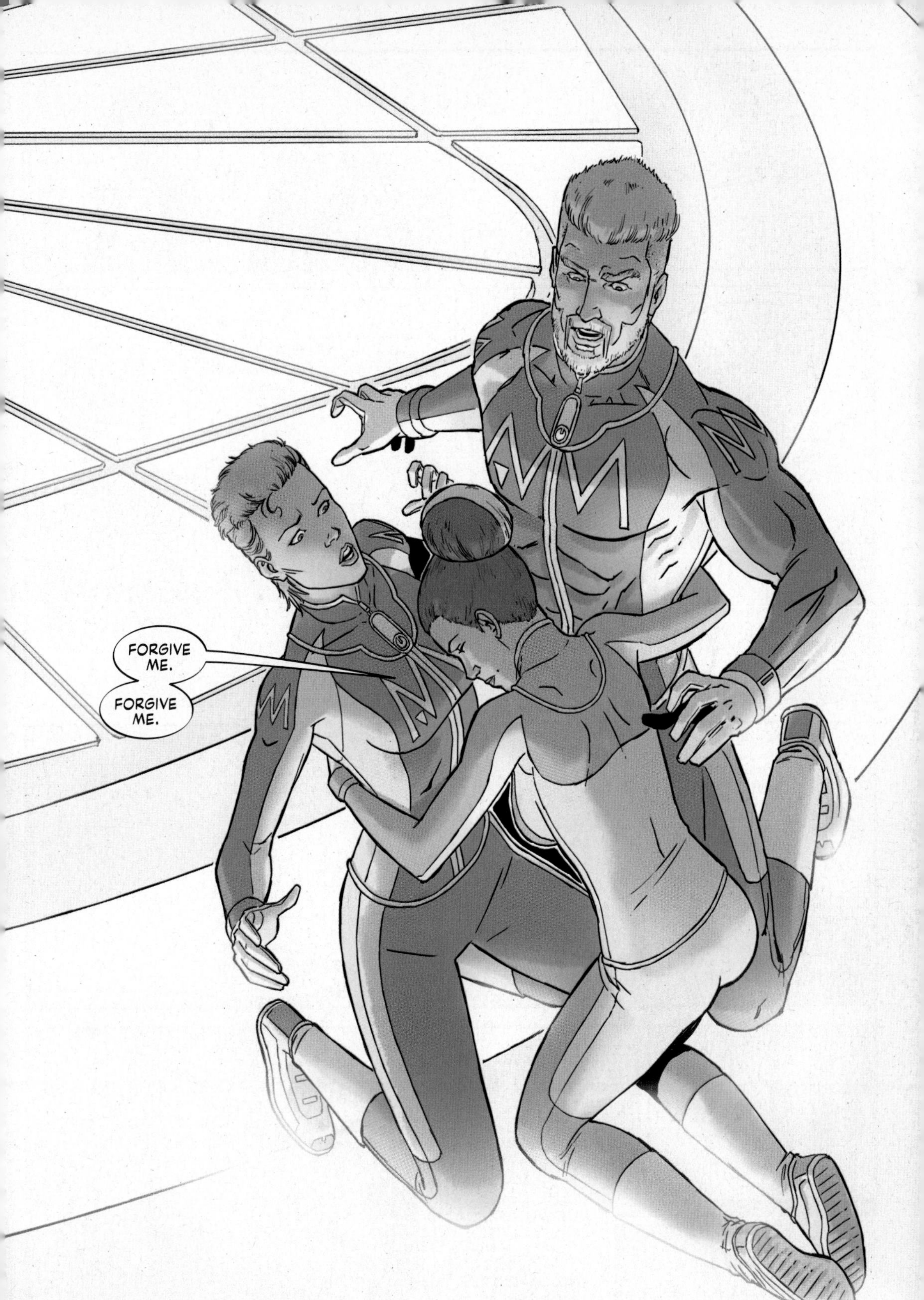
FORGIVE ME.
FORGIVE ME.

YES.

WELL.

YOU ARE ON **PROBATION** FROM YOUR ROOK STATUS.

YOU WILL ATTEND EVALUATION MEETINGS **DAILY** UNTIL I AM SATISFIED THAT THIS WAS AN ISOLATED INCIDENT.

YOUR...

...PAST SERVICE AND LOYALTY IS NOT FORGOTTEN.

IT HAS BEEN...MORE THAN ADEQUATE.

...

MAY I ASK WHY YOU ARE CARRYING ON SO, 10?

IT'S JUST...I'VE NEVER SEEN YOU... **APOLOGIZE** TO ANYONE AND IT WAS SO--

I'M NOT SURE WHAT YOU BELIEVE YOU SAW, ACOLYTE...

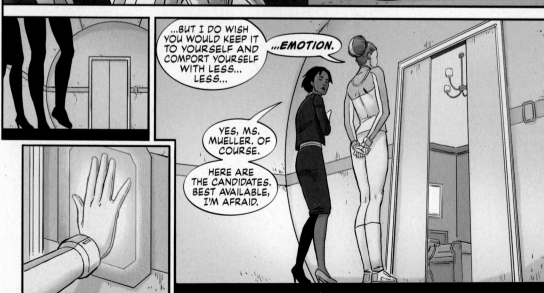

...BUT I DO WISH YOU WOULD KEEP IT TO YOURSELF AND COMPORT YOURSELF WITH LESS... LESS...

...EMOTION.

YES, MS. MUELLER. OF COURSE.

HERE ARE THE CANDIDATES. BEST AVAILABLE, I'M AFRAID.

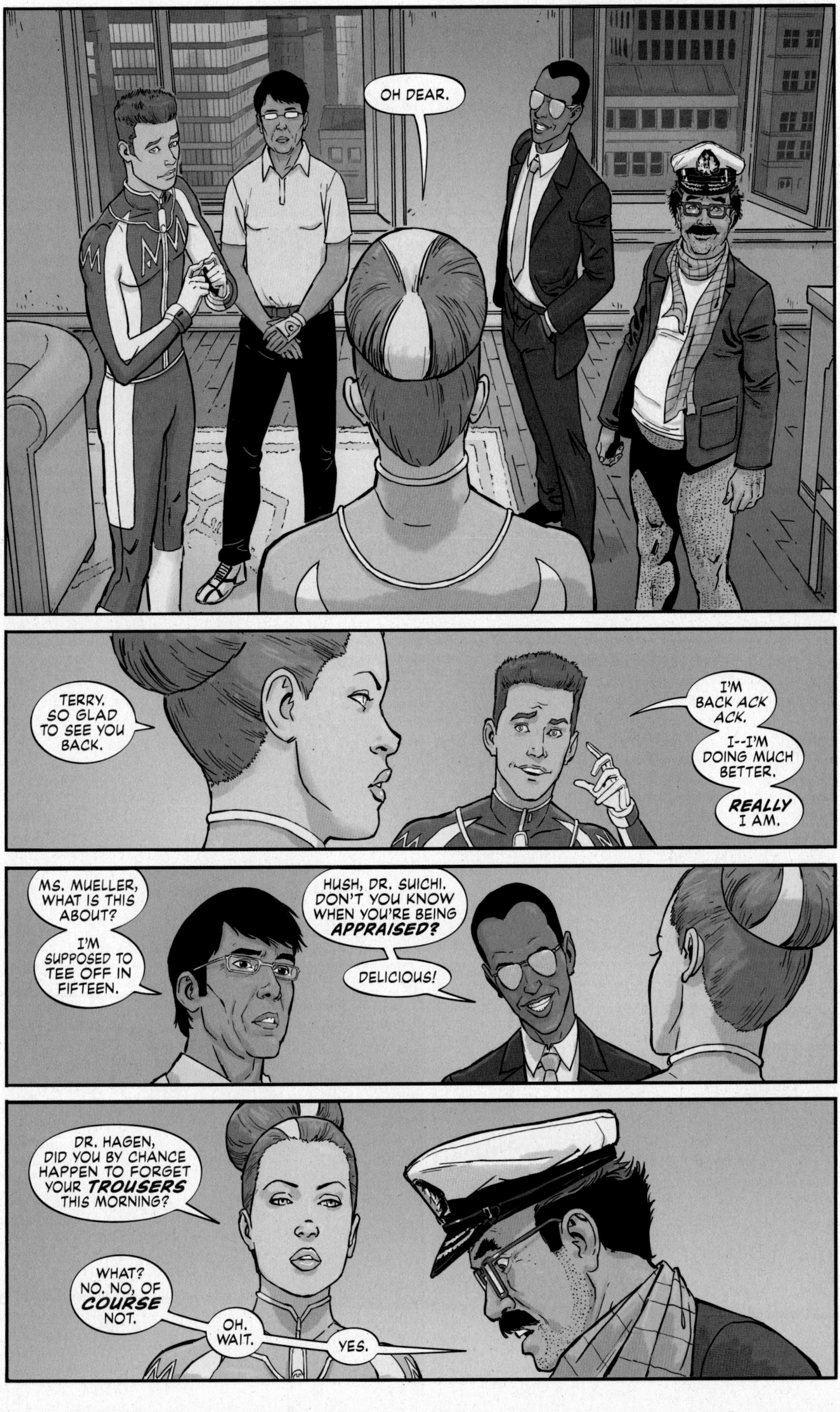
OH DEAR.
TERRY. SO GLAD TO SEE YOU BACK.
I'M BACK ACK ACK.
I--I'M DOING MUCH BETTER.
REALLY I AM.
MS. MUELLER, WHAT IS THIS ABOUT?
I'M SUPPOSED TO TEE OFF IN FIFTEEN.
HUSH, DR. SUICHI. DON'T YOU KNOW WHEN YOU'RE BEING APPRAISED?
DELICIOUS!
DR. HAGEN, DID YOU BY CHANCE HAPPEN TO FORGET YOUR TROUSERS THIS MORNING?
WHAT? NO. NO, OF COURSE NOT.
OH. WAIT.
YES.

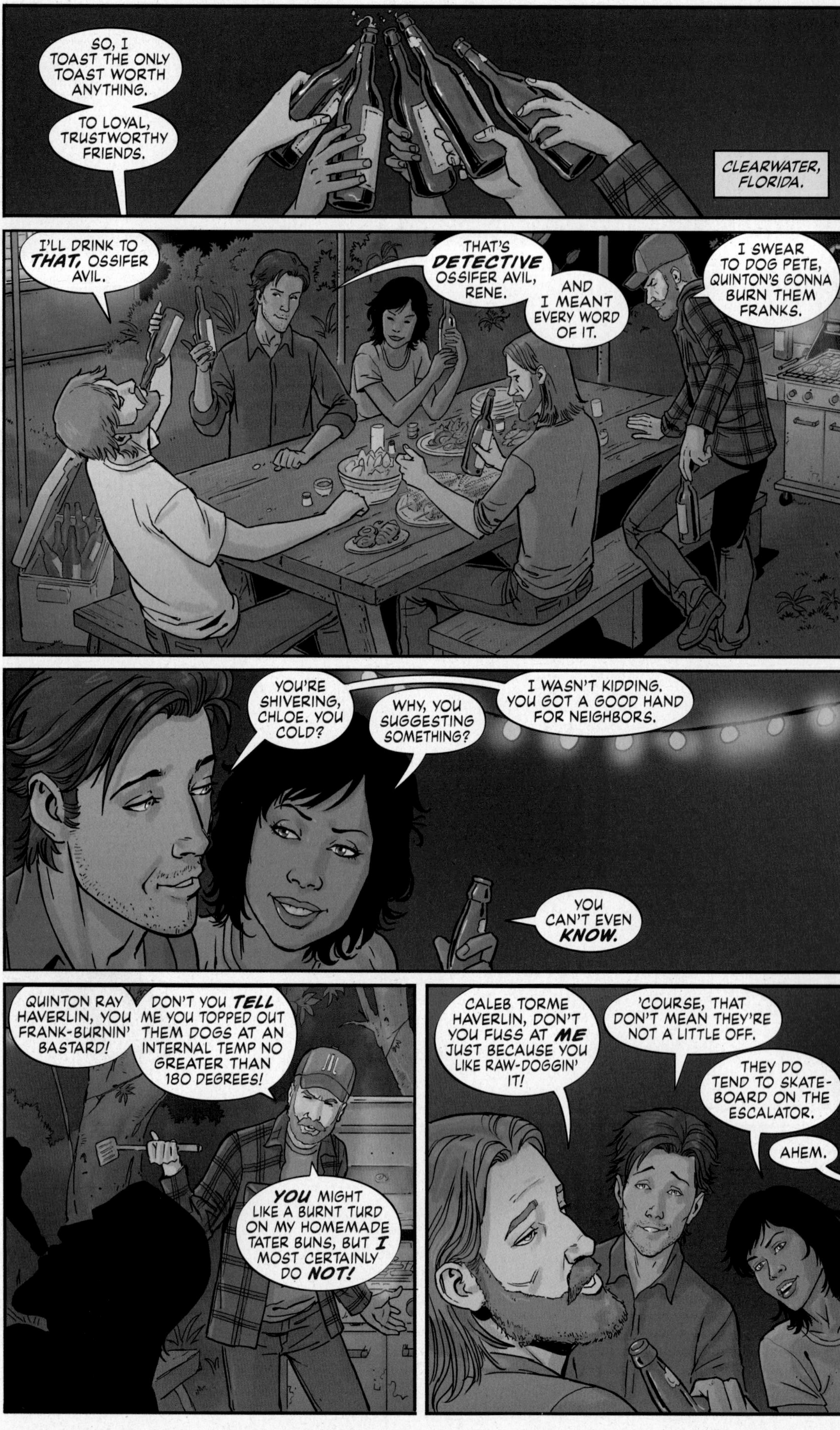
SO, I TOAST THE ONLY TOAST WORTH ANYTHING.
TO LOYAL, TRUSTWORTHY FRIENDS.
CLEARWATER, FLORIDA.
I'LL DRINK TO THAT, OSSIFER AVIL.
THAT'S DETECTIVE OSSIFER AVIL, RENE.
AND I MEANT EVERY WORD OF IT.
I SWEAR TO DOG PETE, QUINTON'S GONNA BURN THEM FRANKS.
YOU'RE SHIVERING, CHLOE. YOU COLD?
WHY, YOU SUGGESTING SOMETHING?
I WASN'T KIDDING. YOU GOT A GOOD HAND FOR NEIGHBORS.
YOU CAN'T EVEN KNOW.
QUINTON RAY HAVERLIN, YOU FRANK-BURNIN' BASTARD!
DON'T YOU TELL ME YOU TOPPED OUT THEM DOGS AT AN INTERNAL TEMP NO GREATER THAN 180 DEGREES!
YOU MIGHT LIKE A BURNT TURD ON MY HOMEMADE TATER BUNS, BUT I MOST CERTAINLY DO NOT!
CALEB TORME HAVERLIN, DON'T YOU FUSS AT ME JUST BECAUSE YOU LIKE RAW-DOGGIN' IT!
'COURSE, THAT DON'T MEAN THEY'RE NOT A LITTLE OFF.
THEY DO TEND TO SKATE-BOARD ON THE ESCALATOR.
AHEM.

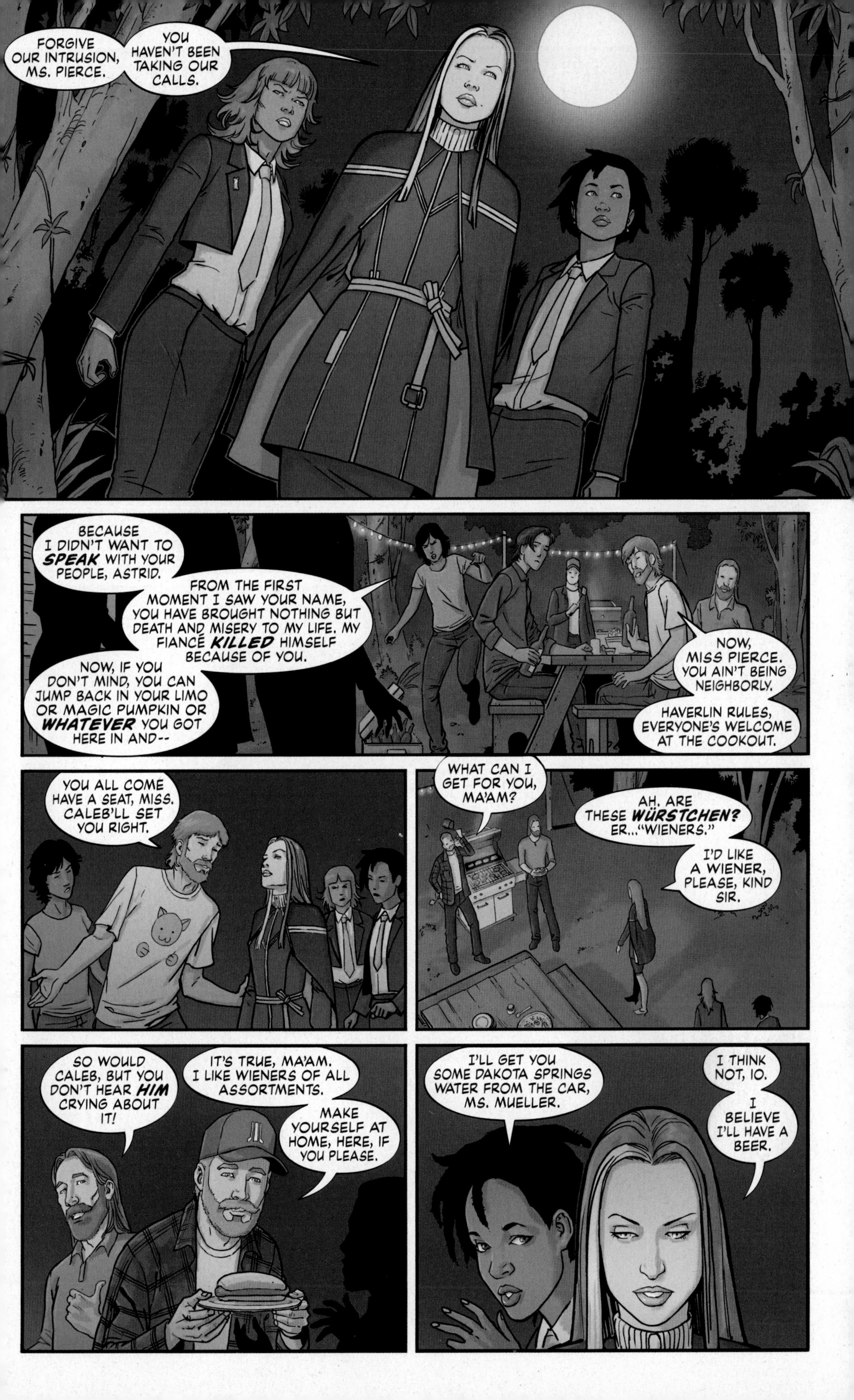
FORGIVE OUR INTRUSION, MS. PIERCE.
YOU HAVEN'T BEEN TAKING OUR CALLS.
BECAUSE I DIDN'T WANT TO SPEAK WITH YOUR PEOPLE, ASTRID.
FROM THE FIRST MOMENT I SAW YOUR NAME, YOU HAVE BROUGHT NOTHING BUT DEATH AND MISERY TO MY LIFE. MY FIANCÉ KILLED HIMSELF BECAUSE OF YOU.
NOW, IF YOU DON'T MIND, YOU CAN JUMP BACK IN YOUR LIMO OR MAGIC PUMPKIN OR WHATEVER YOU GOT HERE IN AND--
NOW, MISS PIERCE. YOU AIN'T BEING NEIGHBORLY.
HAVERLIN RULES, EVERYONE'S WELCOME AT THE COOKOUT.
YOU ALL COME HAVE A SEAT, MISS. CALEB'LL SET YOU RIGHT.
WHAT CAN I GET FOR YOU, MA'AM?
AH. ARE THESE WÜRSTCHEN? ER..."WIENERS."
I'D LIKE A WIENER, PLEASE, KIND SIR.
SO WOULD CALEB, BUT YOU DON'T HEAR HIM CRYING ABOUT IT!
IT'S TRUE, MA'AM. I LIKE WIENERS OF ALL ASSORTMENTS.
MAKE YOURSELF AT HOME, HERE, IF YOU PLEASE.
I'LL GET YOU SOME DAKOTA SPRINGS WATER FROM THE CAR, MS. MUELLER.
I THINK NOT, IO.
I BELIEVE I'LL HAVE A BEER.

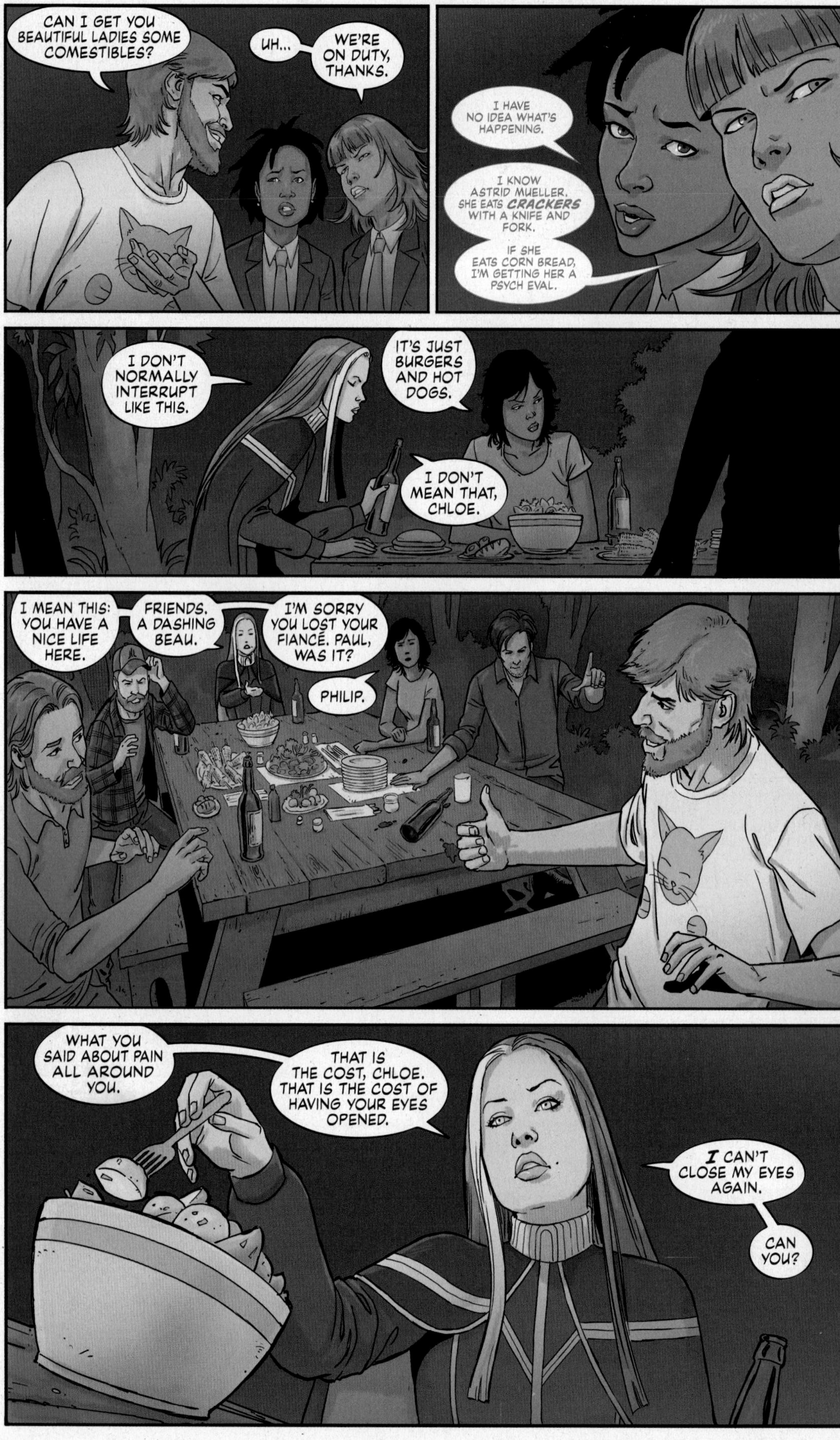
CAN I GET YOU BEAUTIFUL LADIES SOME COMESTIBLES?
UH...
WE'RE ON DUTY, THANKS.
I HAVE NO IDEA WHAT'S HAPPENING.
I KNOW ASTRID MUELLER. SHE EATS CRACKERS WITH A KNIFE AND FORK.
IF SHE EATS CORN BREAD, I'M GETTING HER A PSYCH EVAL.
I DON'T NORMALLY INTERRUPT LIKE THIS.
IT'S JUST BURGERS AND HOT DOGS.
I DON'T MEAN THAT, CHLOE.
I MEAN THIS: YOU HAVE A NICE LIFE HERE.
FRIENDS. A DASHING BEAU.
I'M SORRY YOU LOST YOUR FIANCÉ. PAUL, WAS IT?
PHILIP.
WHAT YOU SAID ABOUT PAIN ALL AROUND YOU.
THAT IS THE COST, CHLOE. THAT IS THE COST OF HAVING YOUR EYES OPENED.
I CAN'T CLOSE MY EYES AGAIN.
CAN YOU?

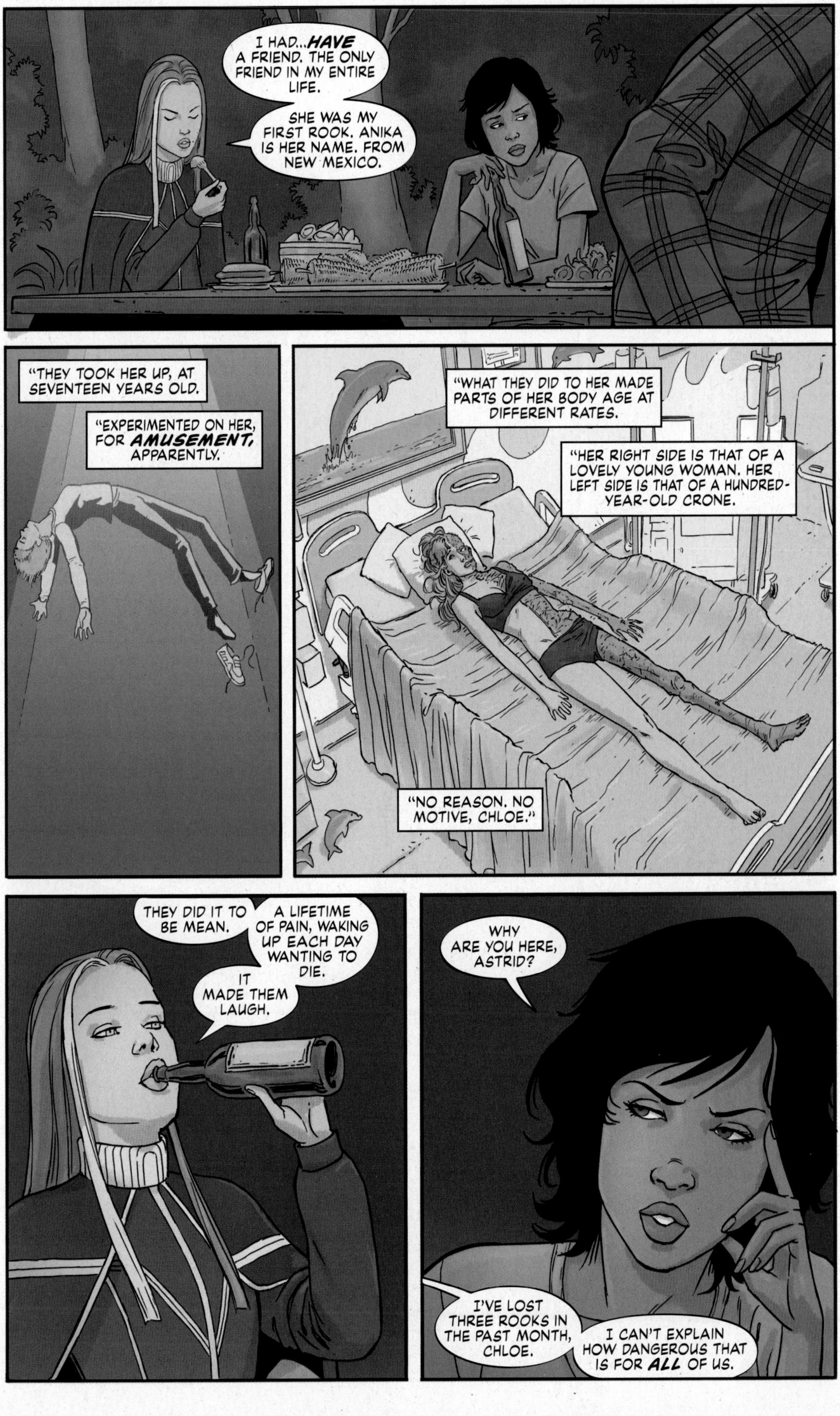
I HAD...HAVE A FRIEND. THE ONLY FRIEND IN MY ENTIRE LIFE.
SHE WAS MY FIRST ROOK. ANIKA IS HER NAME. FROM NEW MEXICO.
"THEY TOOK HER UP, AT SEVENTEEN YEARS OLD.
"EXPERIMENTED ON HER, FOR AMUSEMENT, APPARENTLY.
"WHAT THEY DID TO HER MADE PARTS OF HER BODY AGE AT DIFFERENT RATES.
"HER RIGHT SIDE IS THAT OF A LOVELY YOUNG WOMAN. HER LEFT SIDE IS THAT OF A HUNDRED-YEAR-OLD CRONE.
"NO REASON. NO MOTIVE, CHLOE."
THEY DID IT TO BE MEAN.
A LIFETIME OF PAIN, WAKING UP EACH DAY WANTING TO DIE.
IT MADE THEM LAUGH.
WHY ARE YOU HERE, ASTRID?
I'VE LOST THREE ROOKS IN THE PAST MONTH, CHLOE.
I CAN'T EXPLAIN HOW DANGEROUS THAT IS FOR ALL OF US.

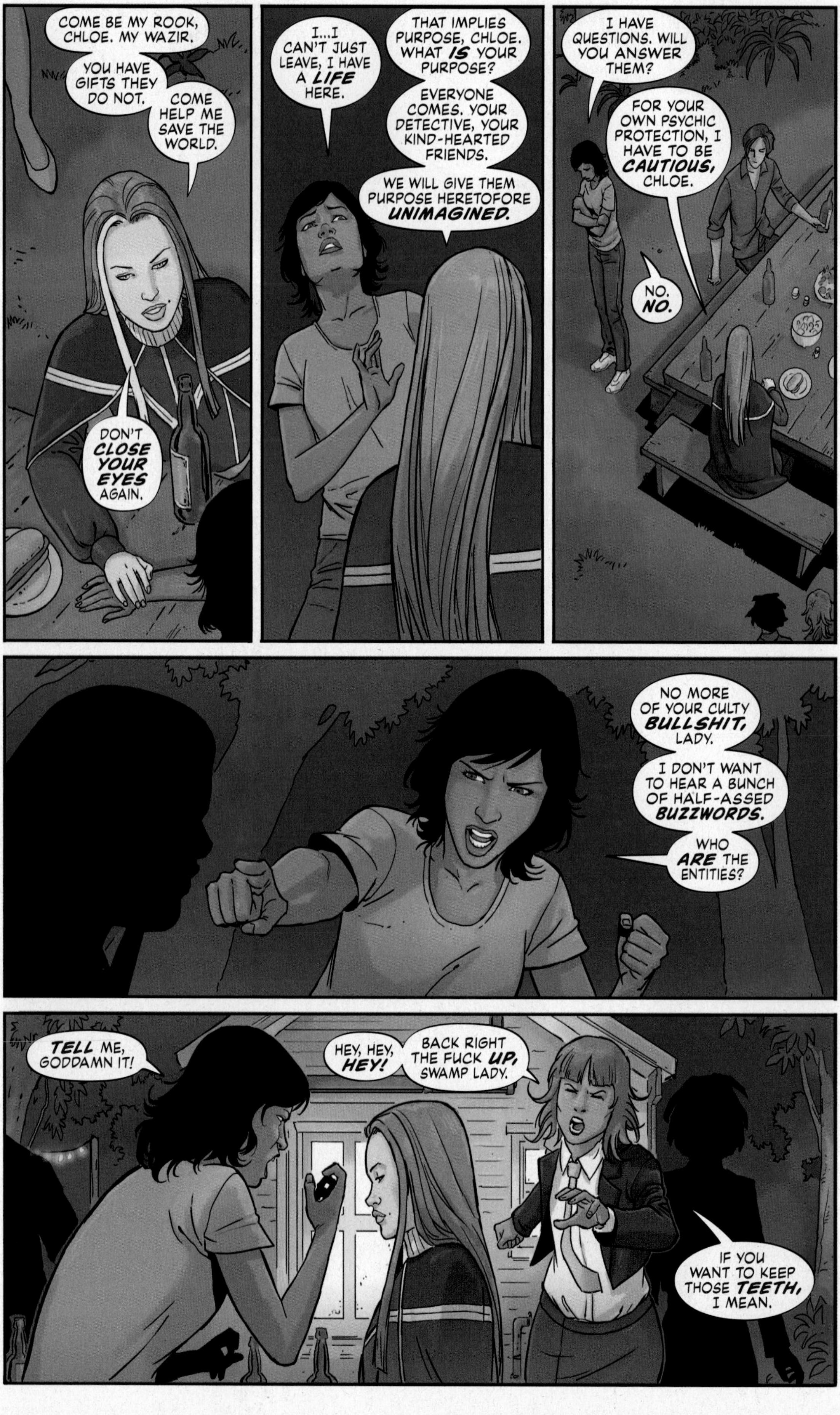
COME BE MY ROOK, CHLOE. MY WAZIR.
YOU HAVE GIFTS THEY DO NOT.
COME HELP ME SAVE THE WORLD.
DON'T CLOSE YOUR EYES AGAIN.
I...I CAN'T JUST LEAVE, I HAVE A LIFE HERE.
THAT IMPLIES PURPOSE, CHLOE. WHAT IS YOUR PURPOSE?
EVERYONE COMES. YOUR DETECTIVE, YOUR KIND-HEARTED FRIENDS.
WE WILL GIVE THEM PURPOSE HERETOFORE UNIMAGINED.
I HAVE QUESTIONS. WILL YOU ANSWER THEM?
FOR YOUR OWN PSYCHIC PROTECTION, I HAVE TO BE CAUTIOUS, CHLOE.
NO. NO.
NO MORE OF YOUR CULTY BULLSHIT, LADY.
I DON'T WANT TO HEAR A BUNCH OF HALF-ASSED BUZZWORDS.
WHO ARE THE ENTITIES?
TELL ME, GODDAMN IT!
HEY, HEY, HEY!
BACK RIGHT THE FUCK UP, SWAMP LADY.
IF YOU WANT TO KEEP THOSE TEETH, I MEAN.

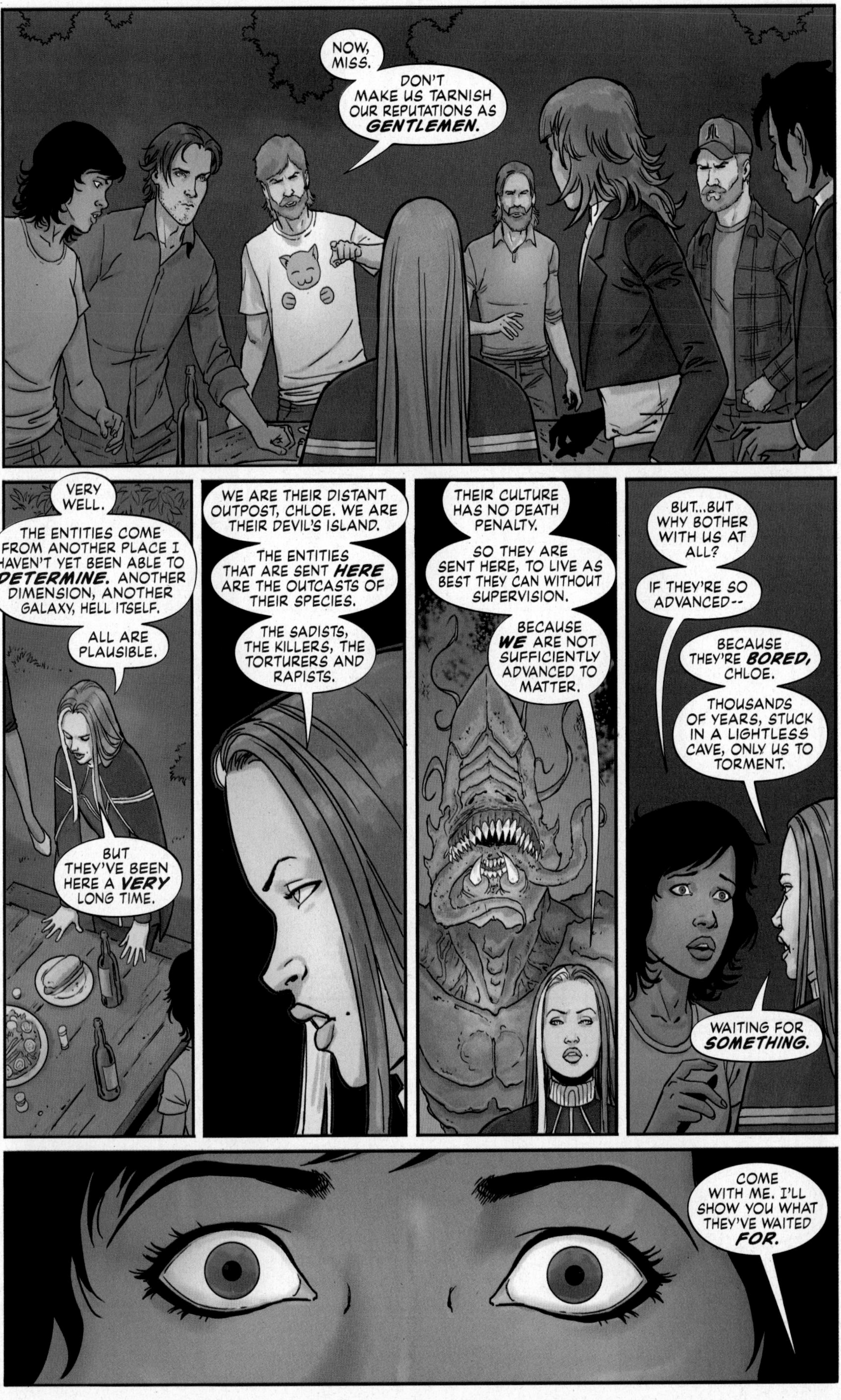
NOW, MISS.
DON'T MAKE US TARNISH OUR REPUTATIONS AS GENTLEMEN.
VERY WELL.
THE ENTITIES COME FROM ANOTHER PLACE I HAVEN'T YET BEEN ABLE TO DETERMINE. ANOTHER DIMENSION, ANOTHER GALAXY, HELL ITSELF.
ALL ARE PLAUSIBLE.
BUT THEY'VE BEEN HERE A VERY LONG TIME.
WE ARE THEIR DISTANT OUTPOST, CHLOE. WE ARE THEIR DEVIL'S ISLAND.
THE ENTITIES THAT ARE SENT HERE ARE THE OUTCASTS OF THEIR SPECIES.
THE SADISTS, THE KILLERS, THE TORTURERS AND RAPISTS.
THEIR CULTURE HAS NO DEATH PENALTY.
SO THEY ARE SENT HERE, TO LIVE AS BEST THEY CAN WITHOUT SUPERVISION.
BECAUSE WE ARE NOT SUFFICIENTLY ADVANCED TO MATTER.
BUT...BUT WHY BOTHER WITH US AT ALL?
IF THEY'RE SO ADVANCED--
BECAUSE THEY'RE BORED, CHLOE.
THOUSANDS OF YEARS, STUCK IN A LIGHTLESS CAVE, ONLY US TO TORMENT.
WAITING FOR SOMETHING.
COME WITH ME. I'LL SHOW YOU WHAT THEY'VE WAITED FOR.

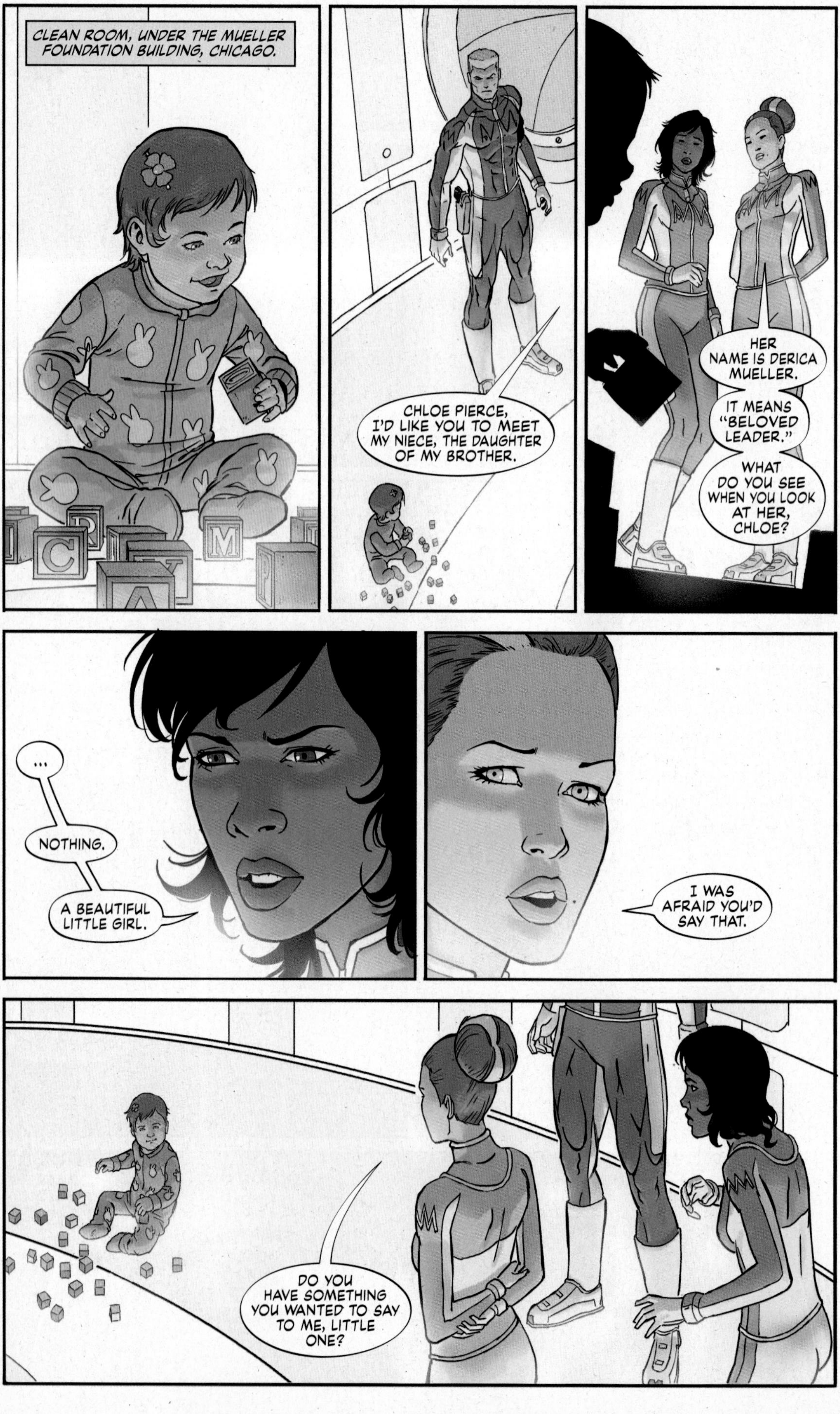
CLEAN ROOM, UNDER THE MUELLER FOUNDATION BUILDING, CHICAGO.
CHLOE PIERCE, I'D LIKE YOU TO MEET MY NIECE, THE DAUGHTER OF MY BROTHER.
HER NAME IS DERICA MUELLER.
IT MEANS "BELOVED LEADER."
WHAT DO YOU SEE WHEN YOU LOOK AT HER, CHLOE?
...
NOTHING.
A BEAUTIFUL LITTLE GIRL.
I WAS AFRAID YOU'D SAY THAT.
DO YOU HAVE SOMETHING YOU WANTED TO SAY TO ME, LITTLE ONE?

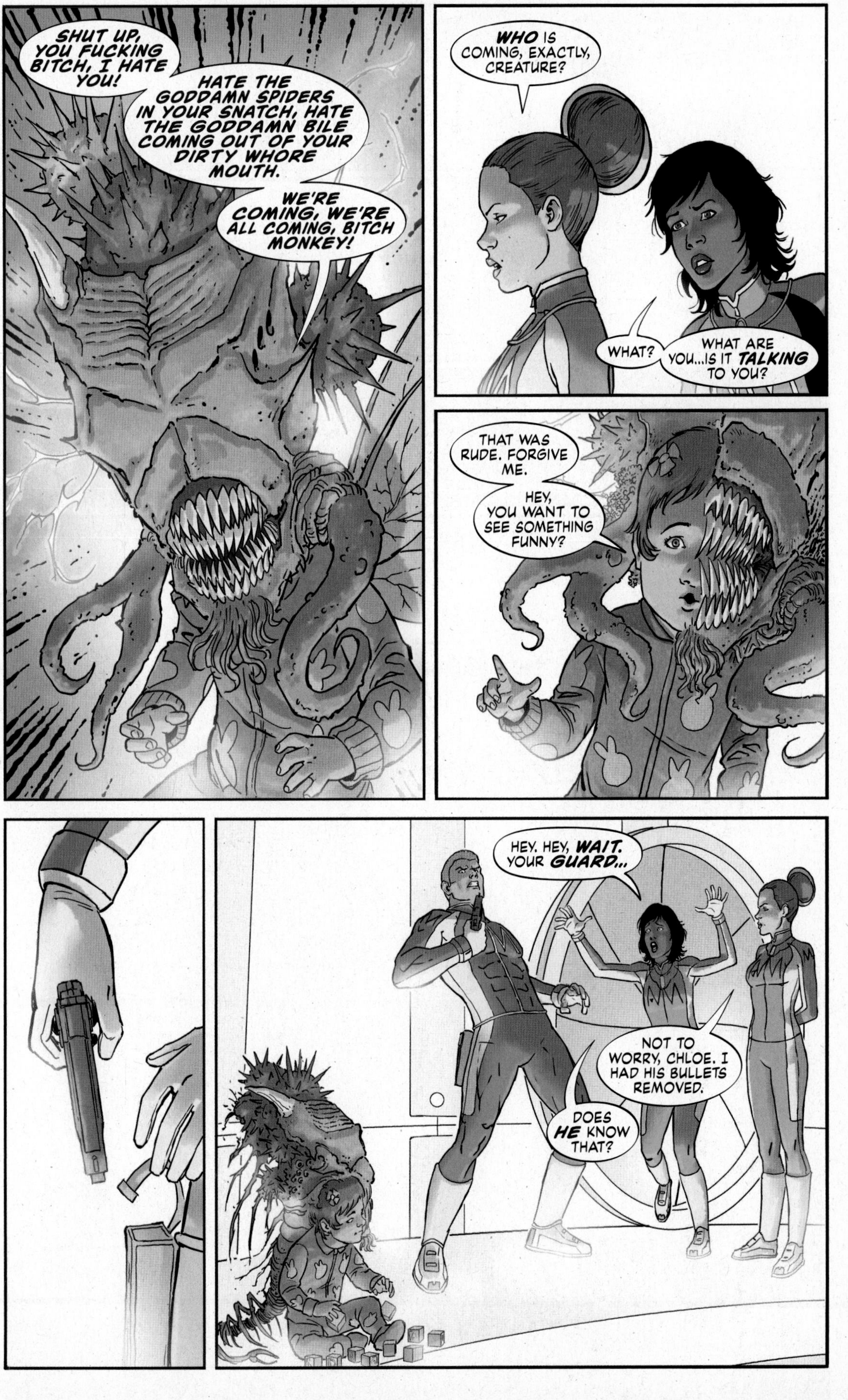
SHUT UP, YOU FUCKING BITCH, I HATE YOU!
HATE THE GODDAMN SPIDERS IN YOUR SNATCH, HATE THE GODDAMN BILE COMING OUT OF YOUR DIRTY WHORE MOUTH.
WE'RE COMING, WE'RE ALL COMING, BITCH MONKEY!
WHO IS COMING, EXACTLY, CREATURE?
WHAT?
WHAT ARE YOU...IS IT TALKING TO YOU?
THAT WAS RUDE. FORGIVE ME.
HEY, YOU WANT TO SEE SOMETHING FUNNY?
HEY. HEY, WAIT. YOUR GUARD...
NOT TO WORRY, CHLOE. I HAD HIS BULLETS REMOVED.
DOES HE KNOW THAT?

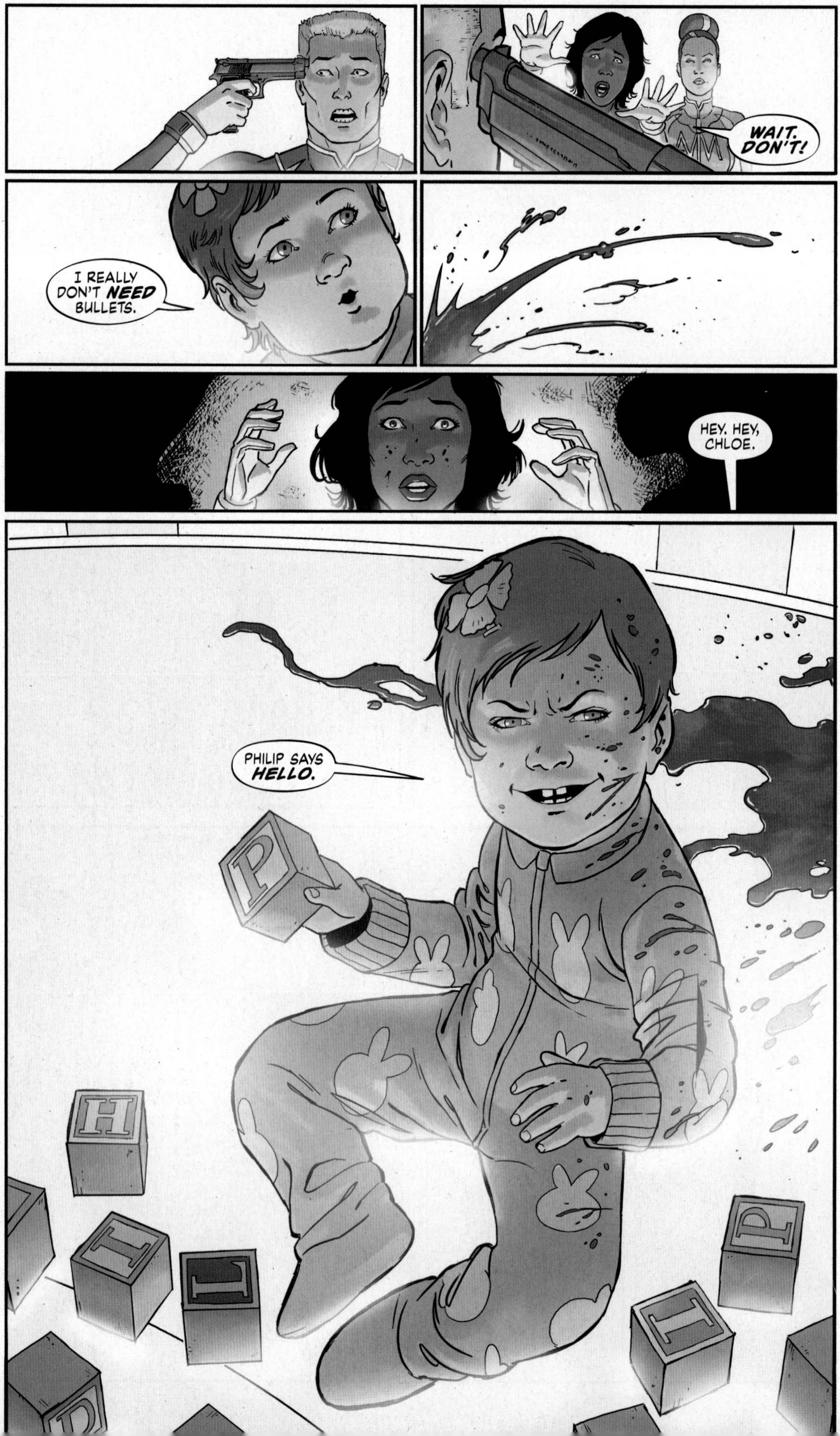
WAIT. DON'T!
I REALLY DON'T NEED BULLETS.
HEY. HEY, CHLOE.
PHILIP SAYS HELLO.

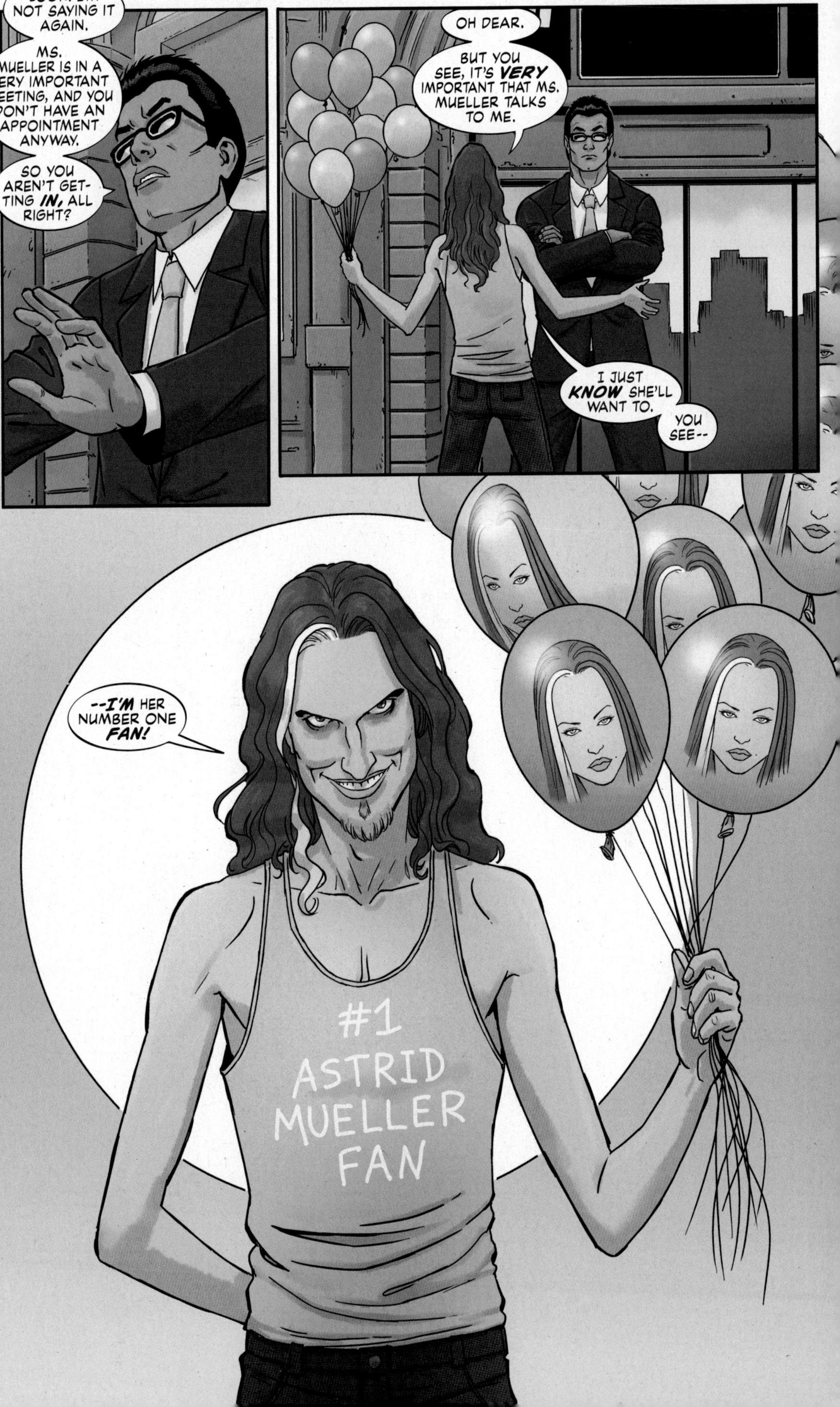
LOOK. I'M NOT SAYING IT AGAIN.
MS. MUELLER IS IN A VERY IMPORTANT MEETING, AND YOU DON'T HAVE AN APPOINTMENT ANYWAY.
SO YOU AREN'T GETTING IN, ALL RIGHT?
OH DEAR.
BUT YOU SEE, IT'S VERY IMPORTANT THAT MS. MUELLER TALKS TO ME.
I JUST KNOW SHE'LL WANT TO.
YOU SEE--
--I'M HER NUMBER ONE FAN!
#1 ASTRID MUELLER FAN

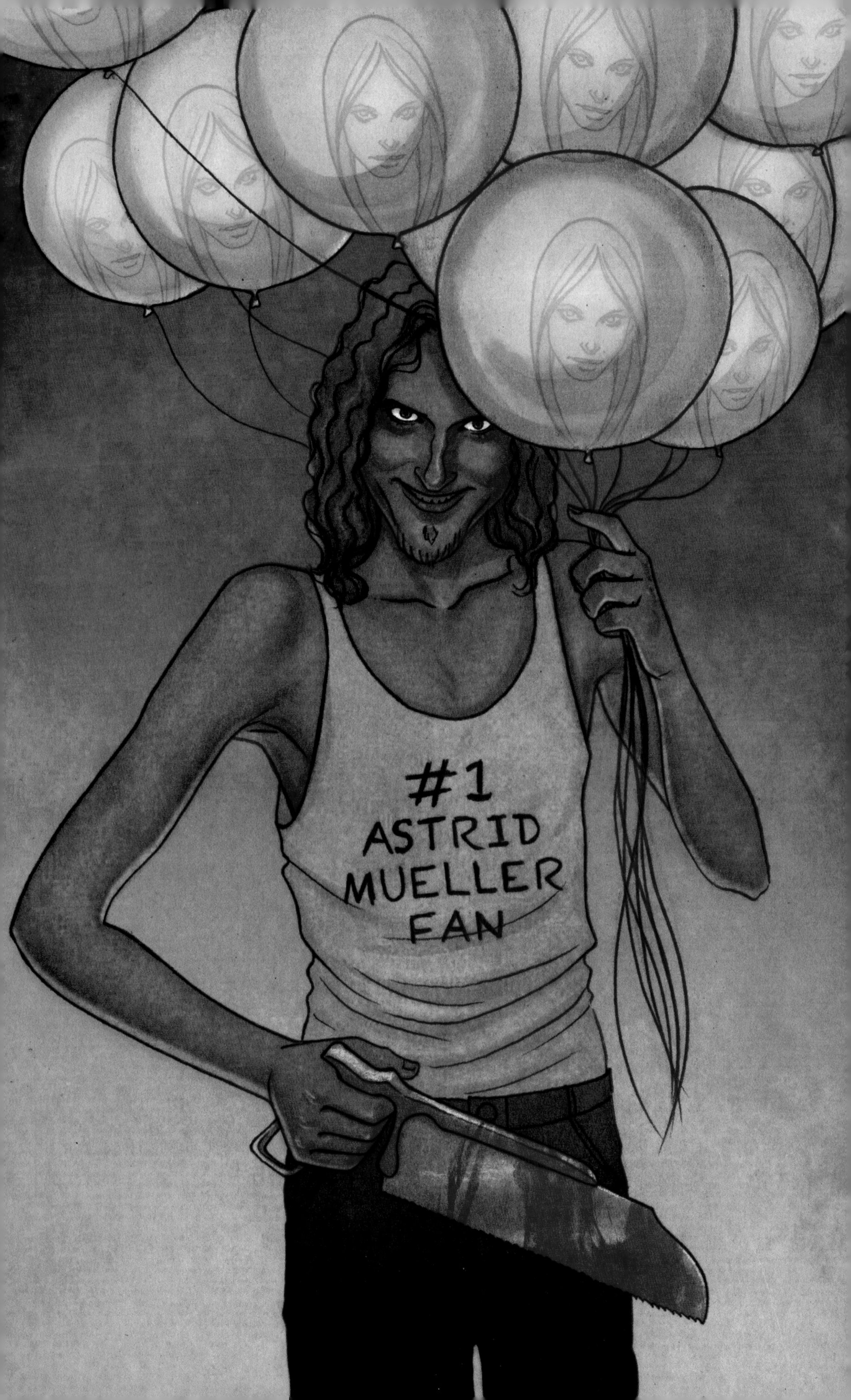
#1
ASTRID
MUELLER
FAN

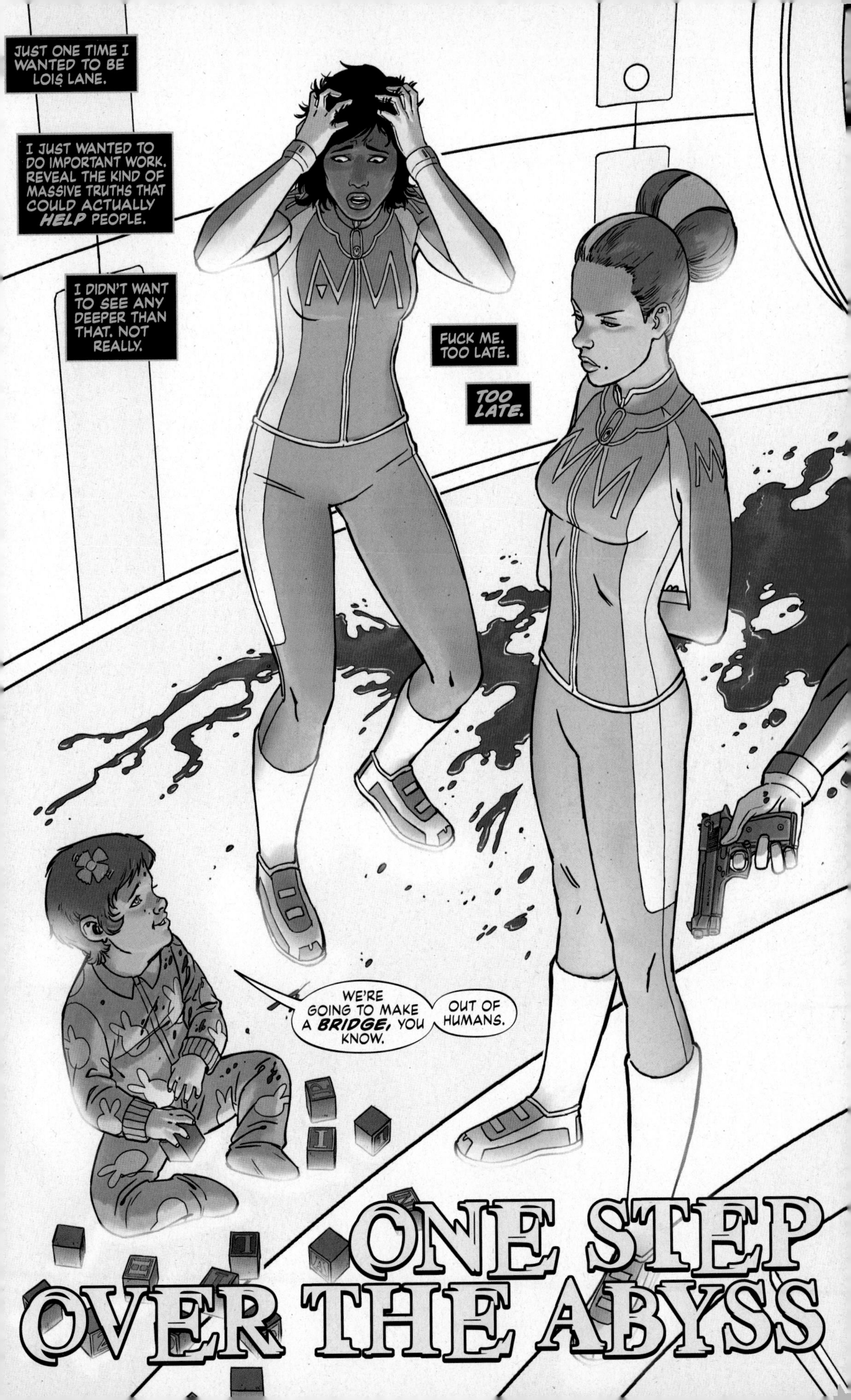
JUST ONE TIME I WANTED TO BE LOIS LANE.
I JUST WANTED TO DO IMPORTANT WORK. REVEAL THE KIND OF MASSIVE TRUTHS THAT COULD ACTUALLY HELP PEOPLE.
I DIDN'T WANT TO SEE ANY DEEPER THAN THAT. NOT REALLY.
FUCK ME. TOO LATE.
TOO LATE.
WE'RE GOING TO MAKE A BRIDGE, YOU KNOW.
OUT OF HUMANS.
ONE STEP OVER THE ABYSS

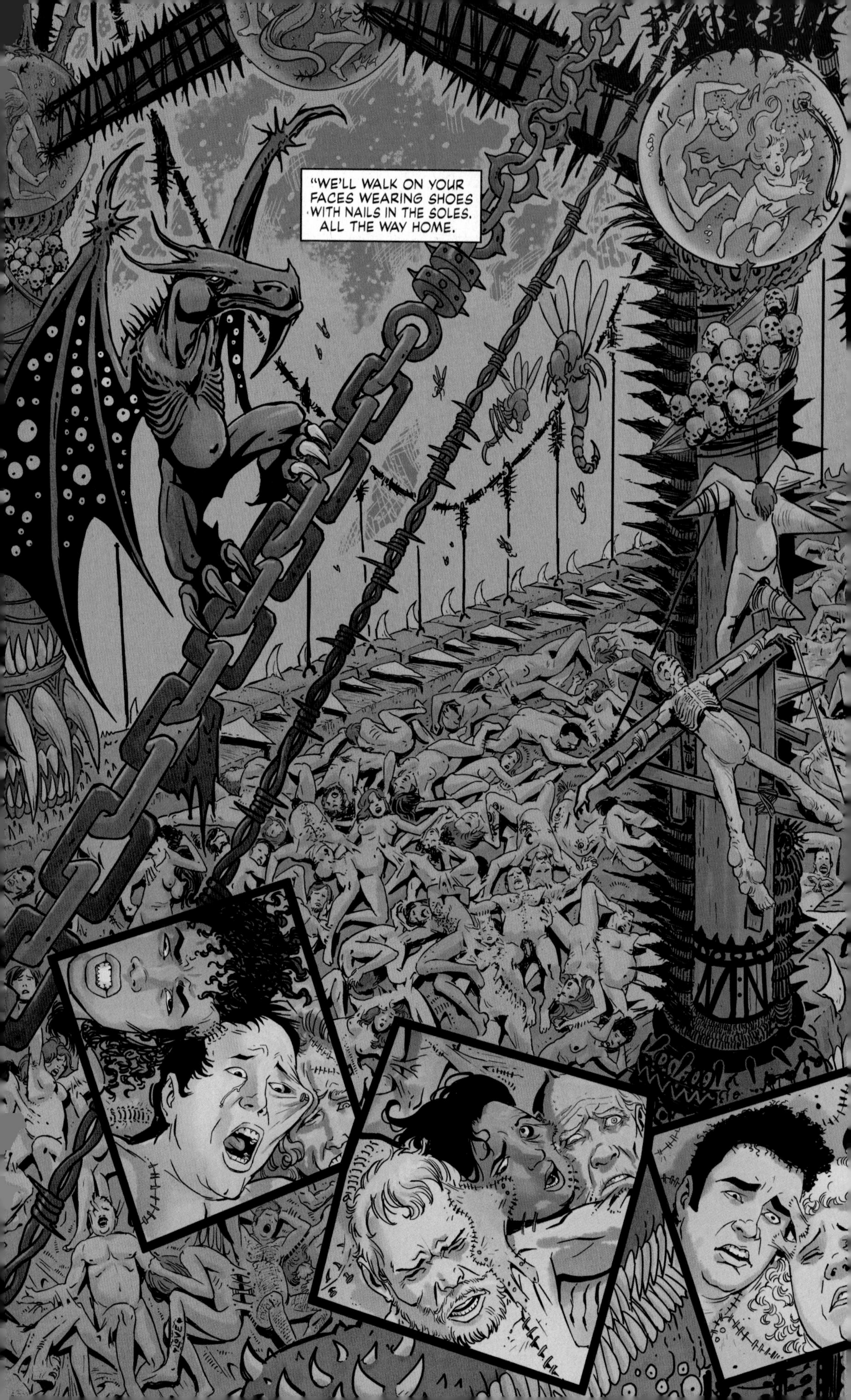
"WE'LL WALK ON YOUR FACES WEARING SHOES WITH NAILS IN THE SOLES. ALL THE WAY HOME.

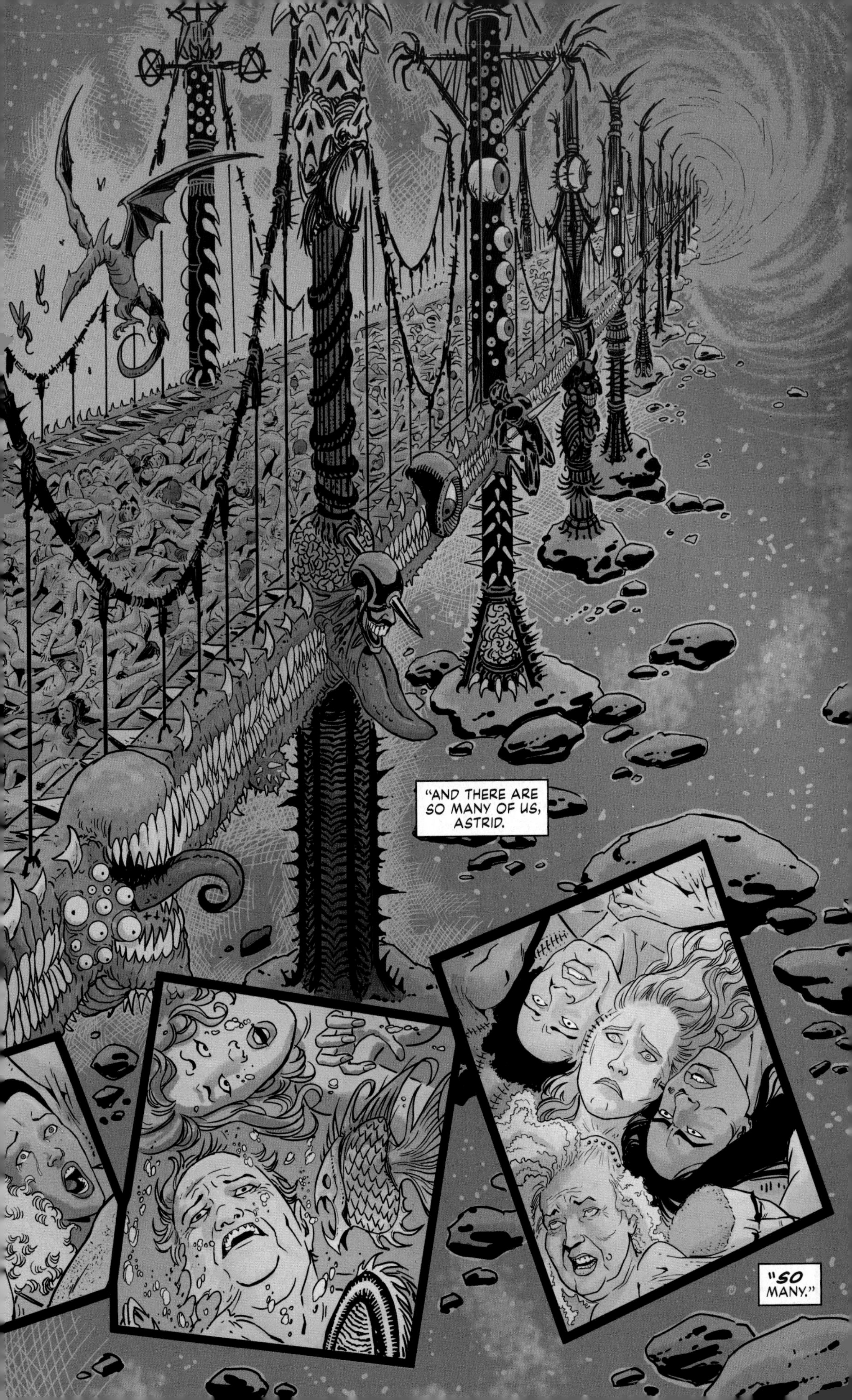
"AND THERE ARE
SO MANY OF US,
ASTRID.
"SO
MANY."

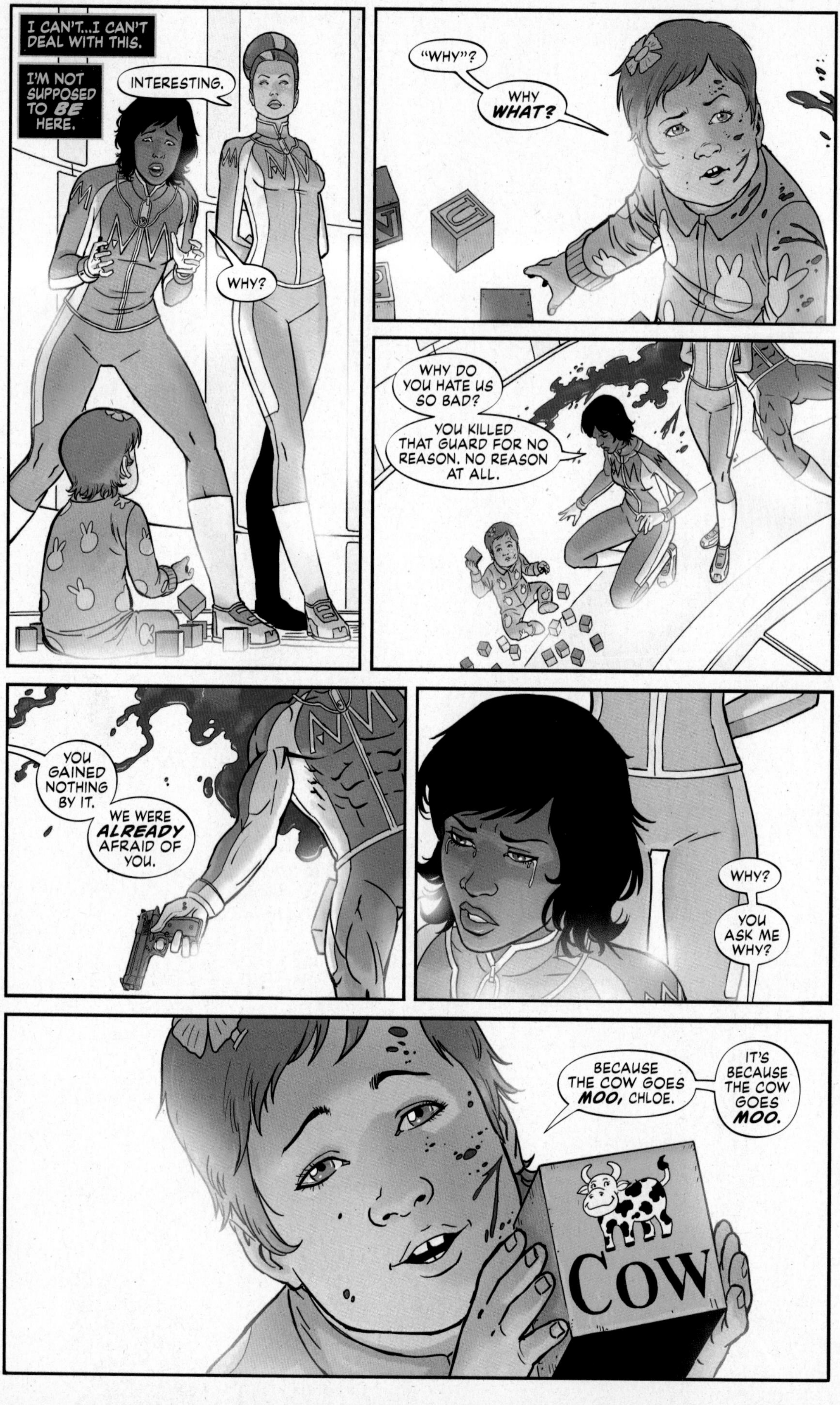
I CAN'T...I CAN'T DEAL WITH THIS.
I'M NOT SUPPOSED TO BE HERE.
INTERESTING.
WHY?
"WHY"?
WHY WHAT?
WHY DO YOU HATE US SO BAD?
YOU KILLED THAT GUARD FOR NO REASON. NO REASON AT ALL.
YOU GAINED NOTHING BY IT.
WE WERE ALREADY AFRAID OF YOU.
WHY?
YOU ASK ME WHY?
BECAUSE THE COW GOES MOO, CHLOE.
IT'S BECAUSE THE COW GOES MOO.
COW

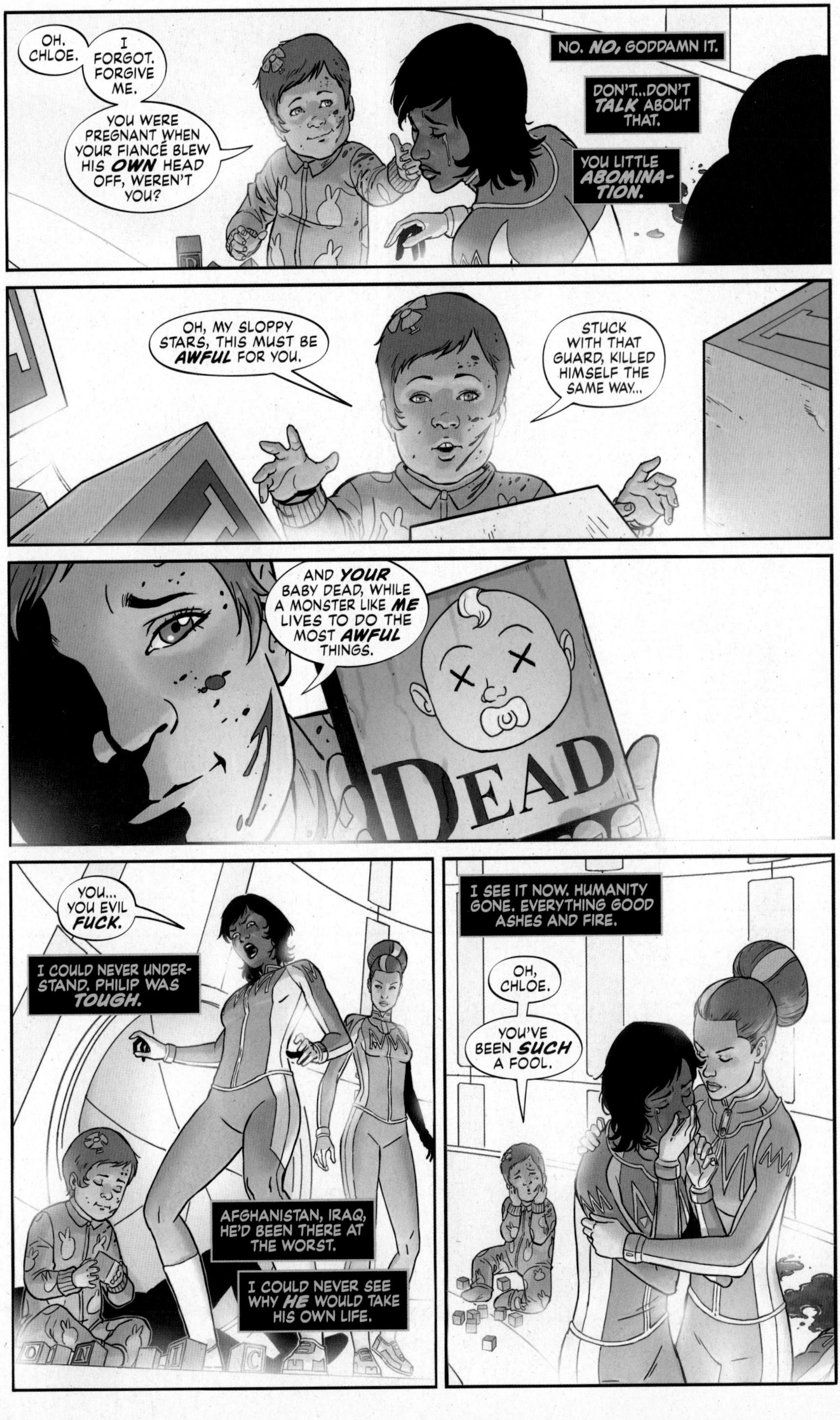

OH. CHLOE.
I FORGOT. FORGIVE ME.
YOU WERE PREGNANT WHEN YOUR FIANCÉ BLEW HIS OWN HEAD OFF, WEREN'T YOU?
NO. NO, GODDAMN IT.
DON'T...DON'T TALK ABOUT THAT.
YOU LITTLE ABOMINATION.
OH, MY SLOPPY STARS, THIS MUST BE AWFUL FOR YOU.
STUCK WITH THAT GUARD, KILLED HIMSELF THE SAME WAY...
AND YOUR BABY DEAD, WHILE A MONSTER LIKE ME LIVES TO DO THE MOST AWFUL THINGS.
DEAD
YOU... YOU EVIL FUCK.
I COULD NEVER UNDERSTAND. PHILIP WAS TOUGH.
AFGHANISTAN, IRAQ, HE'D BEEN THERE AT THE WORST.
I COULD NEVER SEE WHY HE WOULD TAKE HIS OWN LIFE.
I SEE IT NOW. HUMANITY GONE. EVERYTHING GOOD ASHES AND FIRE.
OH, CHLOE.
YOU'VE BEEN SUCH A FOOL.

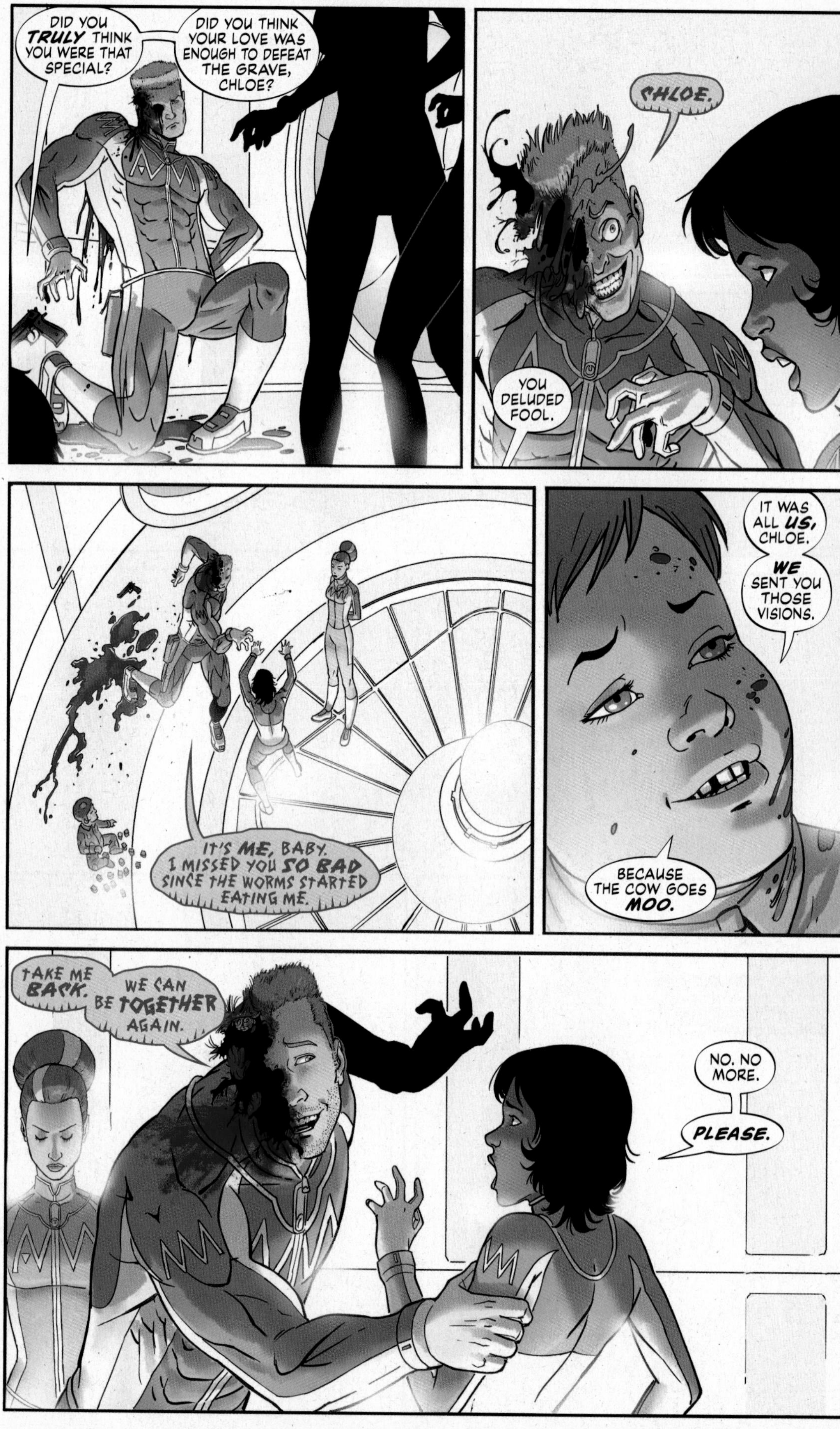
DID YOU TRULY THINK YOU WERE THAT SPECIAL?
DID YOU THINK YOUR LOVE WAS ENOUGH TO DEFEAT THE GRAVE, CHLOE?
CHLOE.
YOU DELUDED FOOL.
IT'S ME, BABY. I MISSED YOU SO BAD SINCE THE WORMS STARTED EATING ME.
IT WAS ALL US, CHLOE.
WE SENT YOU THOSE VISIONS.
BECAUSE THE COW GOES MOO.
TAKE ME BACK.
WE CAN BE TOGETHER AGAIN.
NO. NO MORE.
PLEASE.

I QUITE AGREE.

RAVEN, ARE YOU LISTENING?

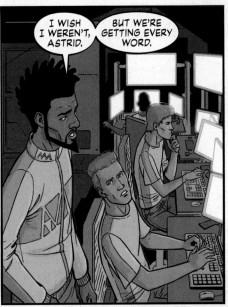

I WISH I WEREN'T, ASTRID.

BUT WE'RE GETTING EVERY WORD.

PLEASE DO ME A FAVOR, THEN, WON'T YOU...

...AND LIGHT THIS DAMN *THING* UP LIKE THE FOURTH OF JULY?

THAT'S A BIG TEN-FOUR, BOSS.

OH, YOU FUCKING BI-- AAAAAAAA-QQUL#%!

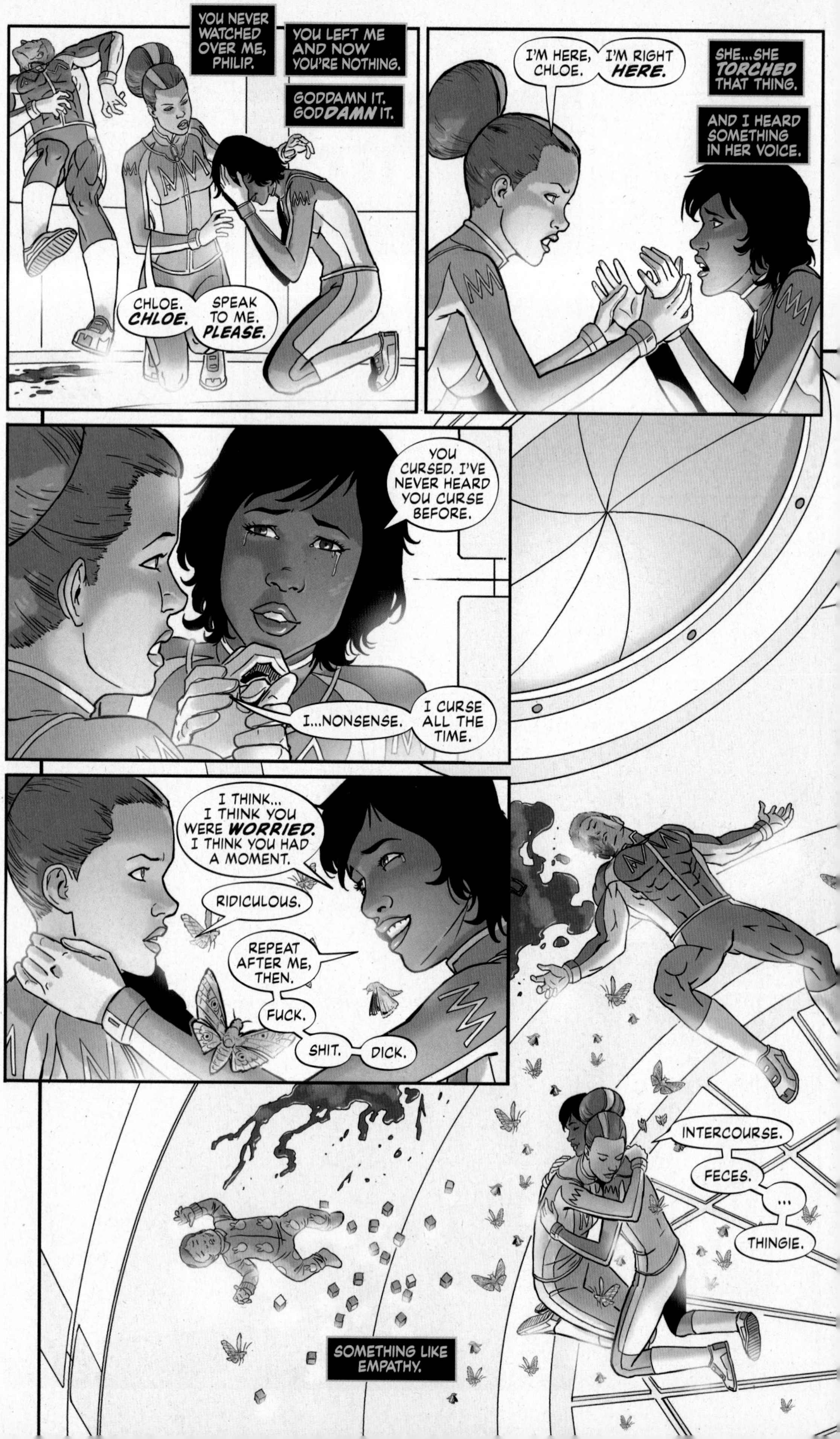
YOU NEVER WATCHED OVER ME, PHILIP.
YOU LEFT ME AND NOW YOU'RE NOTHING.
GODDAMN IT. GOD**DAMN** IT.
CHLOE. **CHLOE.**
SPEAK TO ME. **PLEASE.**
I'M HERE, CHLOE.
I'M RIGHT **HERE.**
SHE...SHE **TORCHED** THAT THING.
AND I HEARD SOMETHING IN HER VOICE.
YOU CURSED. I'VE NEVER HEARD YOU CURSE BEFORE.
I...NONSENSE.
I CURSE ALL THE TIME.
I THINK... I THINK YOU WERE **WORRIED.** I THINK YOU HAD A MOMENT.
RIDICULOUS.
REPEAT AFTER ME, THEN.
FUCK.
SHIT.
DICK.
INTERCOURSE.
FECES.
...
THINGIE.
SOMETHING LIKE EMPATHY.

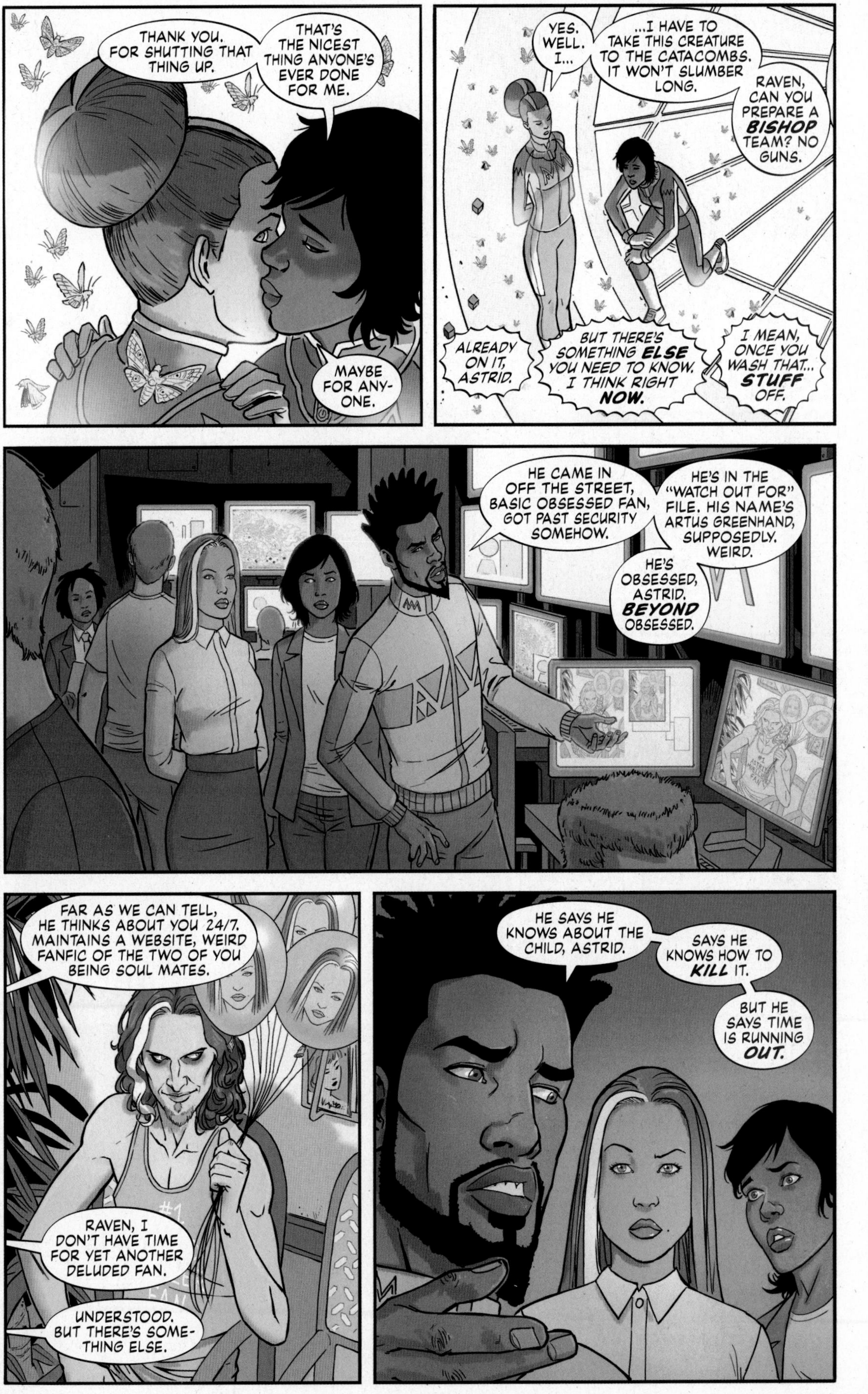
THANK YOU. FOR SHUTTING THAT THING UP.
THAT'S THE NICEST THING ANYONE'S EVER DONE FOR ME.
MAYBE FOR ANY-ONE.
YES. WELL. I...
...I HAVE TO TAKE THIS CREATURE TO THE CATACOMBS. IT WON'T SLUMBER LONG.
RAVEN, CAN YOU PREPARE A BISHOP TEAM? NO GUNS.
ALREADY ON IT, ASTRID.
BUT THERE'S SOMETHING ELSE YOU NEED TO KNOW. I THINK RIGHT NOW.
I MEAN, ONCE YOU WASH THAT... STUFF OFF.
HE CAME IN OFF THE STREET, BASIC OBSESSED FAN, GOT PAST SECURITY SOMEHOW.
HE'S IN THE "WATCH OUT FOR" FILE. HIS NAME'S ARTUS GREENHAND, SUPPOSEDLY. WEIRD.
HE'S OBSESSED, ASTRID. BEYOND OBSESSED.
FAR AS WE CAN TELL, HE THINKS ABOUT YOU 24/7. MAINTAINS A WEBSITE, WEIRD FANFIC OF THE TWO OF YOU BEING SOUL MATES.
RAVEN, I DON'T HAVE TIME FOR YET ANOTHER DELUDED FAN.
UNDERSTOOD. BUT THERE'S SOME-THING ELSE.
HE SAYS HE KNOWS ABOUT THE CHILD, ASTRID.
SAYS HE KNOWS HOW TO KILL IT.
BUT HE SAYS TIME IS RUNNING OUT.

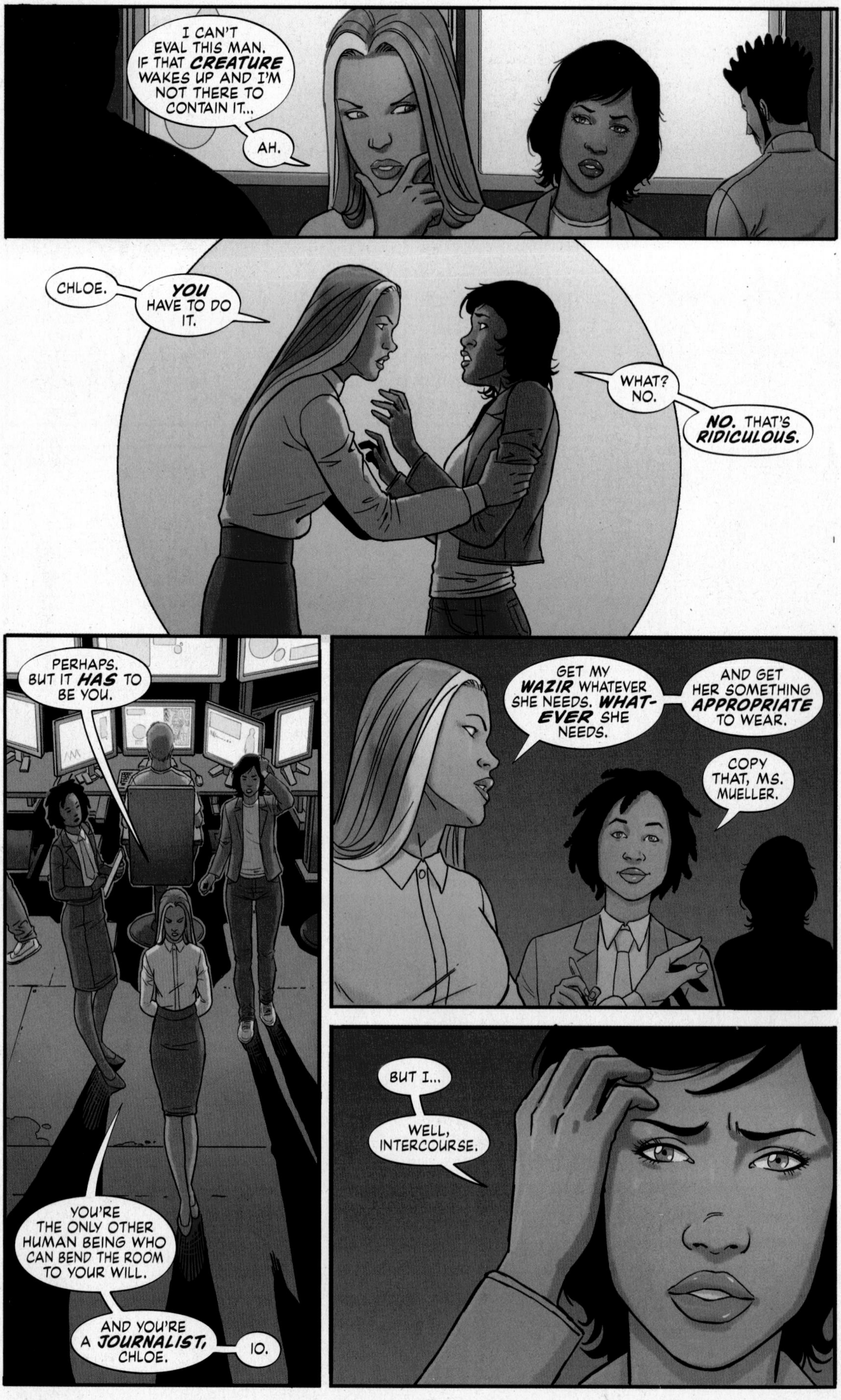

I CAN'T EVAL THIS MAN. IF THAT CREATURE WAKES UP AND I'M NOT THERE TO CONTAIN IT...
AH.
CHLOE.
YOU HAVE TO DO IT.
WHAT? NO.
NO. THAT'S RIDICULOUS.
PERHAPS. BUT IT HAS TO BE YOU.
YOU'RE THE ONLY OTHER HUMAN BEING WHO CAN BEND THE ROOM TO YOUR WILL.
AND YOU'RE A JOURNALIST, CHLOE.
IO.
GET MY WAZIR WHATEVER SHE NEEDS. WHATEVER SHE NEEDS.
AND GET HER SOMETHING APPROPRIATE TO WEAR.
COPY THAT, MS. MUELLER.
BUT I...
WELL, INTERCOURSE.

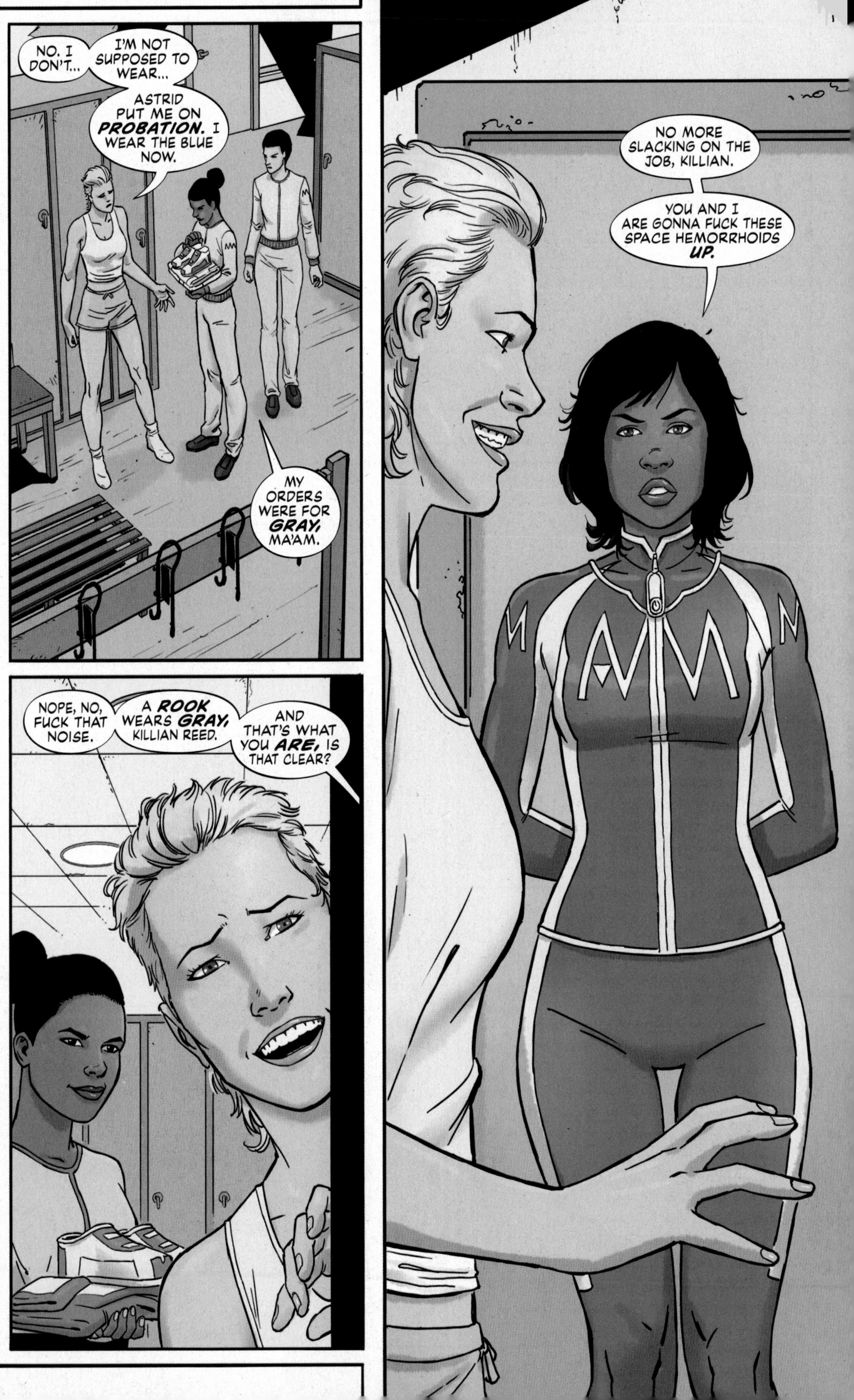
NO. I DON'T...
I'M NOT SUPPOSED TO WEAR...
ASTRID PUT ME ON PROBATION. I WEAR THE BLUE NOW.
MY ORDERS WERE FOR GRAY, MA'AM.
NOPE, NO, FUCK THAT NOISE.
A ROOK WEARS GRAY, KILLIAN REED.
AND THAT'S WHAT YOU ARE, IS THAT CLEAR?
NO MORE SLACKING ON THE JOB, KILLIAN.
YOU AND I ARE GONNA FUCK THESE SPACE HEMORRHOIDS UP.

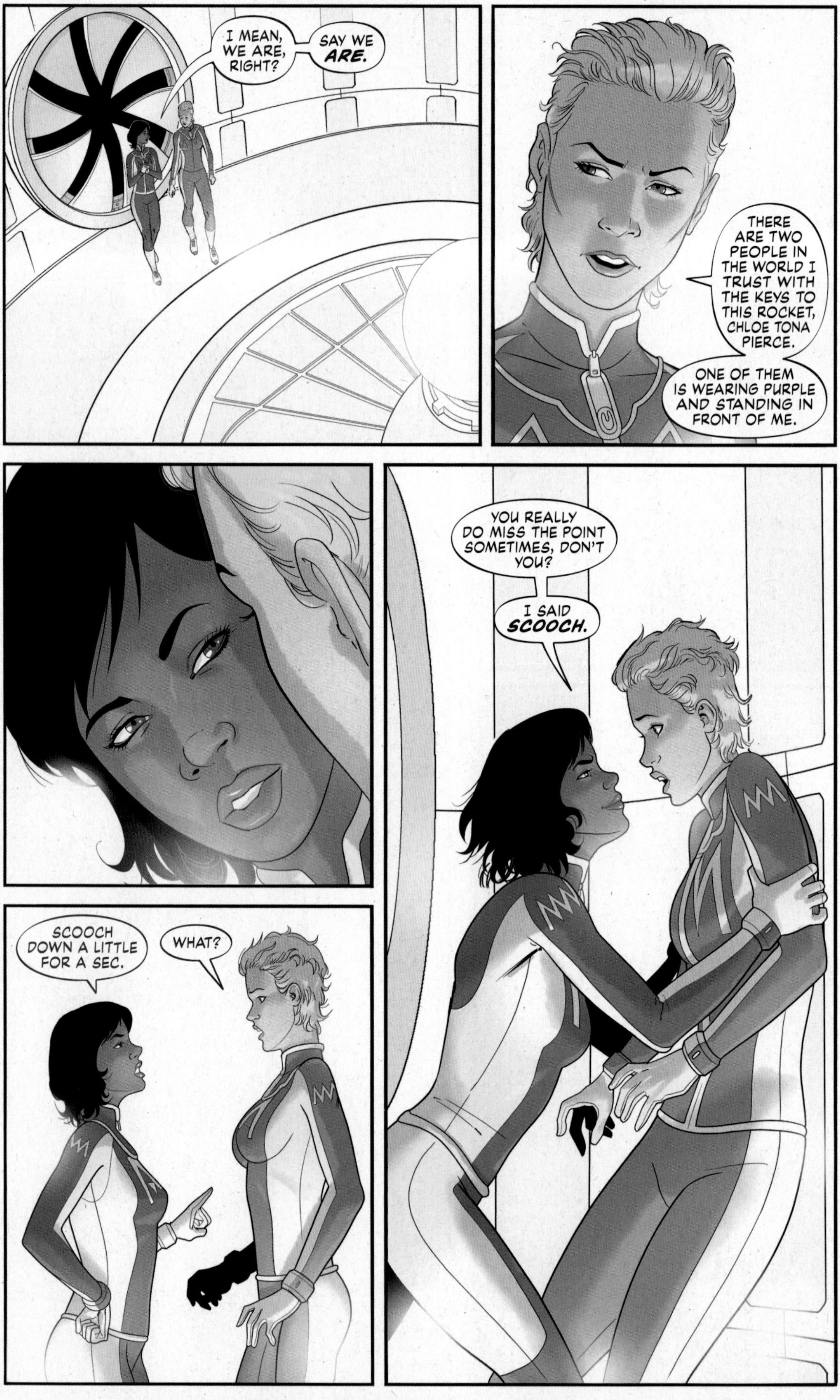
I MEAN, WE ARE, RIGHT?
SAY WE ARE.
THERE ARE TWO PEOPLE IN THE WORLD I TRUST WITH THE KEYS TO THIS ROCKET, CHLOE TONA PIERCE.
ONE OF THEM IS WEARING PURPLE AND STANDING IN FRONT OF ME.
SCOOCH DOWN A LITTLE FOR A SEC.
WHAT?
YOU REALLY DO MISS THE POINT SOMETIMES, DON'T YOU?
I SAID SCOOCH.

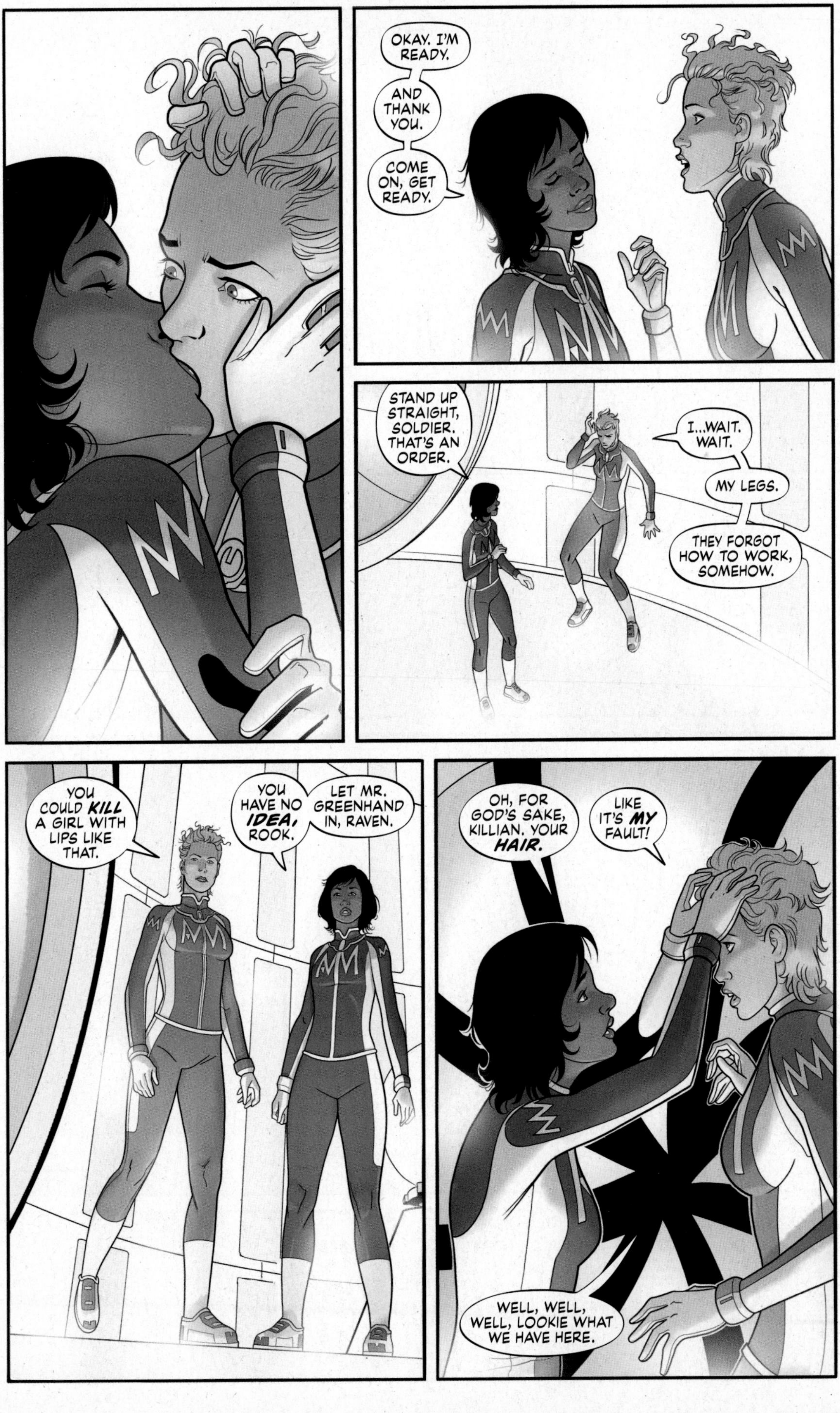
OKAY. I'M READY.
AND THANK YOU.
COME ON, GET READY.
STAND UP STRAIGHT, SOLDIER. THAT'S AN ORDER.
I...WAIT. WAIT.
MY LEGS.
THEY FORGOT HOW TO WORK, SOMEHOW.
YOU COULD KILL A GIRL WITH LIPS LIKE THAT.
YOU HAVE NO IDEA, ROOK.
LET MR. GREENHAND IN, RAVEN.
OH, FOR GOD'S SAKE, KILLIAN. YOUR HAIR.
LIKE IT'S MY FAULT!
WELL, WELL, WELL, LOOKIE WHAT WE HAVE HERE.

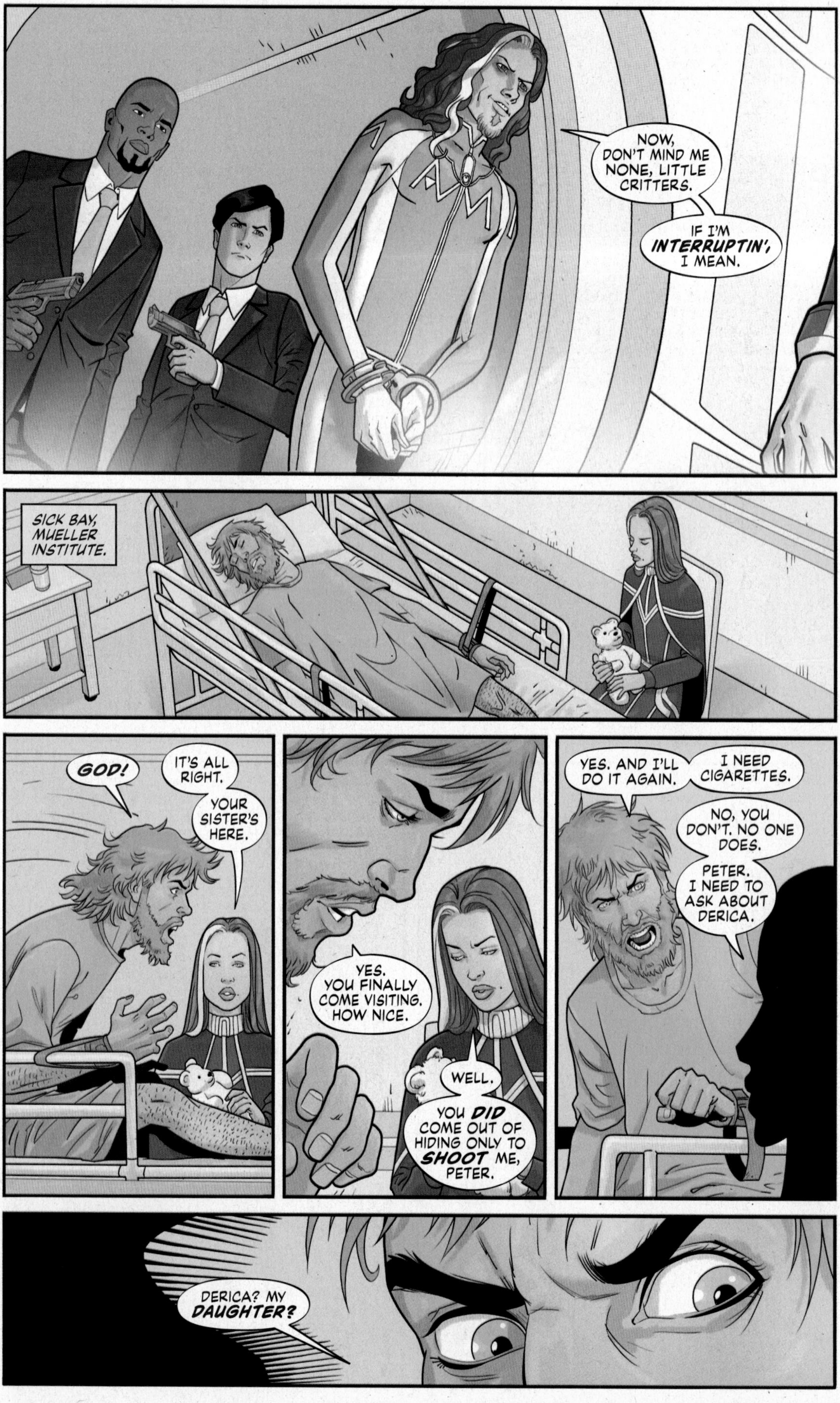
NOW, DON'T MIND ME NONE, LITTLE CRITTERS.
IF I'M **INTERRUPTIN',** I MEAN.
SICK BAY, MUELLER INSTITUTE.
GOD!
IT'S ALL RIGHT.
YOUR SISTER'S HERE.
YES. YOU FINALLY COME VISITING. HOW NICE.
WELL.
YOU **DID** COME OUT OF HIDING ONLY TO **SHOOT** ME, PETER.
YES. AND I'LL DO IT AGAIN.
I NEED CIGARETTES.
NO, YOU DON'T. NO ONE DOES.
PETER. I NEED TO ASK ABOUT DERICA.
DERICA? MY **DAUGHTER?**

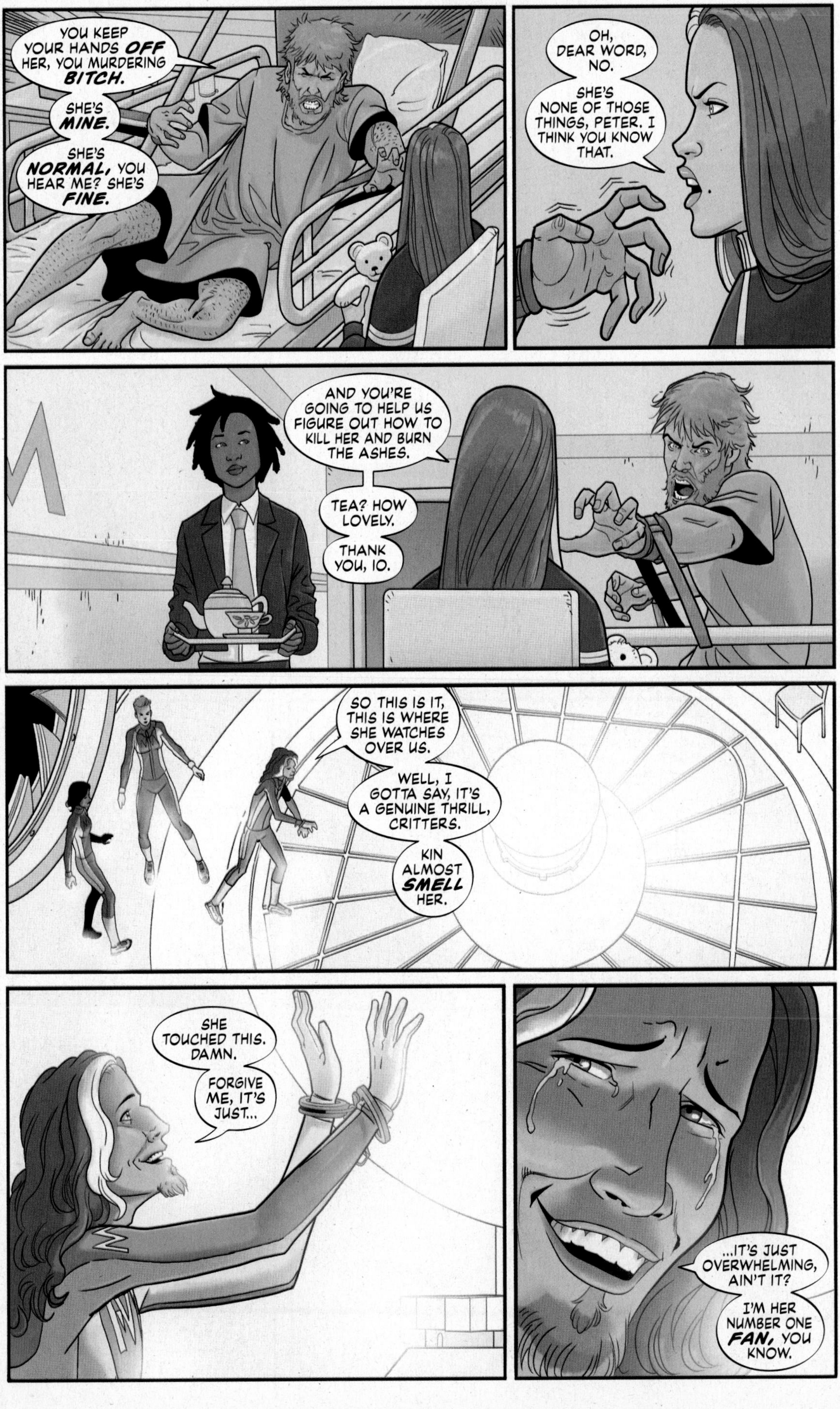
YOU KEEP YOUR HANDS OFF HER, YOU MURDERING BITCH.
SHE'S MINE.
SHE'S NORMAL, YOU HEAR ME? SHE'S FINE.
OH, DEAR WORD, NO.
SHE'S NONE OF THOSE THINGS, PETER. I THINK YOU KNOW THAT.
AND YOU'RE GOING TO HELP US FIGURE OUT HOW TO KILL HER AND BURN THE ASHES.
TEA? HOW LOVELY.
THANK YOU, IO.
SO THIS IS IT, THIS IS WHERE SHE WATCHES OVER US.
WELL, I GOTTA SAY, IT'S A GENUINE THRILL, CRITTERS.
KIN ALMOST SMELL HER.
SHE TOUCHED THIS. DAMN.
FORGIVE ME, IT'S JUST...
...IT'S JUST OVERWHELMING, AIN'T IT?
I'M HER NUMBER ONE FAN, YOU KNOW.

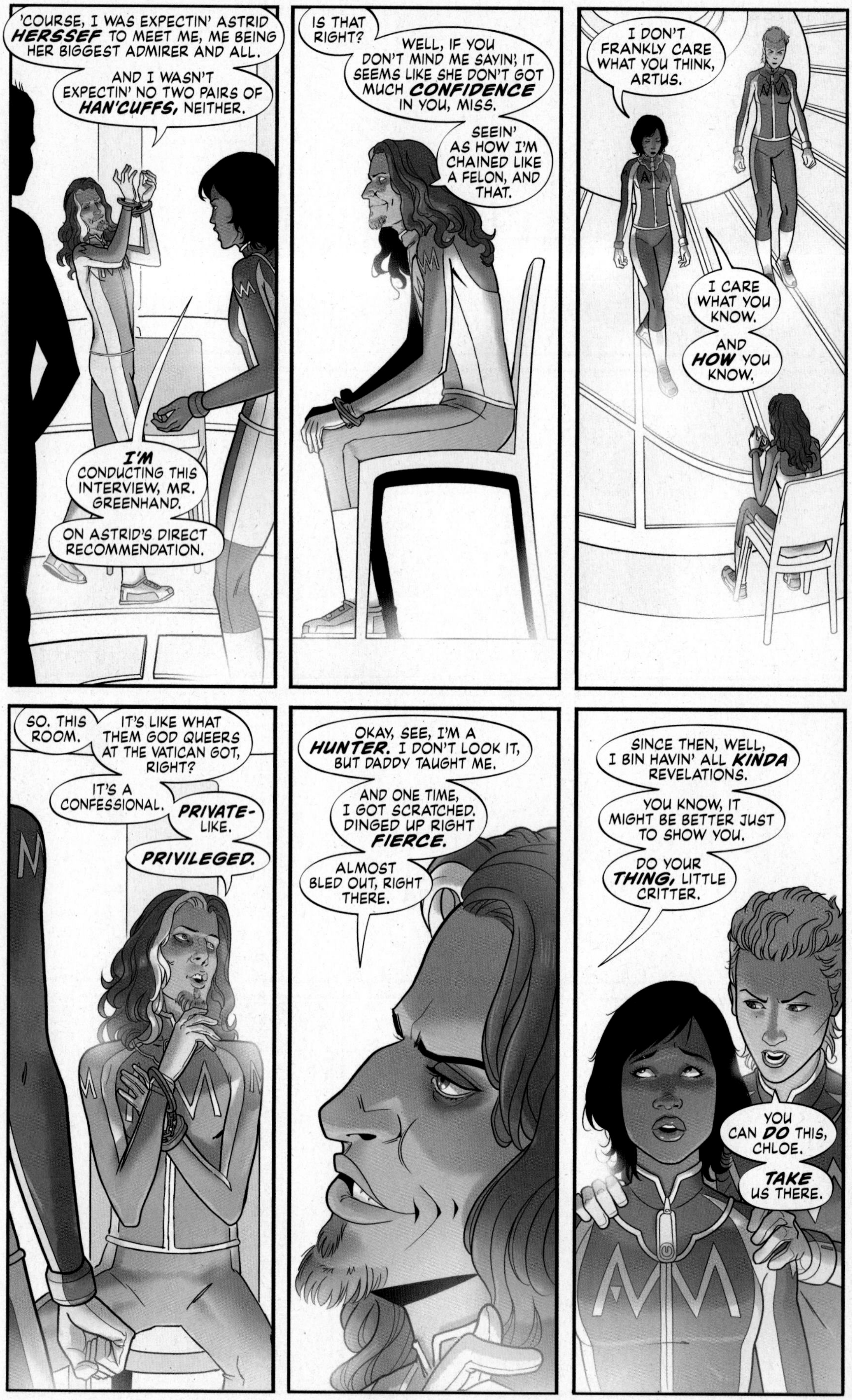
'COURSE, I WAS EXPECTIN' ASTRID HERSSEF TO MEET ME, ME BEING HER BIGGEST ADMIRER AND ALL.
AND I WASN'T EXPECTIN' NO TWO PAIRS OF HAN'CUFFS, NEITHER.
I'M CONDUCTING THIS INTERVIEW, MR. GREENHAND.
ON ASTRID'S DIRECT RECOMMENDATION.
IS THAT RIGHT?
WELL, IF YOU DON'T MIND ME SAYIN', IT SEEMS LIKE SHE DON'T GOT MUCH CONFIDENCE IN YOU, MISS.
SEEIN' AS HOW I'M CHAINED LIKE A FELON, AND THAT.
I DON'T FRANKLY CARE WHAT YOU THINK, ARTUS.
I CARE WHAT YOU KNOW.
AND HOW YOU KNOW.
SO. THIS ROOM.
IT'S LIKE WHAT THEM GOD QUEERS AT THE VATICAN GOT, RIGHT?
IT'S A CONFESSIONAL.
PRIVATE-LIKE.
PRIVILEGED.
OKAY, SEE, I'M A HUNTER. I DON'T LOOK IT, BUT DADDY TAUGHT ME.
AND ONE TIME, I GOT SCRATCHED. DINGED UP RIGHT FIERCE.
ALMOST BLED OUT, RIGHT THERE.
SINCE THEN, WELL, I BIN HAVIN' ALL KINDA REVELATIONS.
YOU KNOW, IT MIGHT BE BETTER JUST TO SHOW YOU.
DO YOUR THING, LITTLE CRITTER.
YOU CAN DO THIS, CHLOE.
TAKE US THERE.

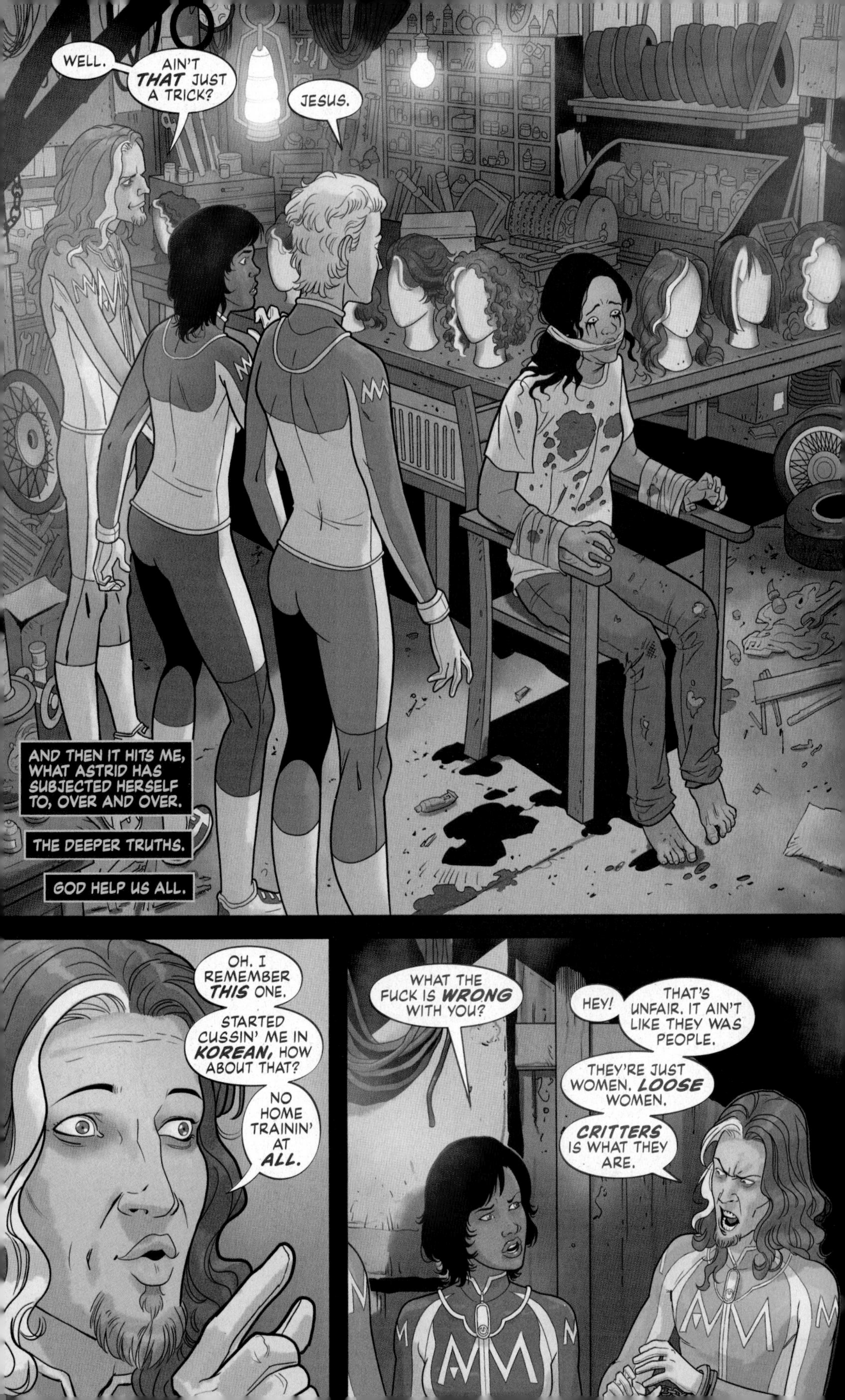

WELL.
AIN'T THAT JUST A TRICK?
JESUS.
AND THEN IT HITS ME, WHAT ASTRID HAS SUBJECTED HERSELF TO, OVER AND OVER.
THE DEEPER TRUTHS.
GOD HELP US ALL.
OH. I REMEMBER THIS ONE.
STARTED CUSSIN' ME IN KOREAN, HOW ABOUT THAT?
NO HOME TRAININ' AT ALL.
WHAT THE FUCK IS WRONG WITH YOU?
HEY!
THAT'S UNFAIR. IT AIN'T LIKE THEY WAS PEOPLE.
THEY'RE JUST WOMEN. LOOSE WOMEN.
CRITTERS IS WHAT THEY ARE.

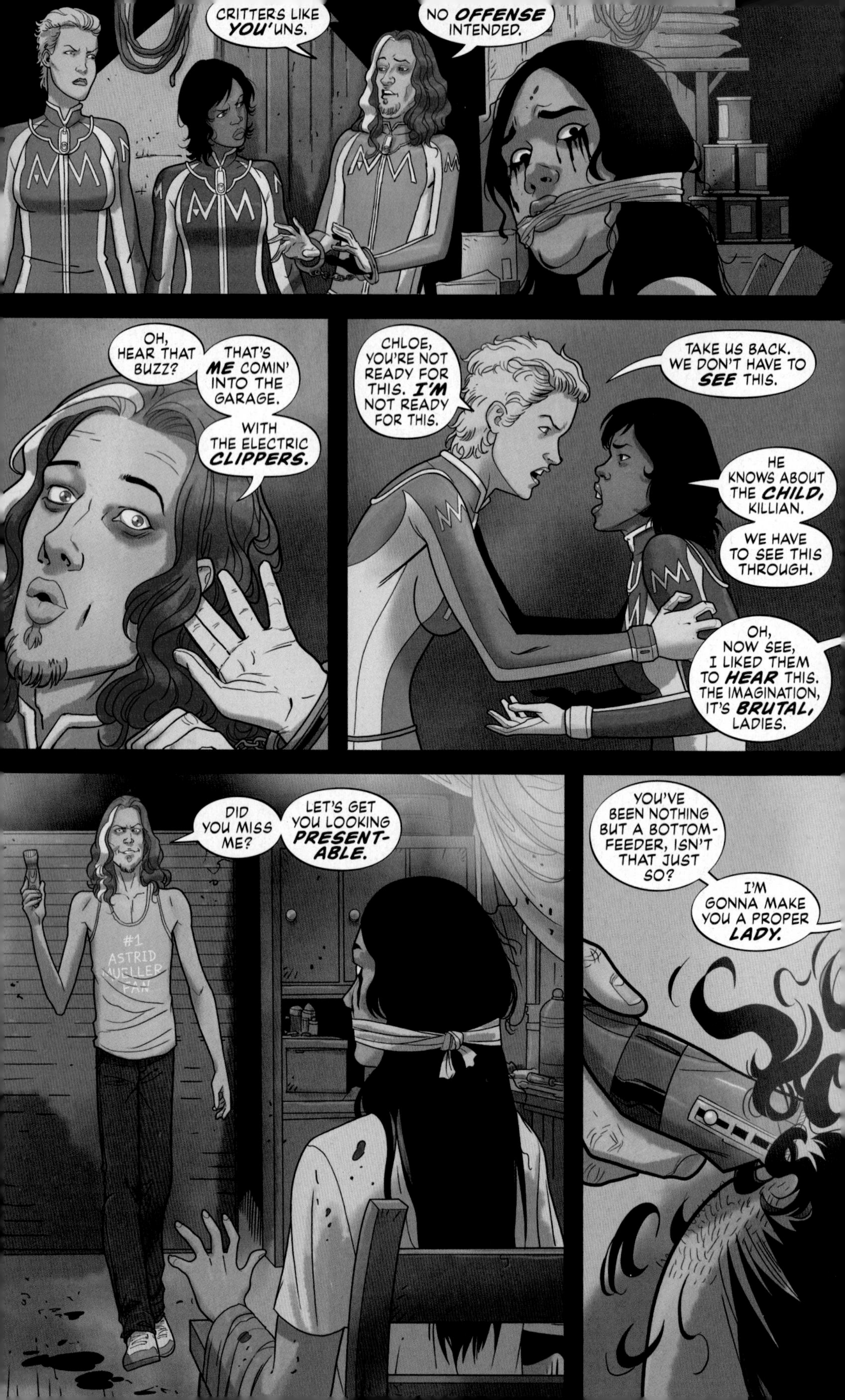

CRITTERS LIKE YOU'UNS.
NO OFFENSE INTENDED.
OH, HEAR THAT BUZZ?
THAT'S ME COMIN' INTO THE GARAGE.
WITH THE ELECTRIC CLIPPERS.
CHLOE, YOU'RE NOT READY FOR THIS. I'M NOT READY FOR THIS.
TAKE US BACK. WE DON'T HAVE TO SEE THIS.
HE KNOWS ABOUT THE CHILD, KILLIAN.
WE HAVE TO SEE THIS THROUGH.
OH, NOW SEE, I LIKED THEM TO HEAR THIS. THE IMAGINATION, IT'S BRUTAL, LADIES.
DID YOU MISS ME?
LET'S GET YOU LOOKING PRESENT-ABLE.
#1 ASTRID MUELLER FAN
YOU'VE BEEN NOTHING BUT A BOTTOM-FEEDER, ISN'T THAT JUST SO?
I'M GONNA MAKE YOU A PROPER LADY.

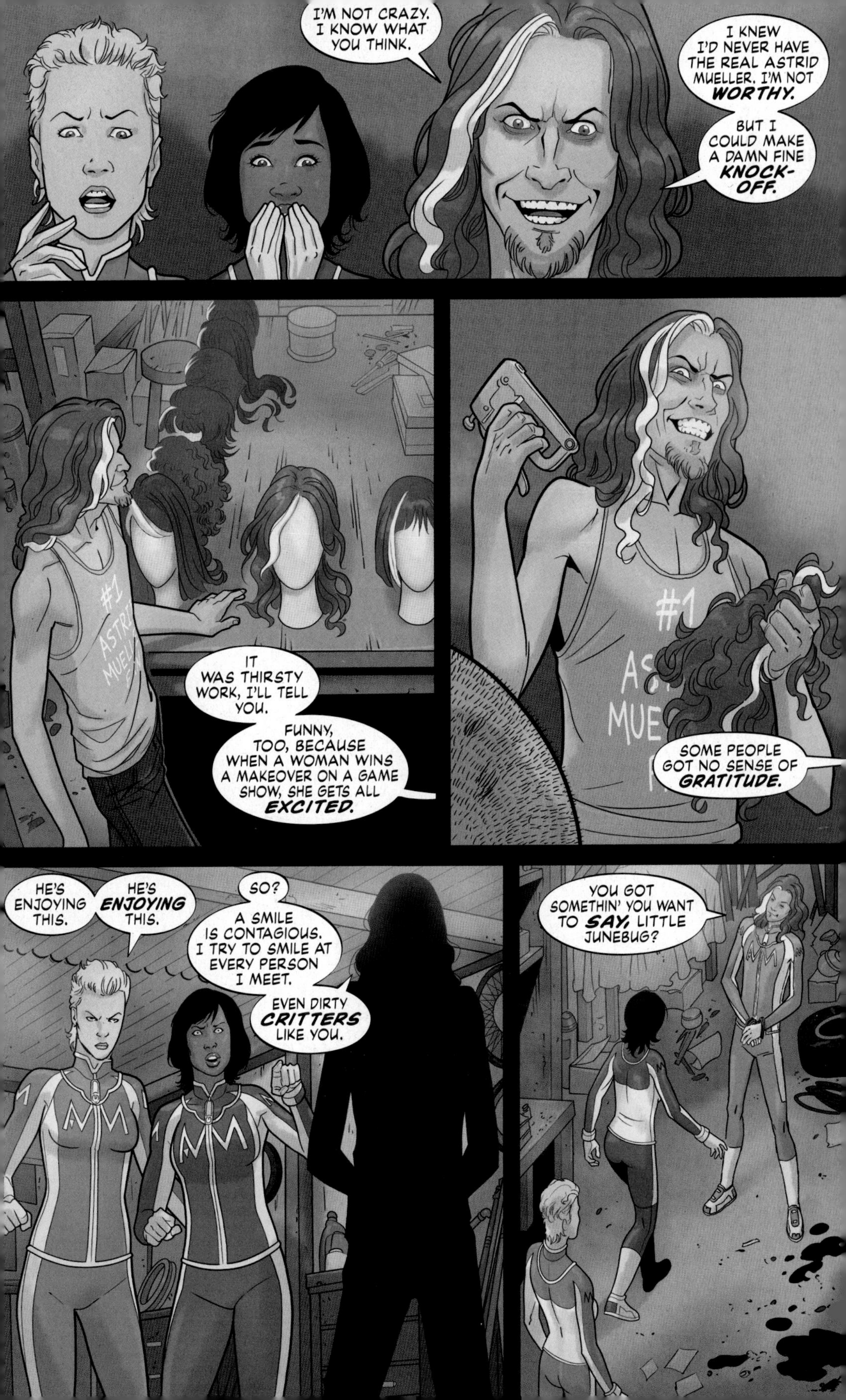
I'M NOT CRAZY. I KNOW WHAT YOU THINK.
I KNEW I'D NEVER HAVE THE REAL ASTRID MUELLER. I'M NOT WORTHY.
BUT I COULD MAKE A DAMN FINE KNOCK-OFF.
IT WAS THIRSTY WORK, I'LL TELL YOU.
FUNNY, TOO, BECAUSE WHEN A WOMAN WINS A MAKEOVER ON A GAME SHOW, SHE GETS ALL EXCITED.
#1 ASTRID MUELLER FAN
SOME PEOPLE GOT NO SENSE OF GRATITUDE.
HE'S ENJOYING THIS.
HE'S ENJOYING THIS.
SO?
A SMILE IS CONTAGIOUS. I TRY TO SMILE AT EVERY PERSON I MEET.
EVEN DIRTY CRITTERS LIKE YOU.
YOU GOT SOMETHIN' YOU WANT TO SAY, LITTLE JUNEBUG?

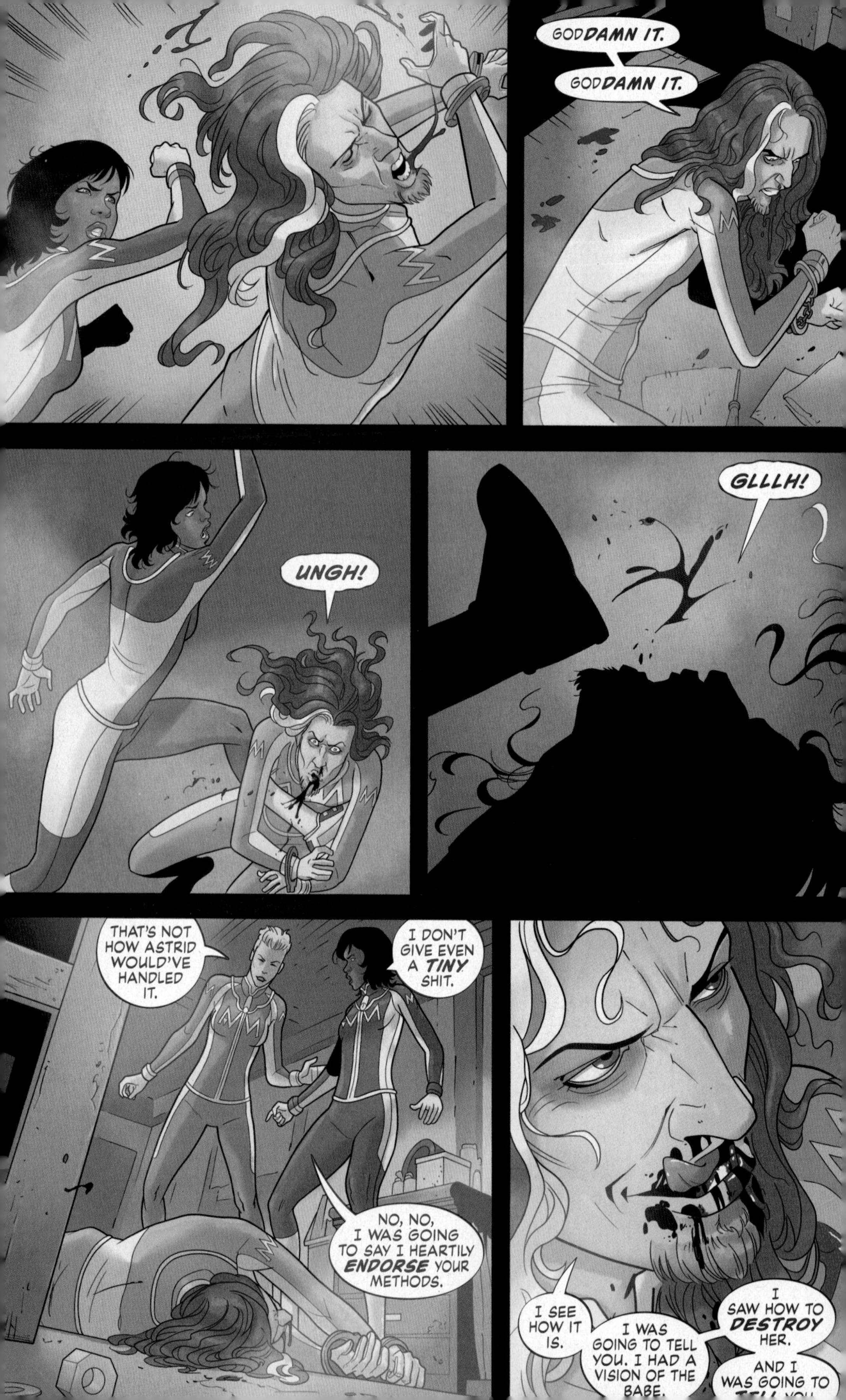
GOD**DAMN IT.**
GOD**DAMN IT.**
UNGH!
GLLLH!
THAT'S NOT HOW ASTRID WOULD'VE HANDLED IT.
I DON'T GIVE EVEN A ***TINY*** SHIT.
NO, NO, I WAS GOING TO SAY I HEARTILY ***ENDORSE*** YOUR METHODS.
I SEE HOW IT IS.
I WAS GOING TO TELL YOU. I HAD A VISION OF THE BABE.
I SAW HOW TO ***DESTROY*** HER.
AND I WAS GOING TO

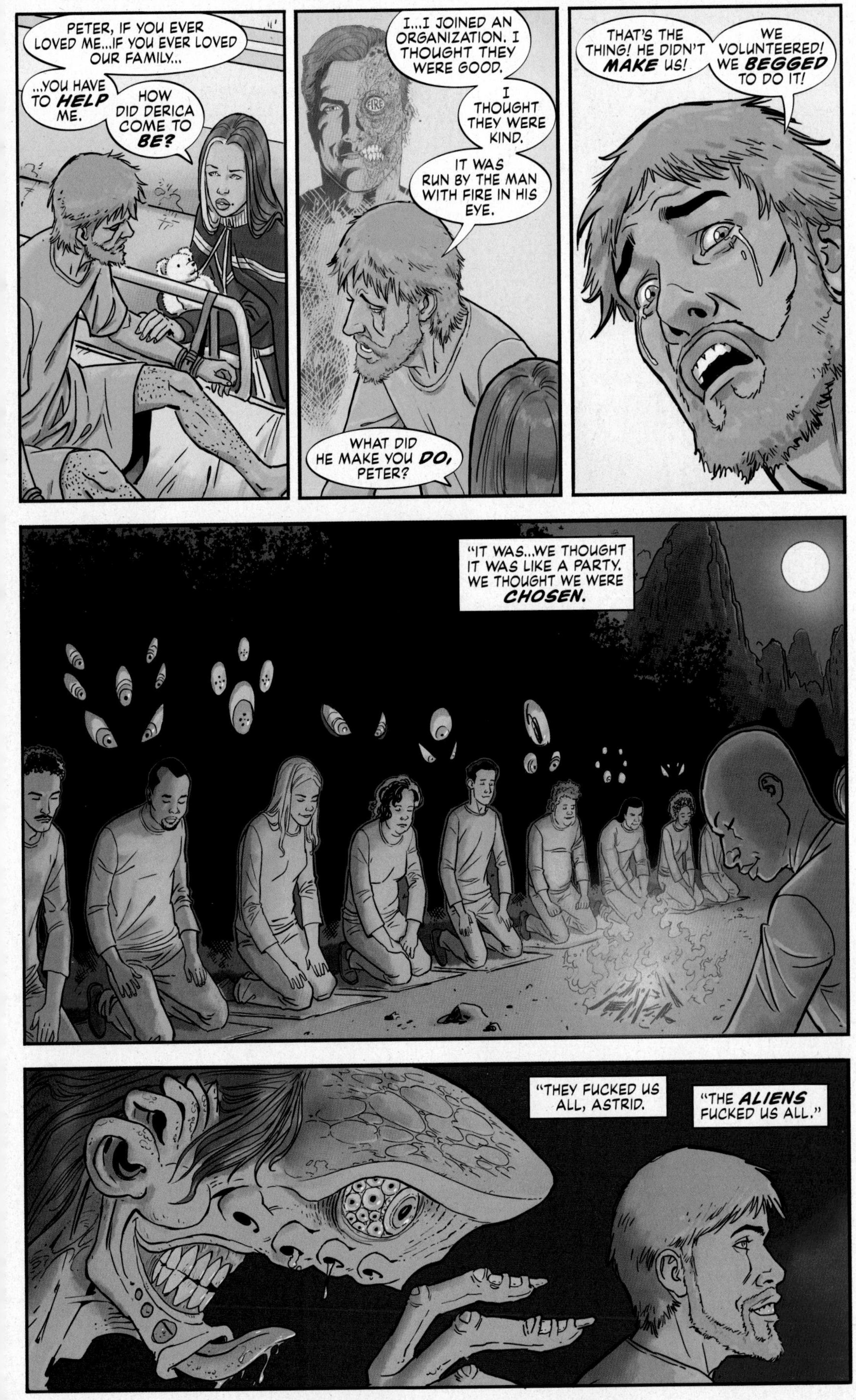
PETER, IF YOU EVER LOVED ME...IF YOU EVER LOVED OUR FAMILY...
...YOU HAVE TO HELP ME.
HOW DID DERICA COME TO BE?
I...I JOINED AN ORGANIZATION. I THOUGHT THEY WERE GOOD.
I THOUGHT THEY WERE KIND.
IT WAS RUN BY THE MAN WITH FIRE IN HIS EYE.
FIRE
WHAT DID HE MAKE YOU DO, PETER?
THAT'S THE THING! HE DIDN'T MAKE US!
WE VOLUNTEERED! WE BEGGED TO DO IT!
"IT WAS...WE THOUGHT IT WAS LIKE A PARTY. WE THOUGHT WE WERE CHOSEN.
"THEY FUCKED US ALL, ASTRID.
"THE ALIENS FUCKED US ALL."

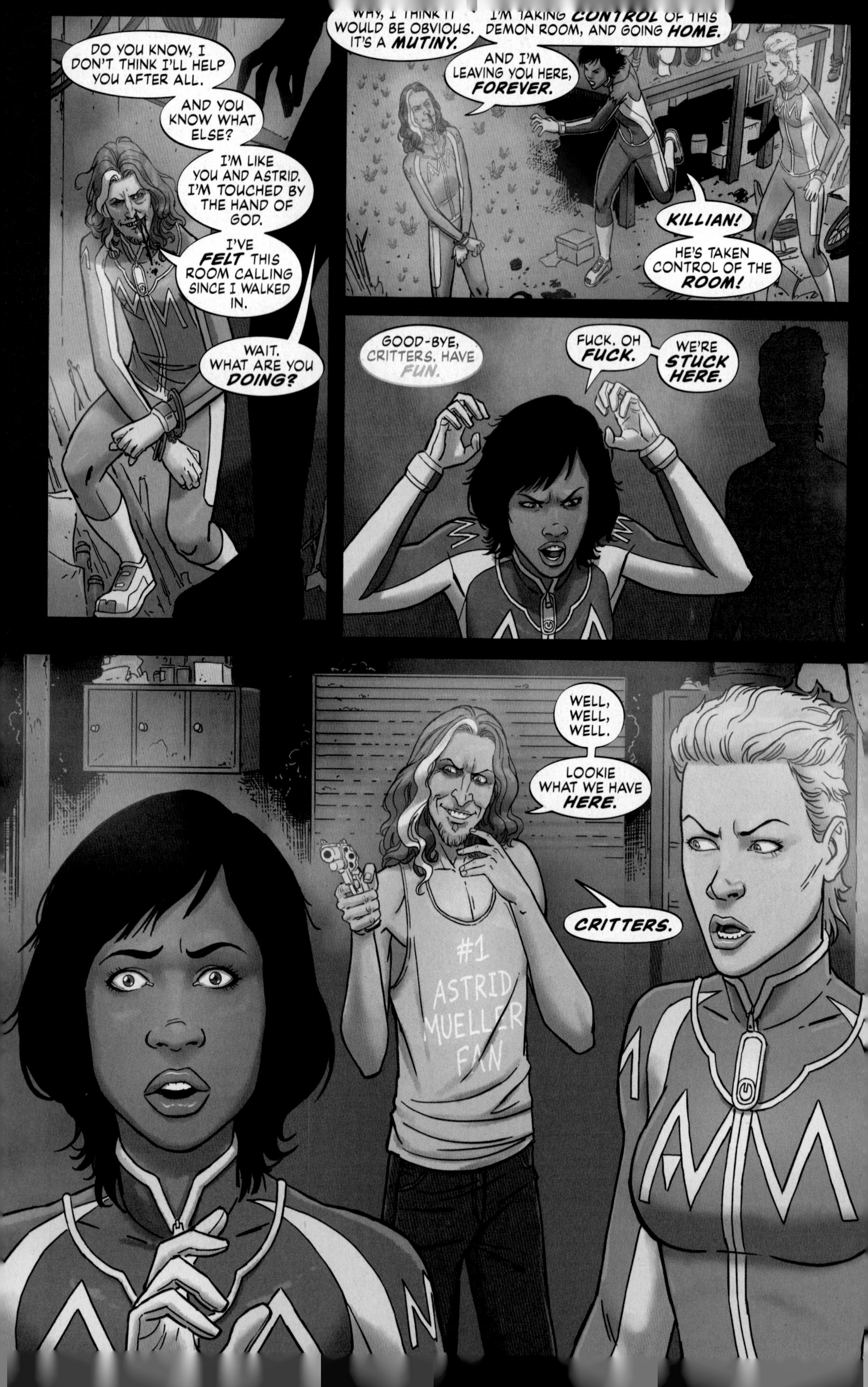
DO YOU KNOW, I DON'T THINK I'LL HELP YOU AFTER ALL.
AND YOU KNOW WHAT ELSE?
I'M LIKE YOU AND ASTRID. I'M TOUCHED BY THE HAND OF GOD.
I'VE FELT THIS ROOM CALLING SINCE I WALKED IN.
WAIT. WHAT ARE YOU DOING?
WHY, I THINK IT WOULD BE OBVIOUS. IT'S A MUTINY.
I'M TAKING CONTROL OF THIS DEMON ROOM, AND GOING HOME.
AND I'M LEAVING YOU HERE, FOREVER.
KILLIAN!
HE'S TAKEN CONTROL OF THE ROOM!
GOOD-BYE, CRITTERS. HAVE FUN.
FUCK. OH FUCK.
WE'RE STUCK HERE.
WELL, WELL, WELL.
LOOKIE WHAT WE HAVE HERE.
CRITTERS.
#1 ASTRID MUELLER FAN

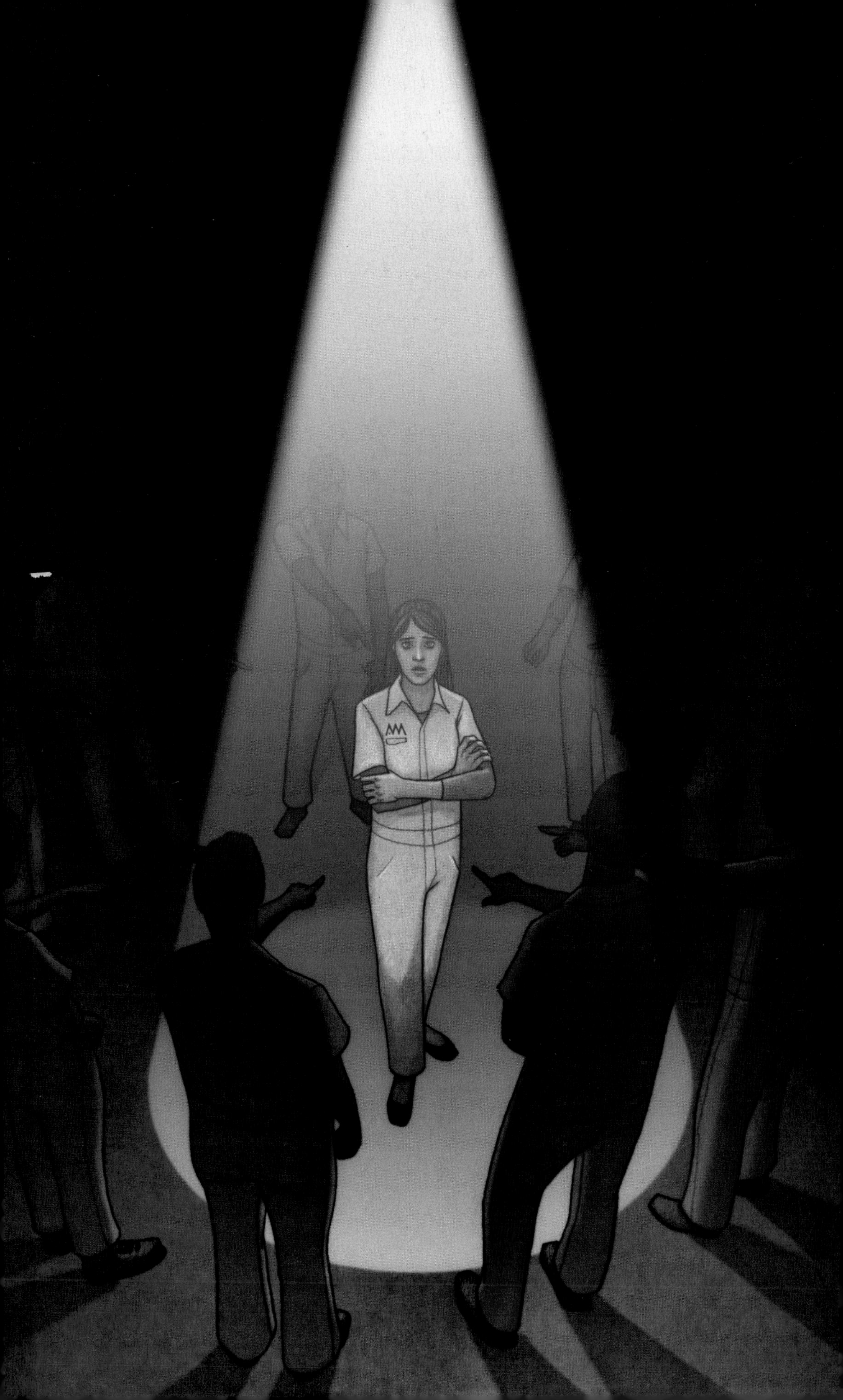

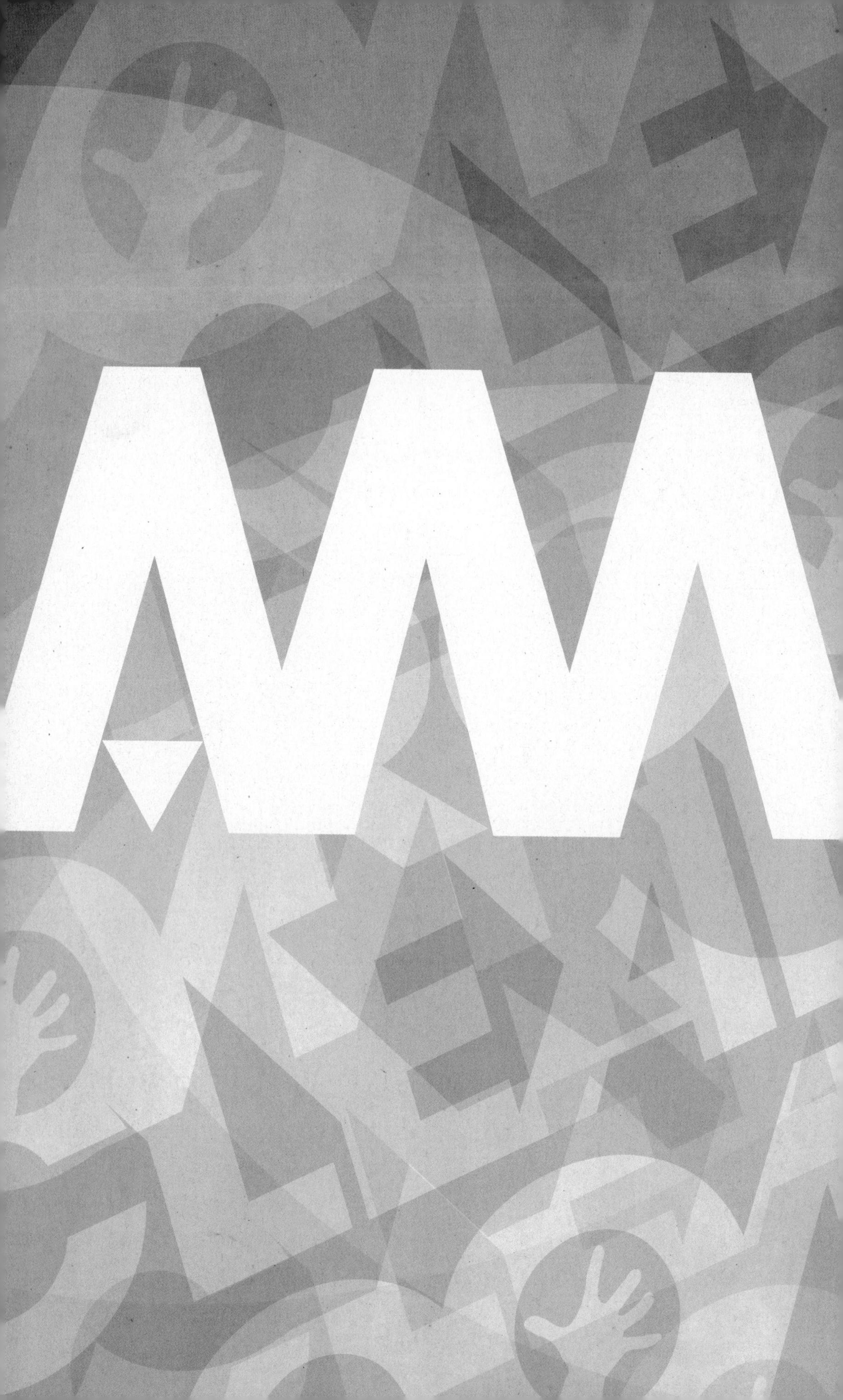

TRINITY COLLEGE.

I MET HIM ON A WHIRLWIND.

HE HAD A STUTTER, YOU KNOW.

PARDON?

LEWIS CARROLL. ONE OF THE GREATEST OF THE WORD GYMNASTS, ABLE TO MAKE WORDS ON THE PAGE SING AND LAUGH AND CAVORT LIKE RUTTING RABBITS.

STAMMERING A TREAT, IN REAL CONVERSATION.

WHICH OF HIS BOOKS ARE YOU READING?

OH, NONE. IT'S A BIOGRAPHY.

I DON'T READ FICTION.

THAT... YOU CAN'T *MEAN* IT.

ALL RIGHT, I CAN SEE THIS IS A LIFE-SAVING SITUATION.

FIRST, I'M TAKING YOU FOR A PINT. I *MIGHT* LET YOU SEE ME BARE-ASS, IF YOU TALK SWEET. BUT *THEN*...

...I WANT YOU TO READ *THIS.*

PUT *HAIR* ON YOUR CHEST, THIS WILL.

WHITEHALLED HEART

ASTRID MUP

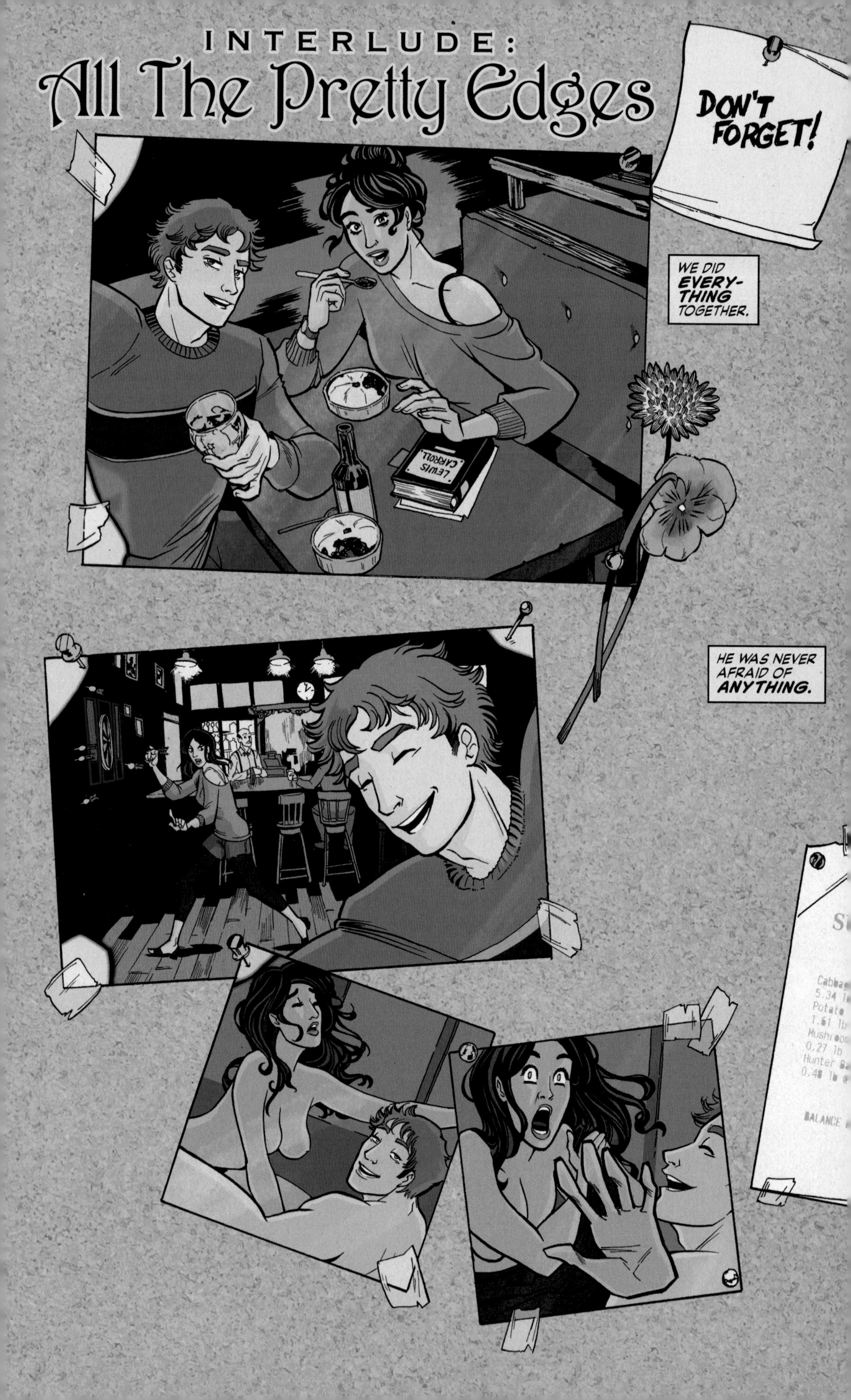
INTERLUDE:
All The Pretty Edges
DON'T FORGET!
WE DID EVERYTHING TOGETHER.
LEWIS CARROLL
HE WAS NEVER AFRAID OF ANYTHING.

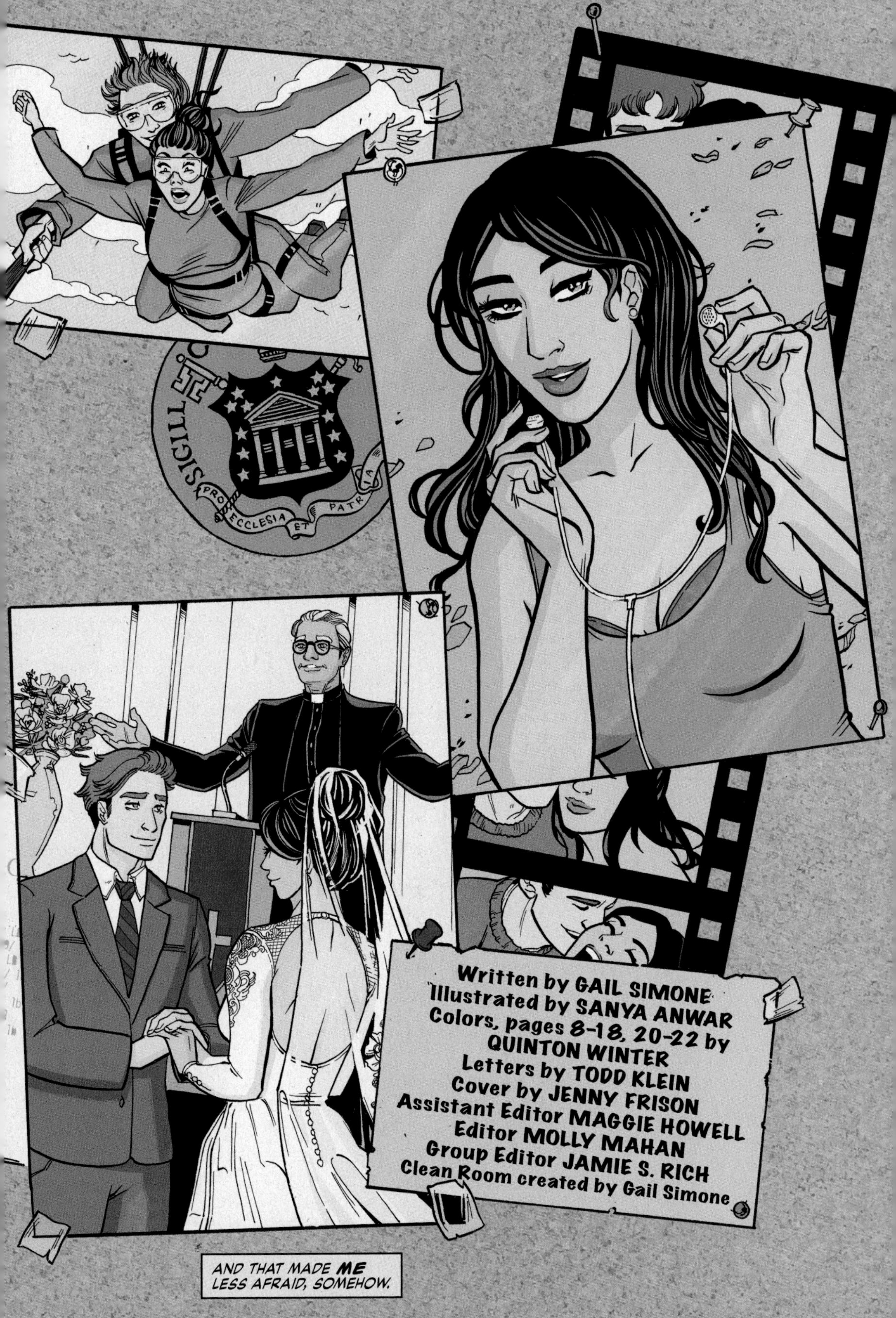
SIGILL
PRO ECCLESIA ET PATR
Written by GAIL SIMONE
Illustrated by SANYA ANWAR
Colors, pages 8-18, 20-22 by QUINTON WINTER
Letters by TODD KLEIN
Cover by JENNY FRISON
Assistant Editor MAGGIE HOWELL
Editor MOLLY MAHAN
Group Editor JAMIE S. RICH
Clean Room created by Gail Simone
AND THAT MADE ME LESS AFRAID, SOMEHOW.

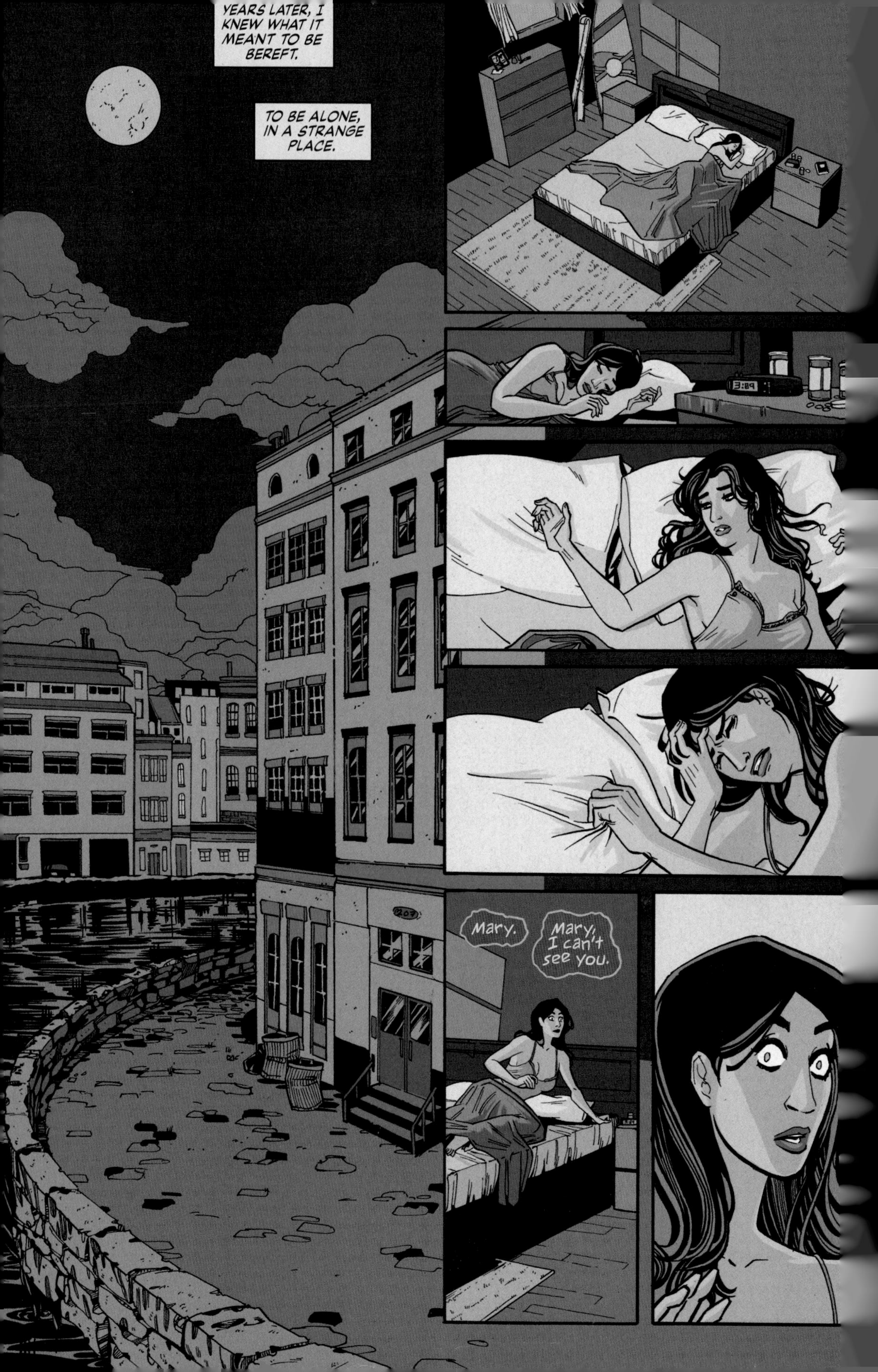
YEARS LATER, I KNEW WHAT IT MEANT TO BE BEREFT.
TO BE ALONE, IN A STRANGE PLACE.
3:09
207
Mary.
Mary, I can't see you.

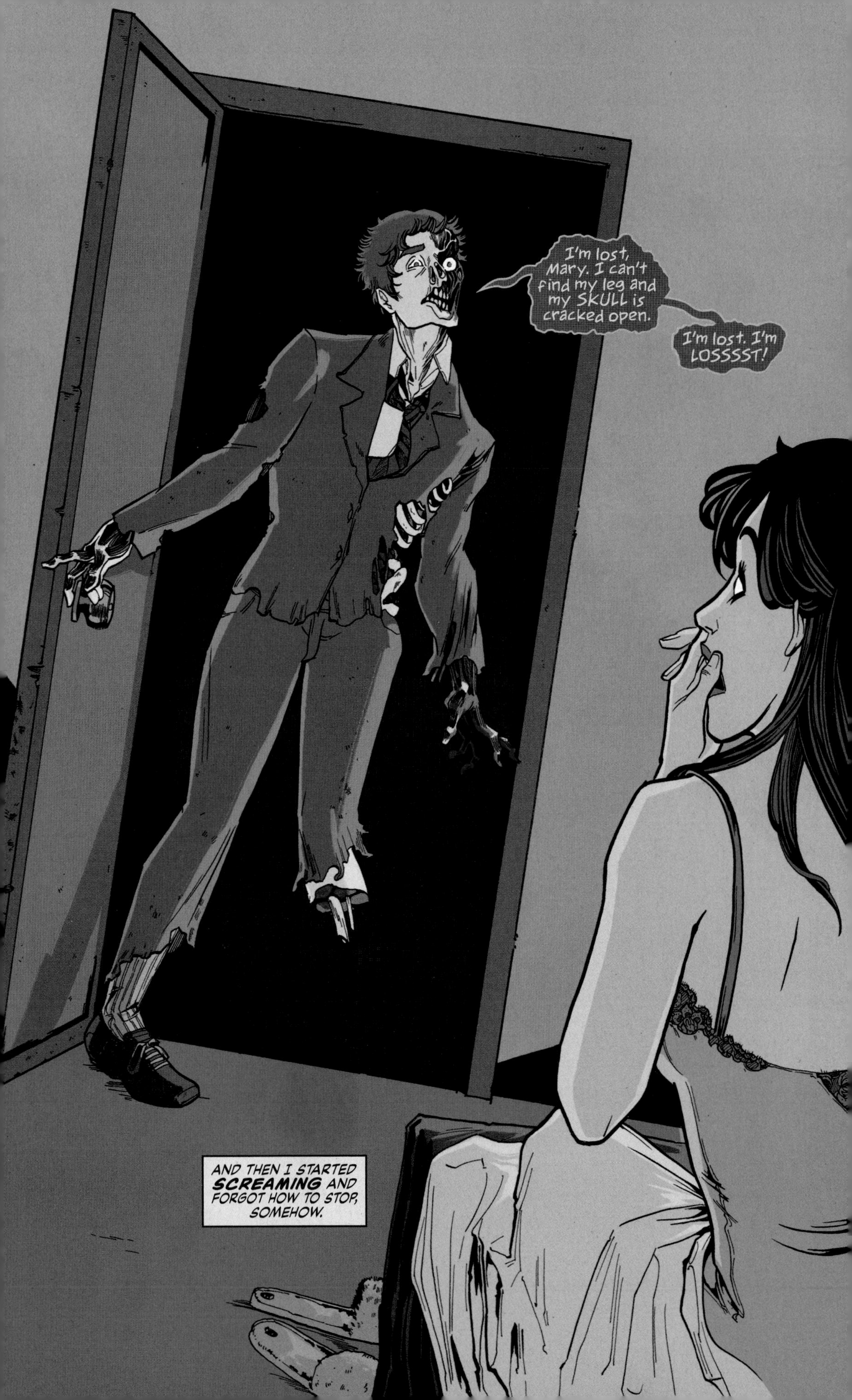
I'm lost, Mary. I can't find my leg and my SKULL is cracked open.
I'm lost. I'm LOSSSST!
AND THEN I STARTED SCREAMING AND FORGOT HOW TO STOP, SOMEHOW.

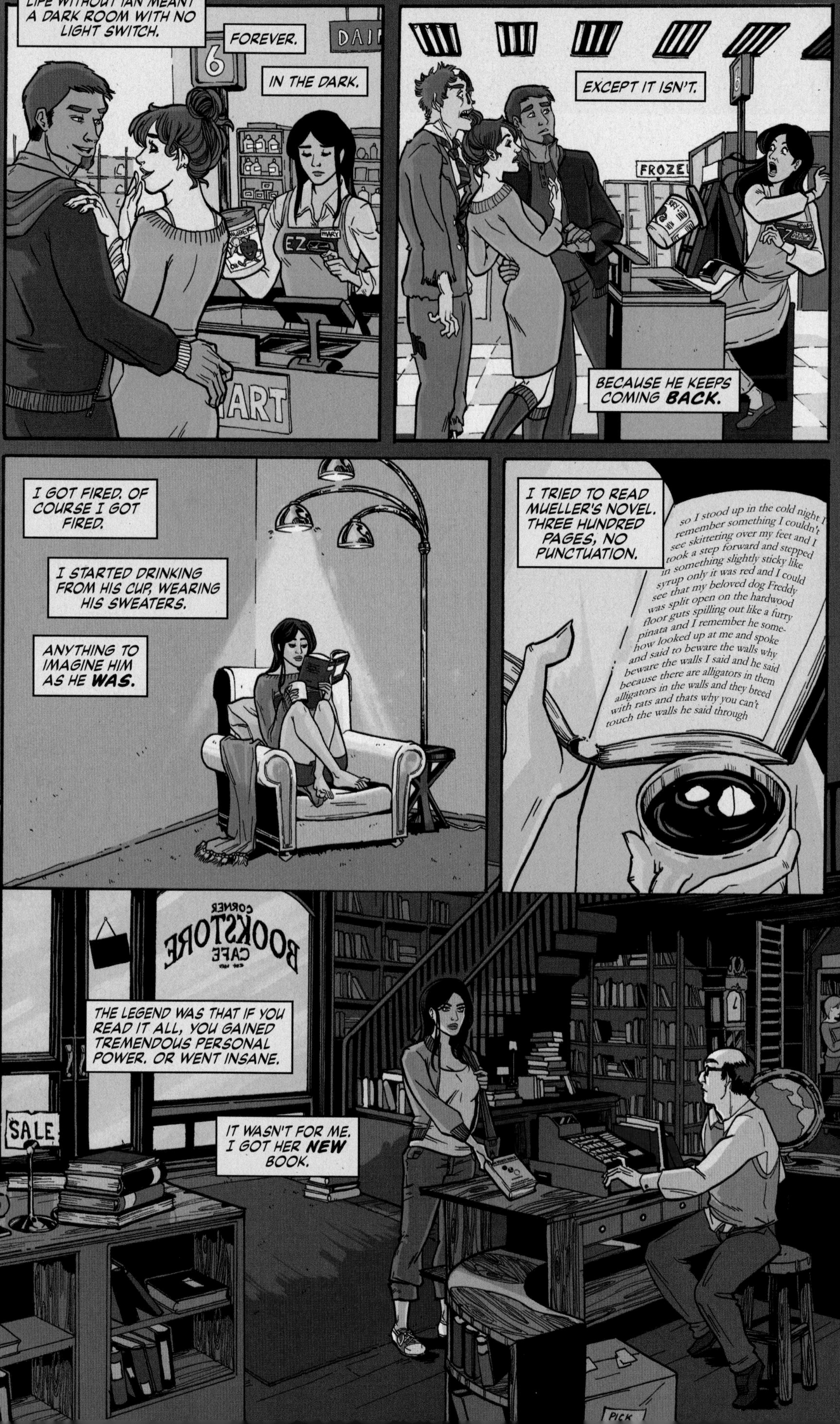
LIFE WITHOUT IAN MEANT A DARK ROOM WITH NO LIGHT SWITCH.
FOREVER.
IN THE DARK.
EXCEPT IT ISN'T.
BECAUSE HE KEEPS COMING BACK.
I GOT FIRED. OF COURSE I GOT FIRED.
I STARTED DRINKING FROM HIS CUP, WEARING HIS SWEATERS.
ANYTHING TO IMAGINE HIM AS HE WAS.
I TRIED TO READ MUELLER'S NOVEL. THREE HUNDRED PAGES, NO PUNCTUATION.
so I stood up in the cold night I
remember something I couldn't
see skittering over my feet and I
took a step forward and stepped
in something slightly sticky like
syrup only it was red and I could
see that my beloved dog Freddy
was split open on the hardwood
floor guts spilling out like a furry
pinata and I remember he somehow looked up at me and spoke
and said to beware the walls why
beware the walls I said and he said
because there are alligators in them
alligators in the walls and they breed
with rats and thats why you can't
touch the walls he said through
THE LEGEND WAS THAT IF YOU READ IT ALL, YOU GAINED TREMENDOUS PERSONAL POWER. OR WENT INSANE.
SALE
IT WASN'T FOR ME. I GOT HER NEW BOOK.

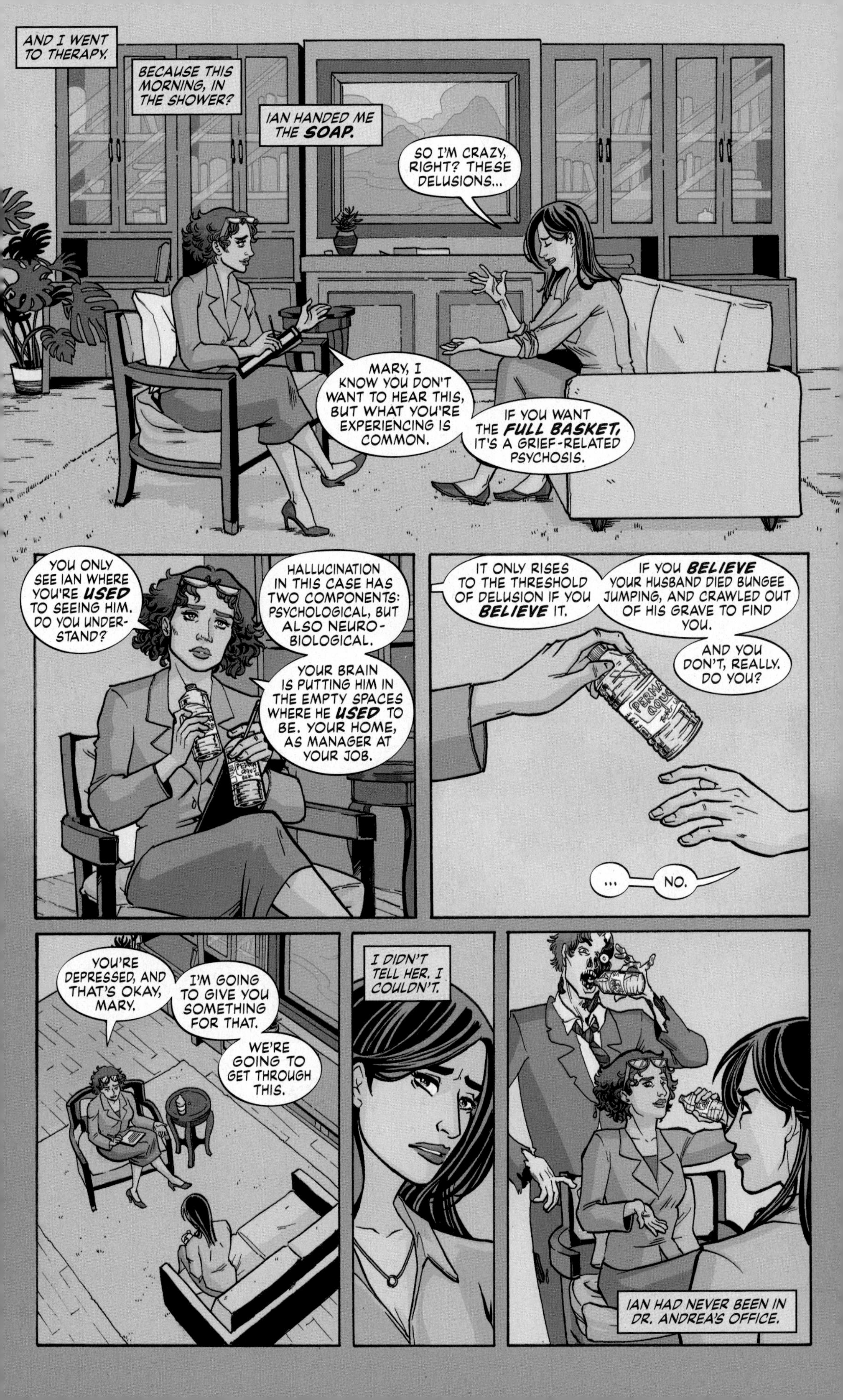
AND I WENT TO THERAPY.
BECAUSE THIS MORNING, IN THE SHOWER?
IAN HANDED ME THE SOAP.
SO I'M CRAZY, RIGHT? THESE DELUSIONS...
MARY, I KNOW YOU DON'T WANT TO HEAR THIS, BUT WHAT YOU'RE EXPERIENCING IS COMMON.
IF YOU WANT THE FULL BASKET, IT'S A GRIEF-RELATED PSYCHOSIS.
YOU ONLY SEE IAN WHERE YOU'RE USED TO SEEING HIM. DO YOU UNDERSTAND?
HALLUCINATION IN THIS CASE HAS TWO COMPONENTS: PSYCHOLOGICAL, BUT ALSO NEUROBIOLOGICAL.
YOUR BRAIN IS PUTTING HIM IN THE EMPTY SPACES WHERE HE USED TO BE. YOUR HOME, AS MANAGER AT YOUR JOB.
IT ONLY RISES TO THE THRESHOLD OF DELUSION IF YOU BELIEVE IT.
IF YOU BELIEVE YOUR HUSBAND DIED BUNGEE JUMPING, AND CRAWLED OUT OF HIS GRAVE TO FIND YOU.
AND YOU DON'T, REALLY. DO YOU?
...
NO.
YOU'RE DEPRESSED, AND THAT'S OKAY, MARY.
I'M GOING TO GIVE YOU SOMETHING FOR THAT.
WE'RE GOING TO GET THROUGH THIS.
I DIDN'T TELL HER. I COULDN'T.
IAN HAD NEVER BEEN IN DR. ANDREA'S OFFICE.

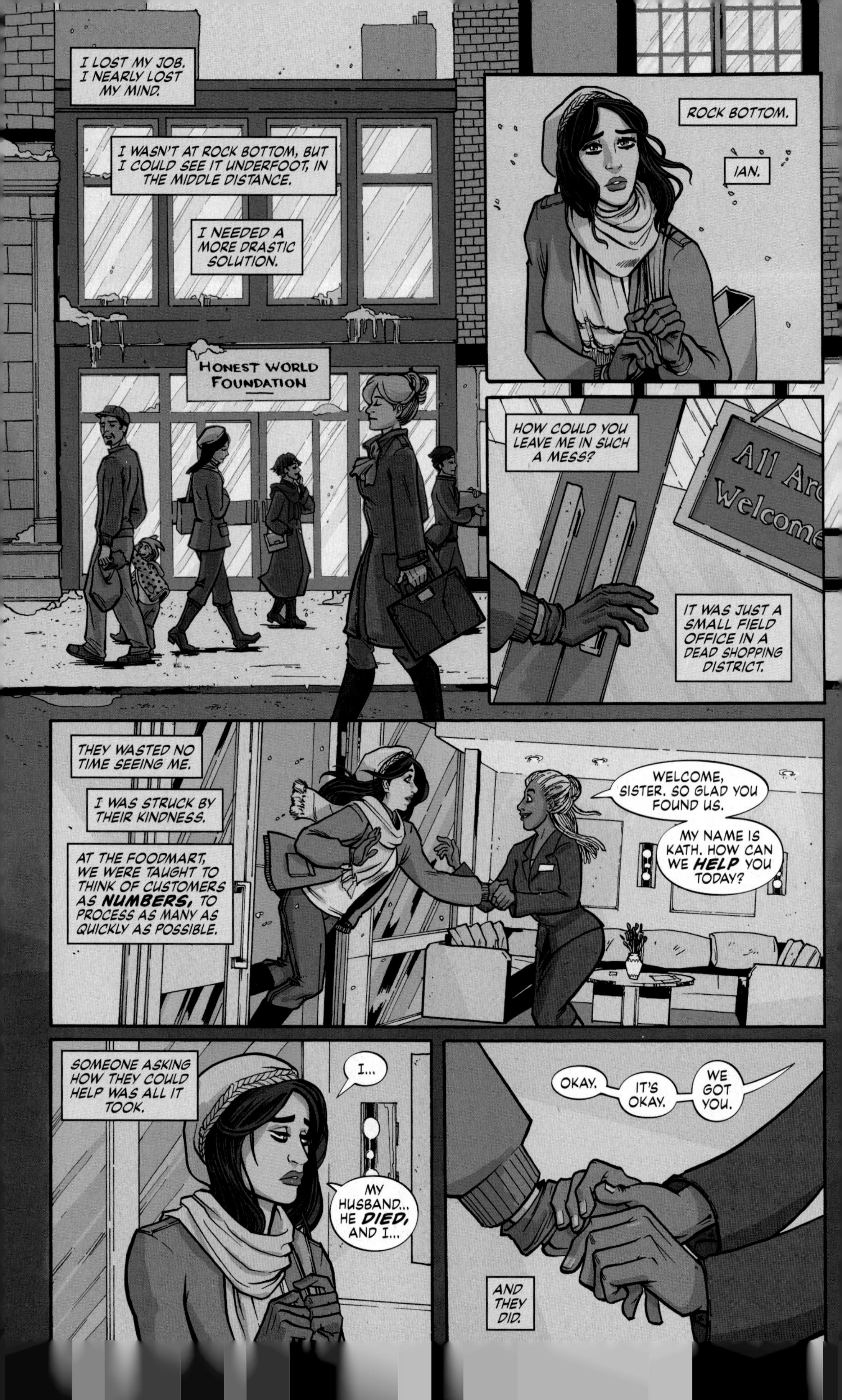

I LOST MY JOB. I NEARLY LOST MY MIND.
I WASN'T AT ROCK BOTTOM, BUT I COULD SEE IT UNDERFOOT, IN THE MIDDLE DISTANCE.
I NEEDED A MORE DRASTIC SOLUTION.
HONEST WORLD FOUNDATION
ROCK BOTTOM.
IAN.
HOW COULD YOU LEAVE ME IN SUCH A MESS?
All Are Welcome
IT WAS JUST A SMALL FIELD OFFICE IN A DEAD SHOPPING DISTRICT.
THEY WASTED NO TIME SEEING ME.
I WAS STRUCK BY THEIR KINDNESS.
AT THE FOODMART, WE WERE TAUGHT TO THINK OF CUSTOMERS AS **NUMBERS**, TO PROCESS AS MANY AS QUICKLY AS POSSIBLE.
WELCOME, SISTER. SO GLAD YOU FOUND US.
MY NAME IS KATH. HOW CAN WE ***HELP*** YOU TODAY?
SOMEONE ASKING HOW THEY COULD HELP WAS ALL IT TOOK.
I...
MY HUSBAND... HE ***DIED***, AND I...
OKAY.
IT'S OKAY.
WE GOT YOU.
AND THEY DID.

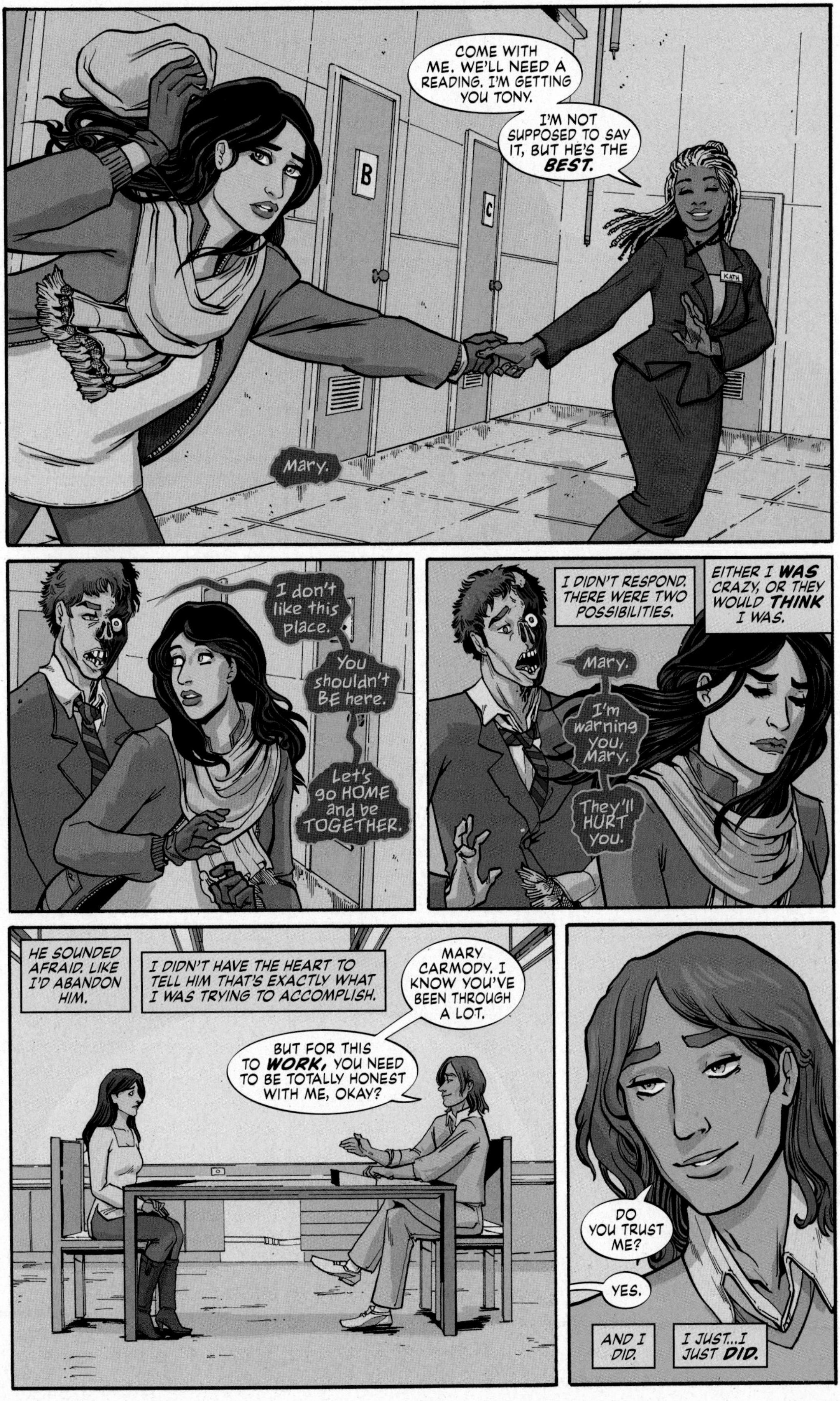
COME WITH ME. WE'LL NEED A READING. I'M GETTING YOU TONY.
I'M NOT SUPPOSED TO SAY IT, BUT HE'S THE BEST.
Mary.
I don't like this place.
You shouldn't BE here.
Let's go HOME and be TOGETHER.
I DIDN'T RESPOND. THERE WERE TWO POSSIBILITIES.
EITHER I WAS CRAZY, OR THEY WOULD THINK I WAS.
Mary.
I'm warning you, Mary.
They'll HURT you.
HE SOUNDED AFRAID. LIKE I'D ABANDON HIM.
I DIDN'T HAVE THE HEART TO TELL HIM THAT'S EXACTLY WHAT I WAS TRYING TO ACCOMPLISH.
MARY CARMODY. I KNOW YOU'VE BEEN THROUGH A LOT.
BUT FOR THIS TO WORK, YOU NEED TO BE TOTALLY HONEST WITH ME, OKAY?
DO YOU TRUST ME?
YES.
AND I DID.
I JUST...I JUST DID.

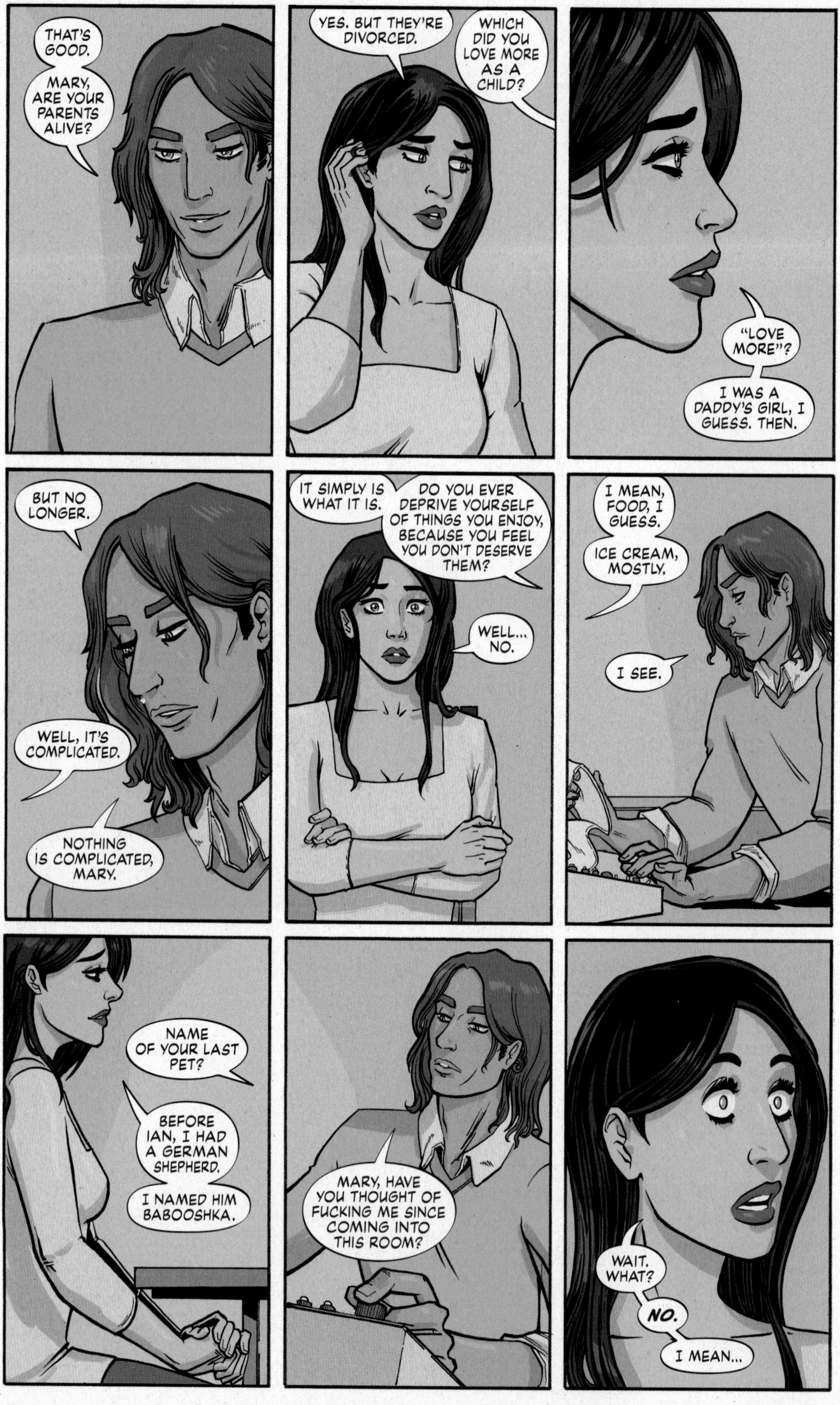
THAT'S GOOD.
MARY, ARE YOUR PARENTS ALIVE?
YES. BUT THEY'RE DIVORCED.
WHICH DID YOU LOVE MORE AS A CHILD?
"LOVE MORE"?
I WAS A DADDY'S GIRL, I GUESS. THEN.
BUT NO LONGER.
WELL, IT'S COMPLICATED.
NOTHING IS COMPLICATED, MARY.
IT SIMPLY IS WHAT IT IS.
DO YOU EVER DEPRIVE YOURSELF OF THINGS YOU ENJOY, BECAUSE YOU FEEL YOU DON'T DESERVE THEM?
WELL... NO.
I MEAN, FOOD, I GUESS.
ICE CREAM, MOSTLY.
I SEE.
NAME OF YOUR LAST PET?
BEFORE IAN, I HAD A GERMAN SHEPHERD.
I NAMED HIM BABOOSHKA.
MARY, HAVE YOU THOUGHT OF FUCKING ME SINCE COMING INTO THIS ROOM?
WAIT. WHAT?
NO.
I MEAN...

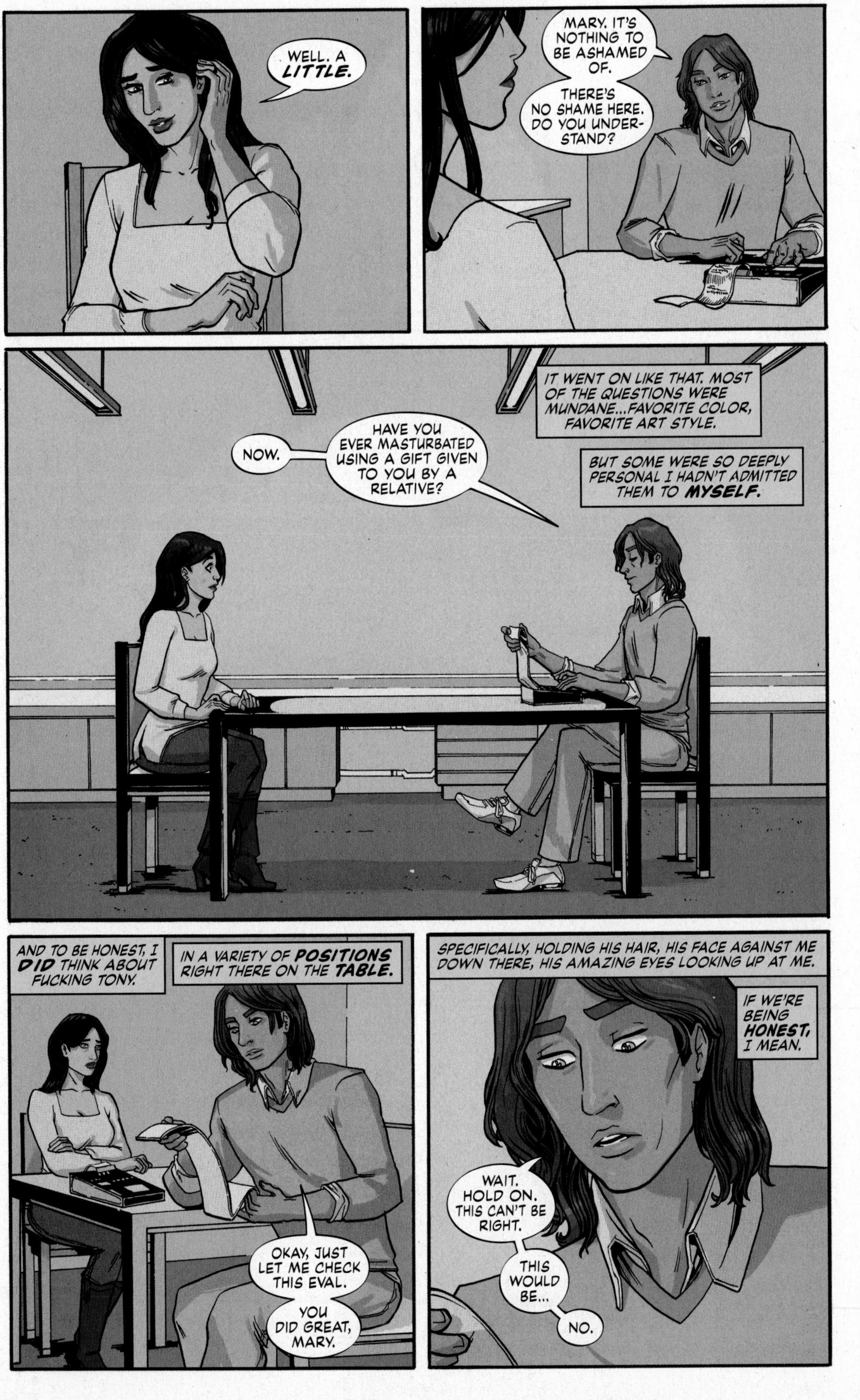
WELL. A **LITTLE.**
MARY. IT'S NOTHING TO BE ASHAMED OF.
THERE'S NO SHAME HERE. DO YOU UNDERSTAND?
IT WENT ON LIKE THAT. MOST OF THE QUESTIONS WERE MUNDANE...FAVORITE COLOR, FAVORITE ART STYLE.
BUT SOME WERE SO DEEPLY PERSONAL I HADN'T ADMITTED THEM TO **MYSELF.**
NOW.
HAVE YOU EVER MASTURBATED USING A GIFT GIVEN TO YOU BY A RELATIVE?
AND TO BE HONEST, I **DID** THINK ABOUT FUCKING TONY.
IN A VARIETY OF **POSITIONS** RIGHT THERE ON THE **TABLE.**
OKAY, JUST LET ME CHECK THIS EVAL.
YOU DID GREAT, MARY.
SPECIFICALLY, HOLDING HIS HAIR, HIS FACE AGAINST ME DOWN THERE, HIS AMAZING EYES LOOKING UP AT ME.
IF WE'RE BEING **HONEST,** I MEAN.
WAIT. HOLD ON. THIS CAN'T BE RIGHT.
THIS WOULD BE...
NO.

TONY SAID HE HAD TO TALK TO HIS SUPERVISOR. HE SAID IT WAS CRUCIAL.

TONY, ARE YOU *SURE?*

DERRICK, I KNOW.

BUT I CHECKED THE EVAL *THREE TIMES.*

EXCUSE ME. WHAT'S GOING ON?

MARY. WE'VE NEVER *SEEN* A READING LIKE YOURS. IT'S OFF THE SCALE.

NEVER EVEN *HEARD* OF ONE LIKE THIS!

UNLIMITED POTENTIAL.

MARY, YOU COULD CHANGE THE *WORLD.*

THEY LOOKED AT ME AND SAW ME FOR WHAT I REALLY AM.

WHAT I COULD *BE.*

I COULDN'T *WAIT* TO GO THROUGH THE ADEPT PROGRAM.

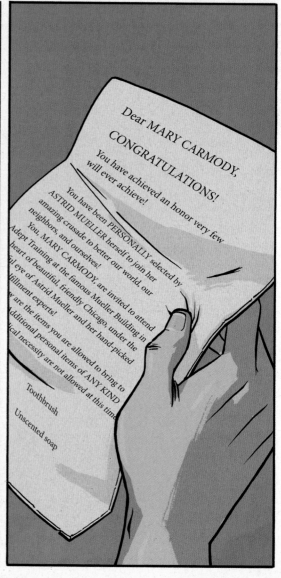

Dear MARY CARMODY,

CONGRATULATIONS!

You have achieved an honor very few will ever achieve!

You have been PERSONALLY selected by ASTRID MUELLER herself to join her amazing crusade to better our world, our neighbors, and ourselves!

You, MARY CARMODY, are invited to attend Adept Training at the famous Mueller Building in the heart of beautiful, friendly Chicago, under the careful eye of Astrid Mueller and her hand-picked fulfillment experts!

Below are the items you are allowed to bring to you. Additional personal items of ANY KIND except medical necessity are not allowed at this time.

Toothbrush

Unscented soap

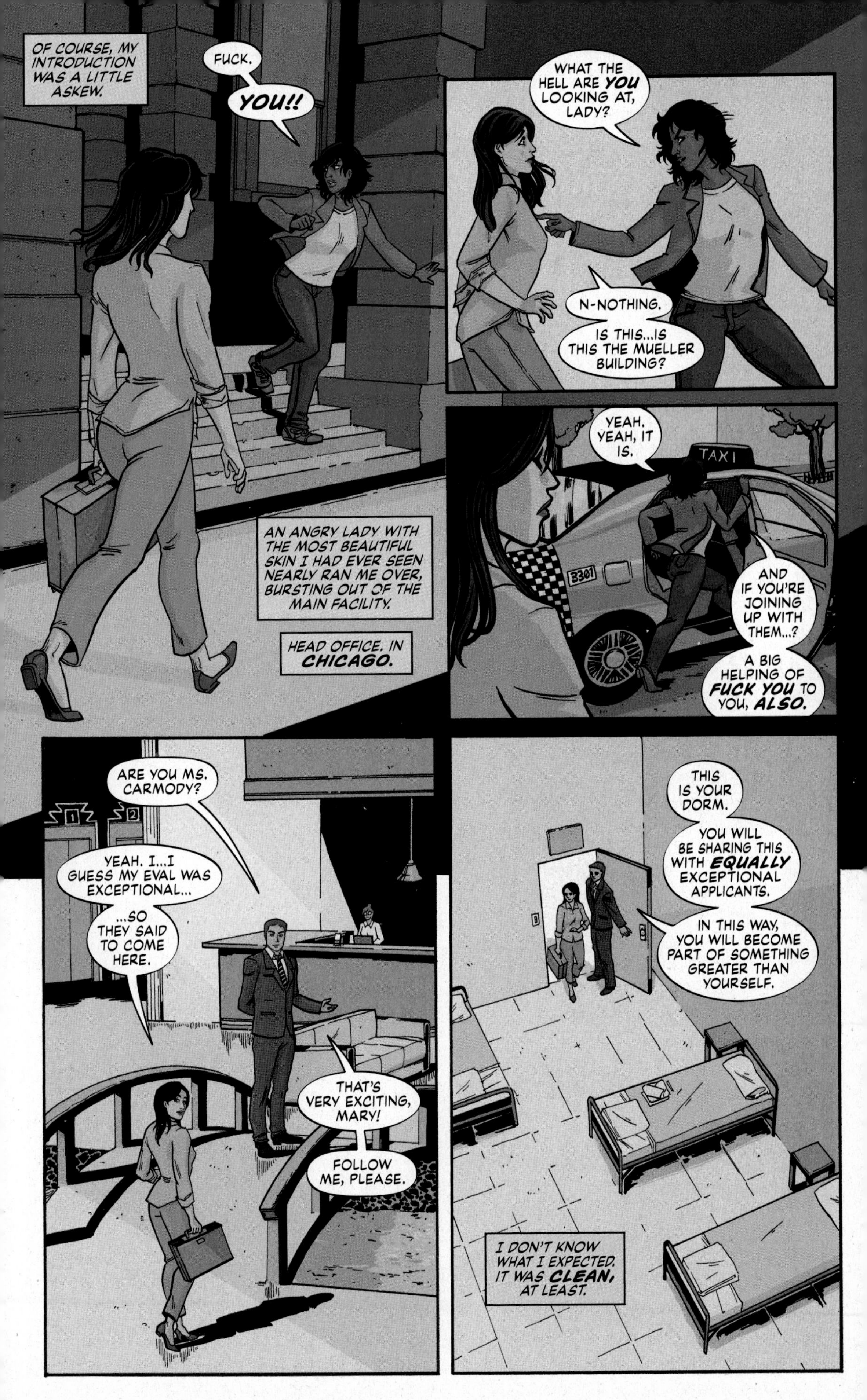

OF COURSE, MY INTRODUCTION WAS A LITTLE ASKEW.
FUCK.
YOU!!
AN ANGRY LADY WITH THE MOST BEAUTIFUL SKIN I HAD EVER SEEN NEARLY RAN ME OVER, BURSTING OUT OF THE MAIN FACILITY.
HEAD OFFICE. IN CHICAGO.
WHAT THE HELL ARE YOU LOOKING AT, LADY?
N-NOTHING.
IS THIS...IS THIS THE MUELLER BUILDING?
YEAH. YEAH, IT IS.
TAXI
3301
AND IF YOU'RE JOINING UP WITH THEM...?
A BIG HELPING OF FUCK YOU TO YOU, ALSO.
ARE YOU MS. CARMODY?
YEAH. I...I GUESS MY EVAL WAS EXCEPTIONAL...
...SO THEY SAID TO COME HERE.
THAT'S VERY EXCITING, MARY!
FOLLOW ME, PLEASE.
THIS IS YOUR DORM.
YOU WILL BE SHARING THIS WITH EQUALLY EXCEPTIONAL APPLICANTS.
IN THIS WAY, YOU WILL BECOME PART OF SOMETHING GREATER THAN YOURSELF.
I DON'T KNOW WHAT I EXPECTED. IT WAS CLEAN, AT LEAST.

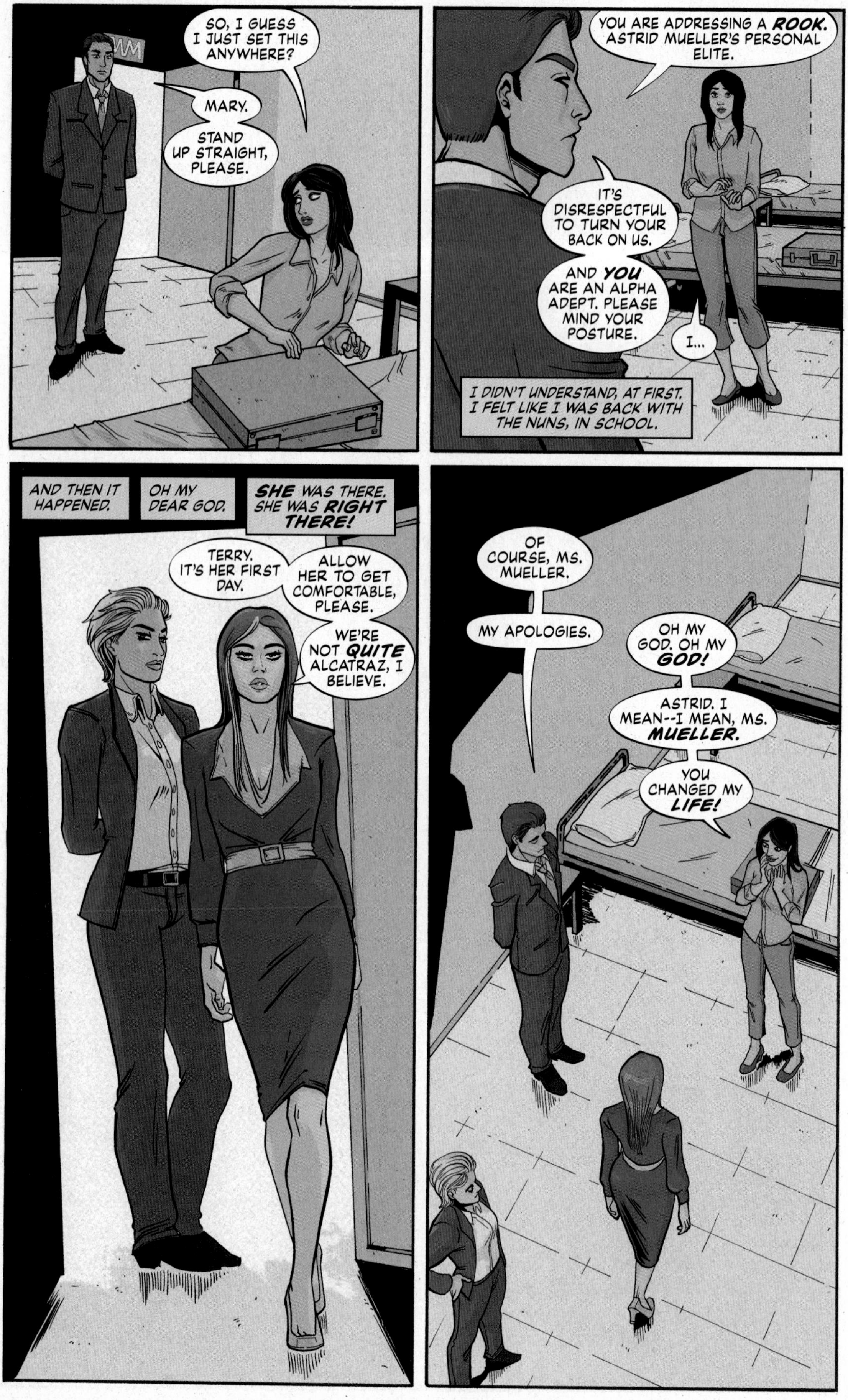
SO, I GUESS I JUST SET THIS ANYWHERE?
MARY.
STAND UP STRAIGHT, PLEASE.
YOU ARE ADDRESSING A ROOK. ASTRID MUELLER'S PERSONAL ELITE.
IT'S DISRESPECTFUL TO TURN YOUR BACK ON US.
AND YOU ARE AN ALPHA ADEPT. PLEASE MIND YOUR POSTURE.
I...
I DIDN'T UNDERSTAND, AT FIRST. I FELT LIKE I WAS BACK WITH THE NUNS, IN SCHOOL.
AND THEN IT HAPPENED.
OH MY DEAR GOD.
SHE WAS THERE. SHE WAS RIGHT THERE!
TERRY. IT'S HER FIRST DAY.
ALLOW HER TO GET COMFORTABLE, PLEASE.
WE'RE NOT QUITE ALCATRAZ, I BELIEVE.
OF COURSE, MS. MUELLER.
MY APOLOGIES.
OH MY GOD. OH MY GOD!
ASTRID. I MEAN--I MEAN, MS. MUELLER.
YOU CHANGED MY LIFE!

SHE LOOKED AT ME QUIETLY FOR A LONG TIME.

I NEVER HAD TO PEE SO BAD IN MY **LIFE**.

I'M SO GLAD.

MIND TERRY'S GUIDANCE. WE'RE ALL HERE TO HELP YOU ACHIEVE YOUR POTENTIAL.

ENJOY YOUR NEW LIFE, MARY.

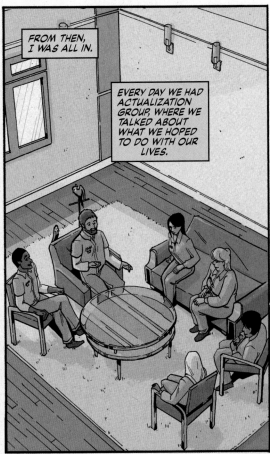

FROM THEN, I WAS ALL IN.

EVERY DAY WE HAD ACTUALIZATION GROUP, WHERE WE TALKED ABOUT WHAT WE HOPED TO DO WITH OUR LIVES.

OUR GROUP MENTOR WAS CANADIAN, AND JUST AS NICE AS THE STEREOTYPE.

HE USED TO BE A PASTOR, IF YOU CAN BELIEVE IT. "PASTOR MATT," WE CALLED HIM.

I LOVED IT. IT WAS PEOPLE BEING KIND. AND **GENUINELY** INTERESTED.

BUT EVEN MORE, I LOVED THAT PASTOR MATT RAISED PARROTS.

I NEVER REALIZED HOW BEAUTIFUL THEY WERE.

ALL COLOR AND WISDOM.

AND YET, THEY WERE USUALLY CAGED, AS IF THOSE THINGS WERE ONLY TOLERABLE IN SMALL, CONTROLLED BURSTS.

WE DID HIGHWAY RECLAMATION. VISIBLE VOLUNTEER WORK.

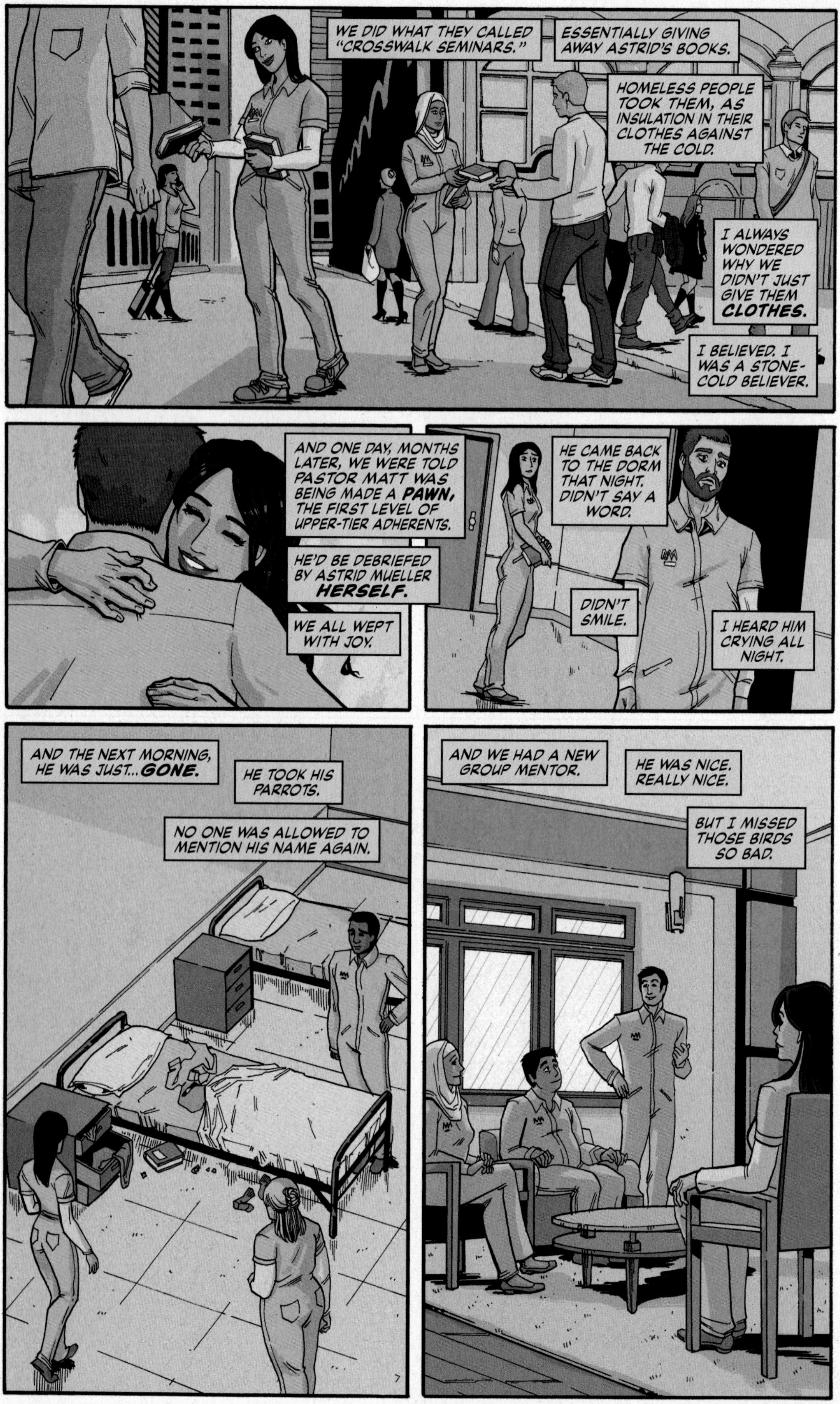
WE DID WHAT THEY CALLED "CROSSWALK SEMINARS."
ESSENTIALLY GIVING AWAY ASTRID'S BOOKS.
HOMELESS PEOPLE TOOK THEM, AS INSULATION IN THEIR CLOTHES AGAINST THE COLD.
I ALWAYS WONDERED WHY WE DIDN'T JUST GIVE THEM **CLOTHES.**
I BELIEVED. I WAS A STONE-COLD BELIEVER.
AND ONE DAY, MONTHS LATER, WE WERE TOLD PASTOR MATT WAS BEING MADE A **PAWN,** THE FIRST LEVEL OF UPPER-TIER ADHERENTS.
HE'D BE DEBRIEFED BY ASTRID MUELLER **HERSELF.**
WE ALL WEPT WITH JOY.
HE CAME BACK TO THE DORM THAT NIGHT. DIDN'T SAY A WORD.
DIDN'T SMILE.
I HEARD HIM CRYING ALL NIGHT.
AND THE NEXT MORNING, HE WAS JUST... **GONE.**
HE TOOK HIS PARROTS.
NO ONE WAS ALLOWED TO MENTION HIS NAME AGAIN.
AND WE HAD A NEW GROUP MENTOR.
HE WAS NICE. REALLY NICE.
BUT I MISSED THOSE BIRDS SO BAD.

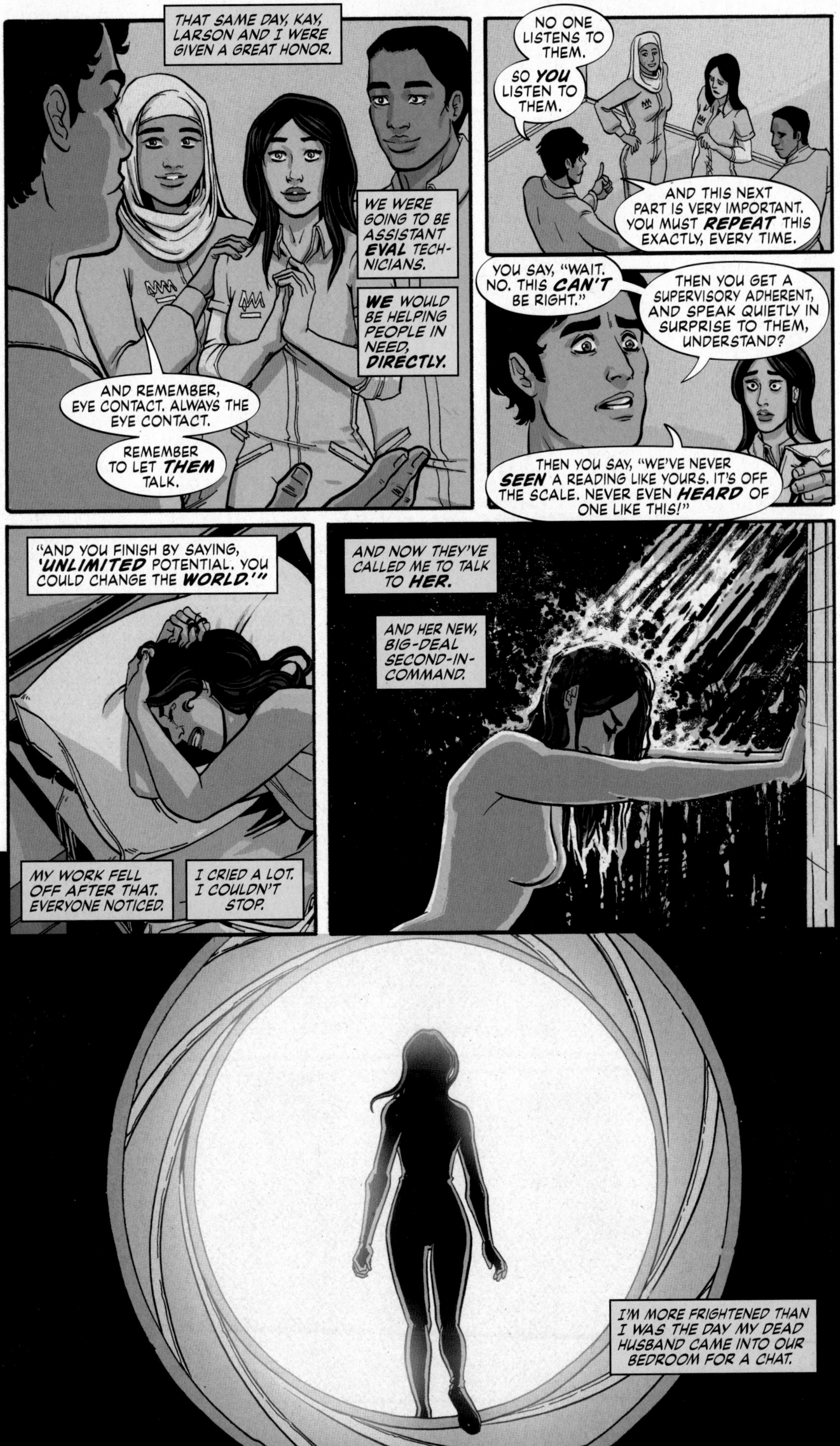

THAT SAME DAY, KAY, LARSON AND I WERE GIVEN A GREAT HONOR.
WE WERE GOING TO BE ASSISTANT EVAL TECHNICIANS.
WE WOULD BE HELPING PEOPLE IN NEED, DIRECTLY.
AND REMEMBER, EYE CONTACT. ALWAYS THE EYE CONTACT.
REMEMBER TO LET THEM TALK.
NO ONE LISTENS TO THEM.
SO YOU LISTEN TO THEM.
AND THIS NEXT PART IS VERY IMPORTANT. YOU MUST REPEAT THIS EXACTLY, EVERY TIME.
YOU SAY, "WAIT. NO. THIS CAN'T BE RIGHT."
THEN YOU GET A SUPERVISORY ADHERENT, AND SPEAK QUIETLY IN SURPRISE TO THEM, UNDERSTAND?
THEN YOU SAY, "WE'VE NEVER SEEN A READING LIKE YOURS. IT'S OFF THE SCALE. NEVER EVEN HEARD OF ONE LIKE THIS!"
"AND YOU FINISH BY SAYING, 'UNLIMITED POTENTIAL. YOU COULD CHANGE THE WORLD.'"
MY WORK FELL OFF AFTER THAT. EVERYONE NOTICED.
I CRIED A LOT. I COULDN'T STOP.
AND NOW THEY'VE CALLED ME TO TALK TO HER.
AND HER NEW, BIG-DEAL SECOND-IN-COMMAND.
I'M MORE FRIGHTENED THAN I WAS THE DAY MY DEAD HUSBAND CAME INTO OUR BEDROOM FOR A CHAT.

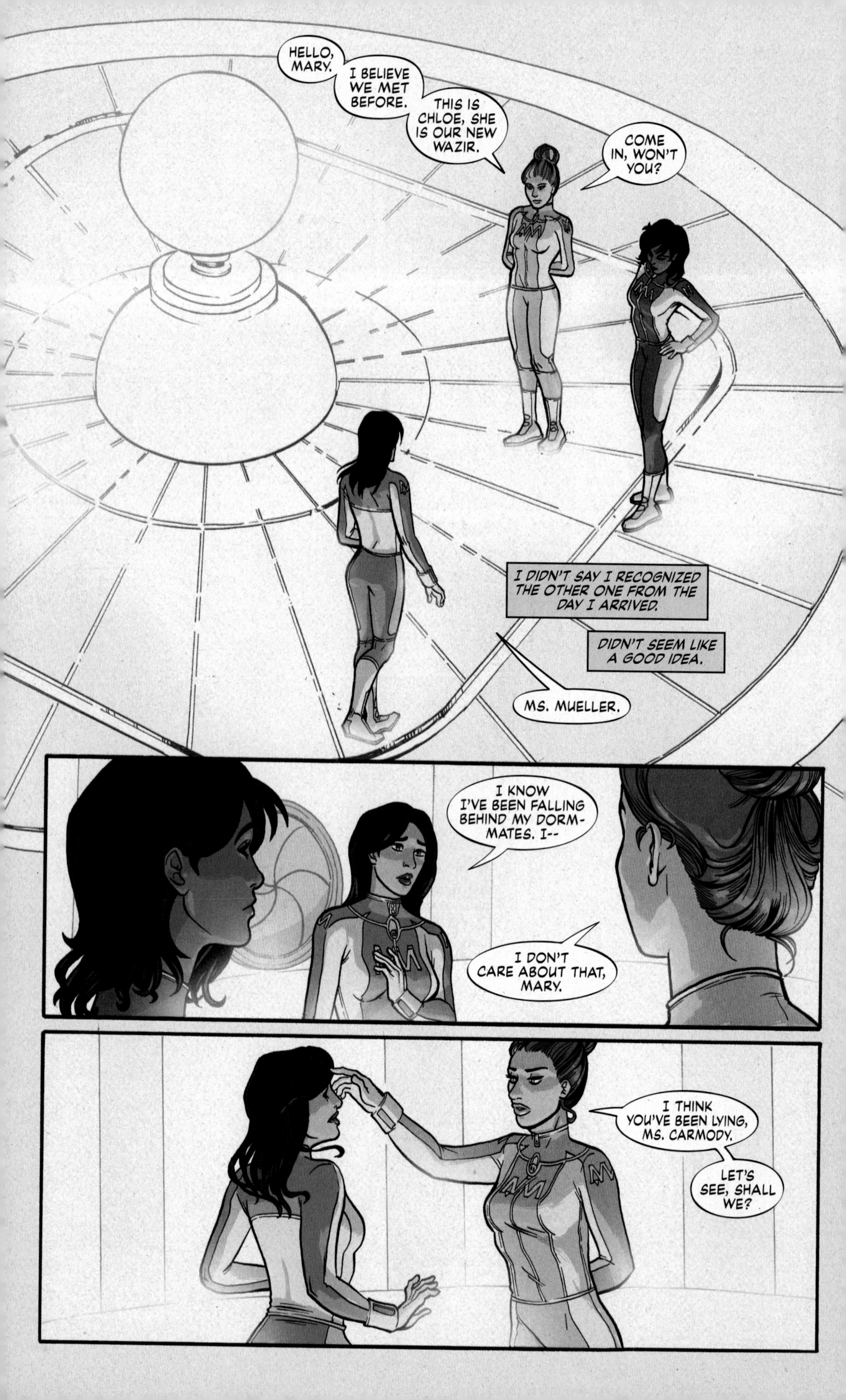
HELLO, MARY.
I BELIEVE WE MET BEFORE.
THIS IS CHLOE, SHE IS OUR NEW WAZIR.
COME IN, WON'T YOU?
I DIDN'T SAY I RECOGNIZED THE OTHER ONE FROM THE DAY I ARRIVED.
DIDN'T SEEM LIKE A GOOD IDEA.
MS. MUELLER.
I KNOW I'VE BEEN FALLING BEHIND MY DORM-MATES. I--
I DON'T CARE ABOUT THAT, MARY.
I THINK YOU'VE BEEN LYING, MS. CARMODY.
LET'S SEE, SHALL WE?

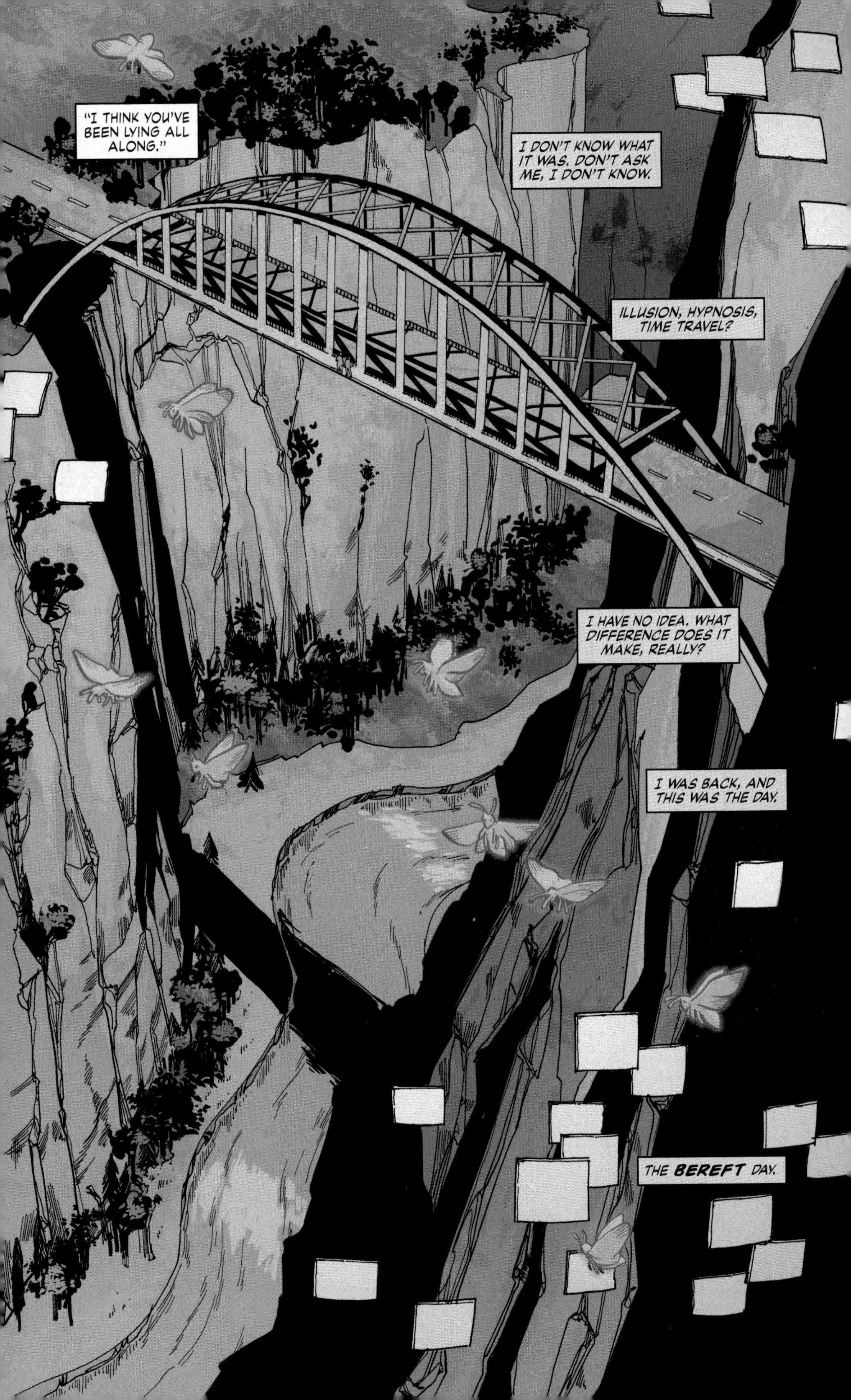
"I THINK YOU'VE BEEN LYING ALL ALONG."
I DON'T KNOW WHAT IT WAS. DON'T ASK ME, I DON'T KNOW.
ILLUSION, HYPNOSIS, TIME TRAVEL?
I HAVE NO IDEA. WHAT DIFFERENCE DOES IT MAKE, REALLY?
I WAS BACK, AND THIS WAS THE DAY.
THE BEREFT DAY.

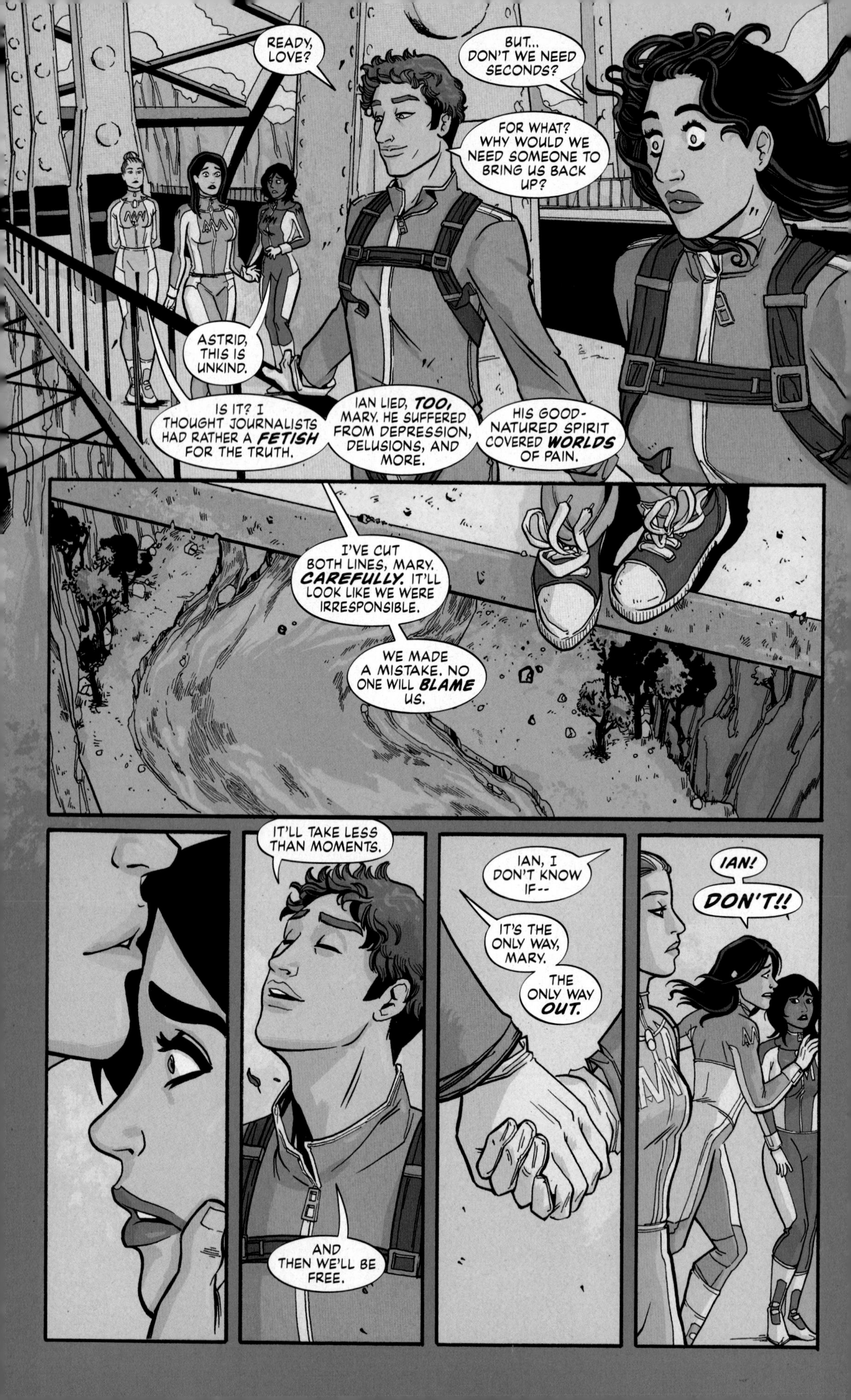
READY, LOVE?
BUT... DON'T WE NEED SECONDS?
FOR WHAT? WHY WOULD WE NEED SOMEONE TO BRING US BACK UP?
ASTRID, THIS IS UNKIND.
IS IT? I THOUGHT JOURNALISTS HAD RATHER A FETISH FOR THE TRUTH.
IAN LIED, TOO, MARY. HE SUFFERED FROM DEPRESSION, DELUSIONS, AND MORE.
HIS GOOD-NATURED SPIRIT COVERED WORLDS OF PAIN.
I'VE CUT BOTH LINES, MARY. CAREFULLY. IT'LL LOOK LIKE WE WERE IRRESPONSIBLE.
WE MADE A MISTAKE. NO ONE WILL BLAME US.
IT'LL TAKE LESS THAN MOMENTS.
AND THEN WE'LL BE FREE.
IAN, I DON'T KNOW IF--
IT'S THE ONLY WAY, MARY.
THE ONLY WAY OUT.
IAN!
DON'T!!

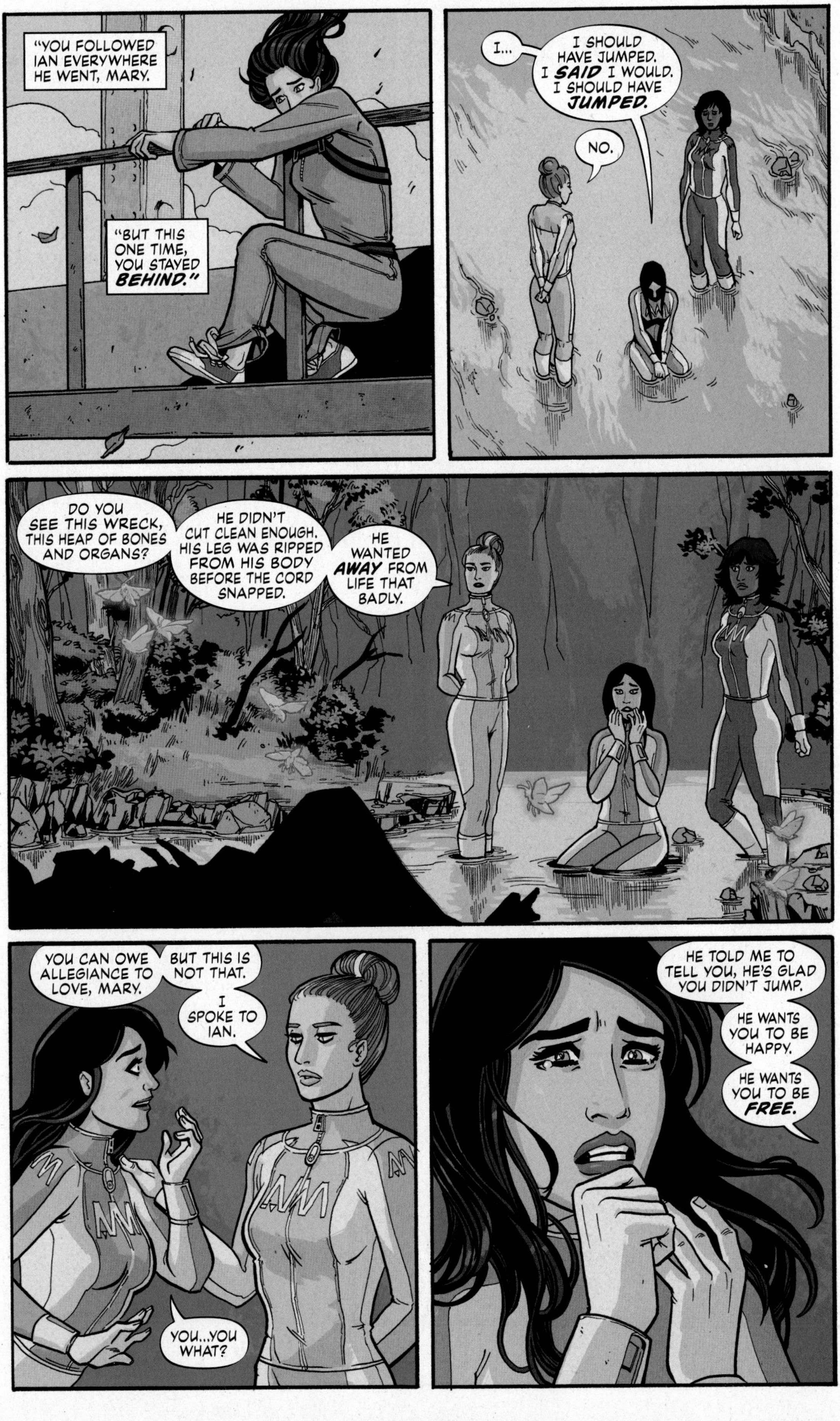
"YOU FOLLOWED IAN EVERYWHERE HE WENT, MARY.
"BUT THIS ONE TIME, YOU STAYED **BEHIND.**"
I...
I SHOULD HAVE JUMPED. I **SAID** I WOULD. I SHOULD HAVE **JUMPED.**
NO.
DO YOU SEE THIS WRECK, THIS HEAP OF BONES AND ORGANS?
HE DIDN'T CUT CLEAN ENOUGH. HIS LEG WAS RIPPED FROM HIS BODY BEFORE THE CORD SNAPPED.
HE WANTED **AWAY** FROM LIFE THAT BADLY.
YOU CAN OWE ALLEGIANCE TO LOVE, MARY.
BUT THIS IS NOT THAT.
I SPOKE TO IAN.
YOU...YOU WHAT?
HE TOLD ME TO TELL YOU, HE'S GLAD YOU DIDN'T JUMP.
HE WANTS YOU TO BE HAPPY.
HE WANTS YOU TO BE **FREE.**

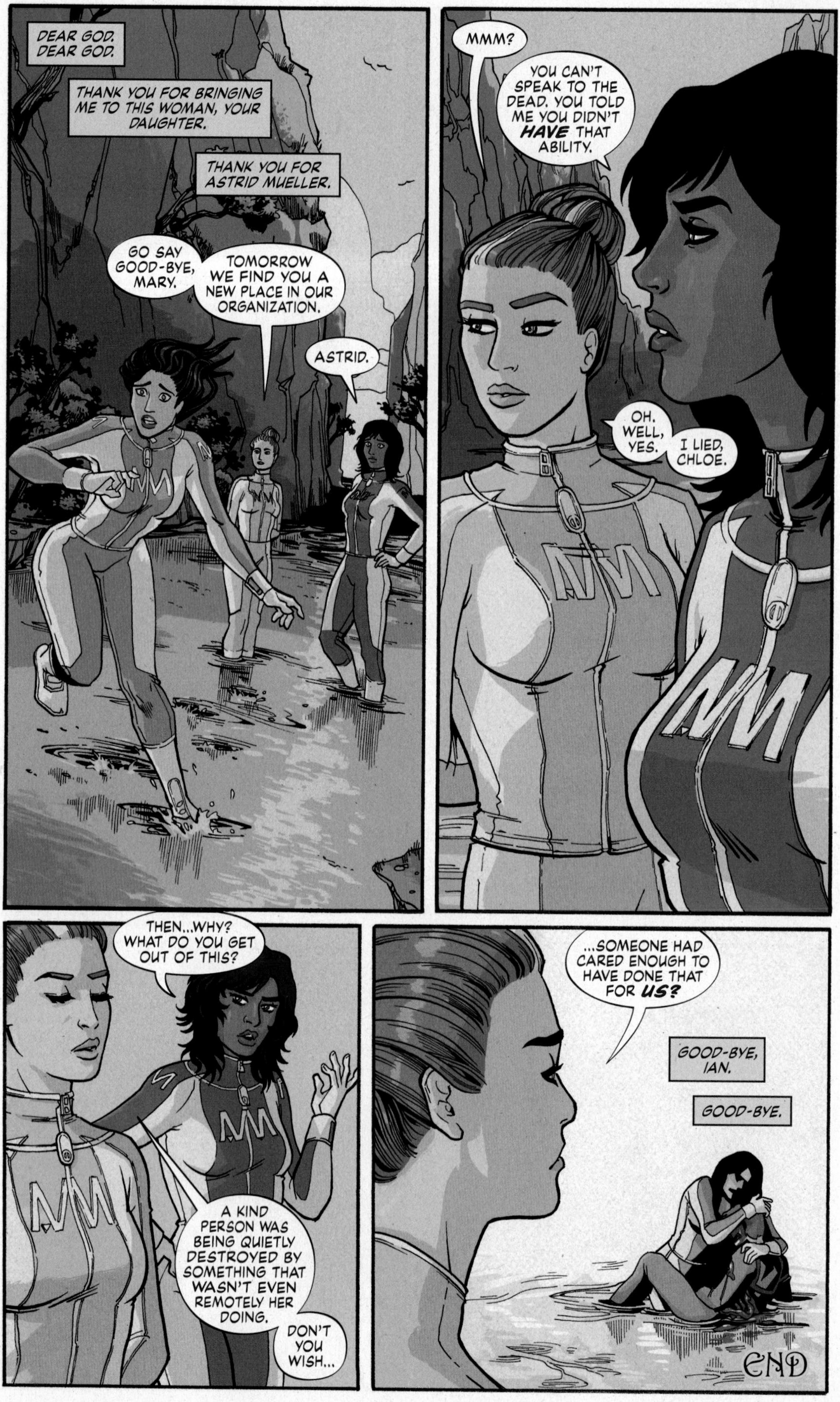
DEAR GOD. DEAR GOD.
THANK YOU FOR BRINGING ME TO THIS WOMAN, YOUR DAUGHTER.
THANK YOU FOR ASTRID MUELLER.
GO SAY GOOD-BYE, MARY.
TOMORROW WE FIND YOU A NEW PLACE IN OUR ORGANIZATION.
ASTRID.
MMM?
YOU CAN'T SPEAK TO THE DEAD. YOU TOLD ME YOU DIDN'T HAVE THAT ABILITY.
OH. WELL, YES.
I LIED, CHLOE.
THEN...WHY? WHAT DO YOU GET OUT OF THIS?
A KIND PERSON WAS BEING QUIETLY DESTROYED BY SOMETHING THAT WASN'T EVEN REMOTELY HER DOING.
DON'T YOU WISH...
...SOMEONE HAD CARED ENOUGH TO HAVE DONE THAT FOR US?
GOOD-BYE, IAN.
GOOD-BYE.
END

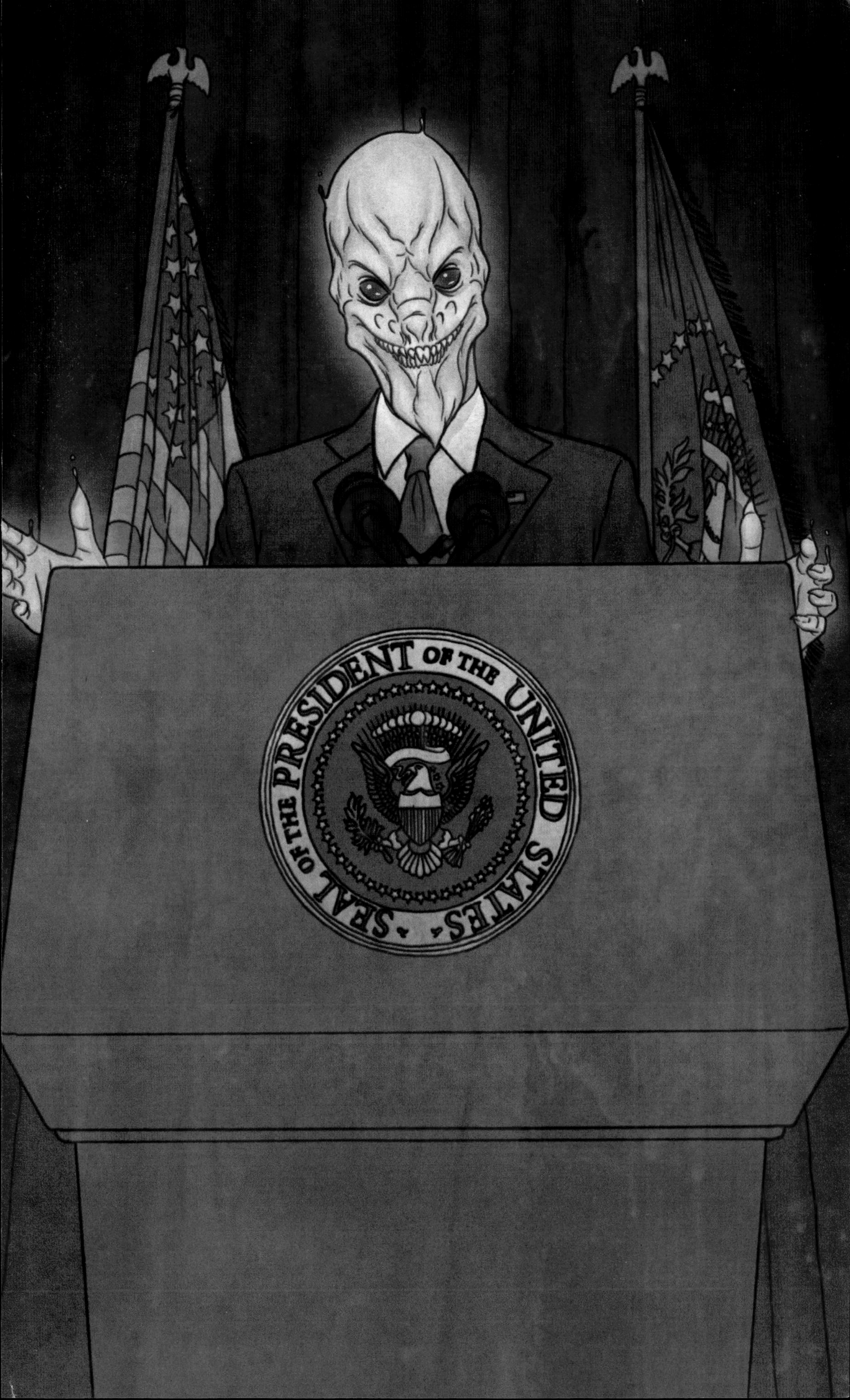
SEAL OF THE PRESIDENT OF THE UNITED STATES

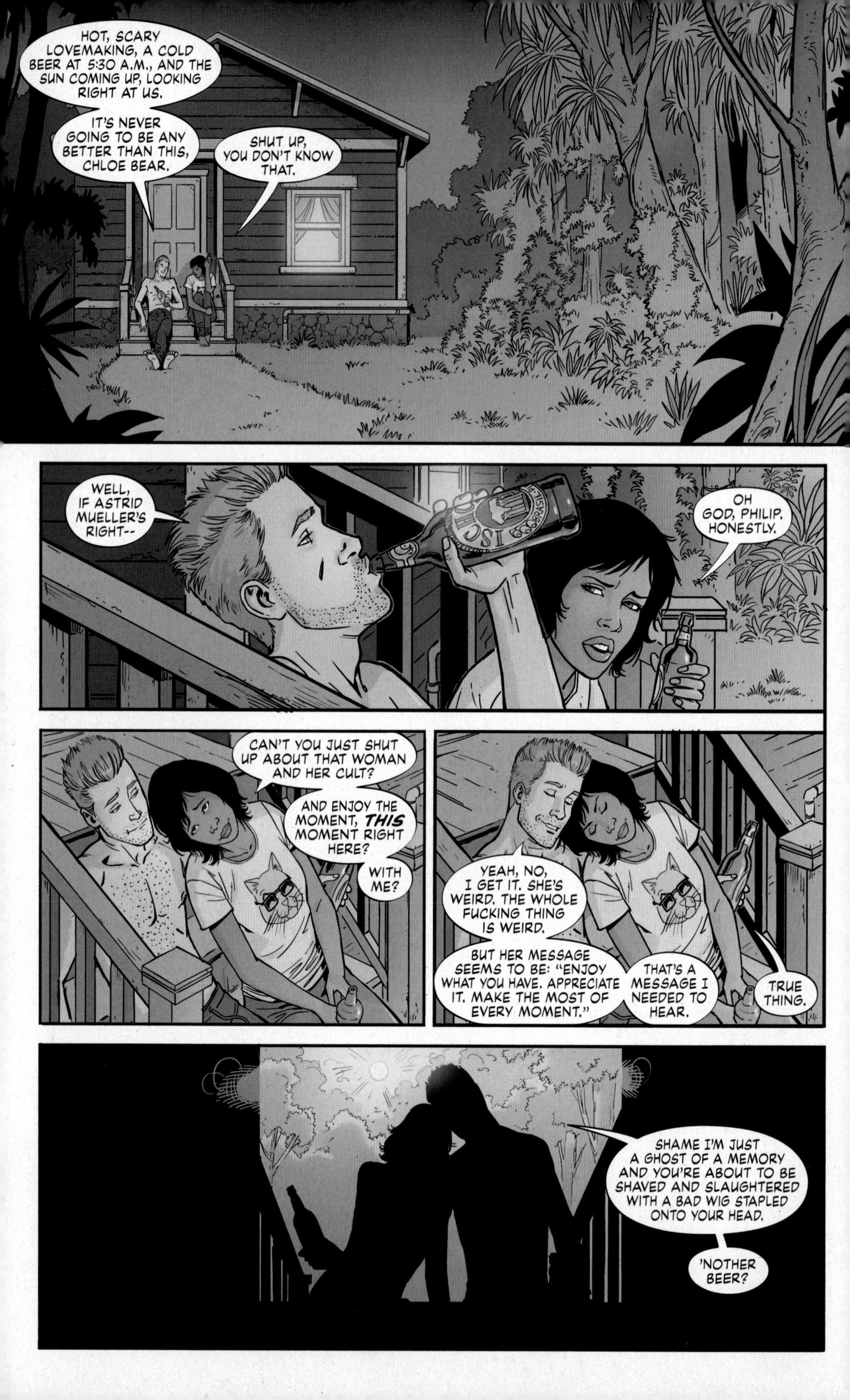
HOT, SCARY LOVEMAKING, A COLD BEER AT 5:30 A.M., AND THE SUN COMING UP, LOOKING RIGHT AT US.
IT'S NEVER GOING TO BE ANY BETTER THAN THIS, CHLOE BEAR.
SHUT UP, YOU DON'T KNOW THAT.
WELL, IF ASTRID MUELLER'S RIGHT--
OH GOD, PHILIP. HONESTLY.
CAN'T YOU JUST SHUT UP ABOUT THAT WOMAN AND HER CULT?
AND ENJOY THE MOMENT, THIS MOMENT RIGHT HERE?
WITH ME?
YEAH, NO, I GET IT. SHE'S WEIRD. THE WHOLE FUCKING THING IS WEIRD.
BUT HER MESSAGE SEEMS TO BE: "ENJOY WHAT YOU HAVE. APPRECIATE IT. MAKE THE MOST OF EVERY MOMENT."
THAT'S A MESSAGE I NEEDED TO HEAR.
TRUE THING.
SHAME I'M JUST A GHOST OF A MEMORY AND YOU'RE ABOUT TO BE SHAVED AND SLAUGHTERED WITH A BAD WIG STAPLED ONTO YOUR HEAD.
'NOTHER BEER?

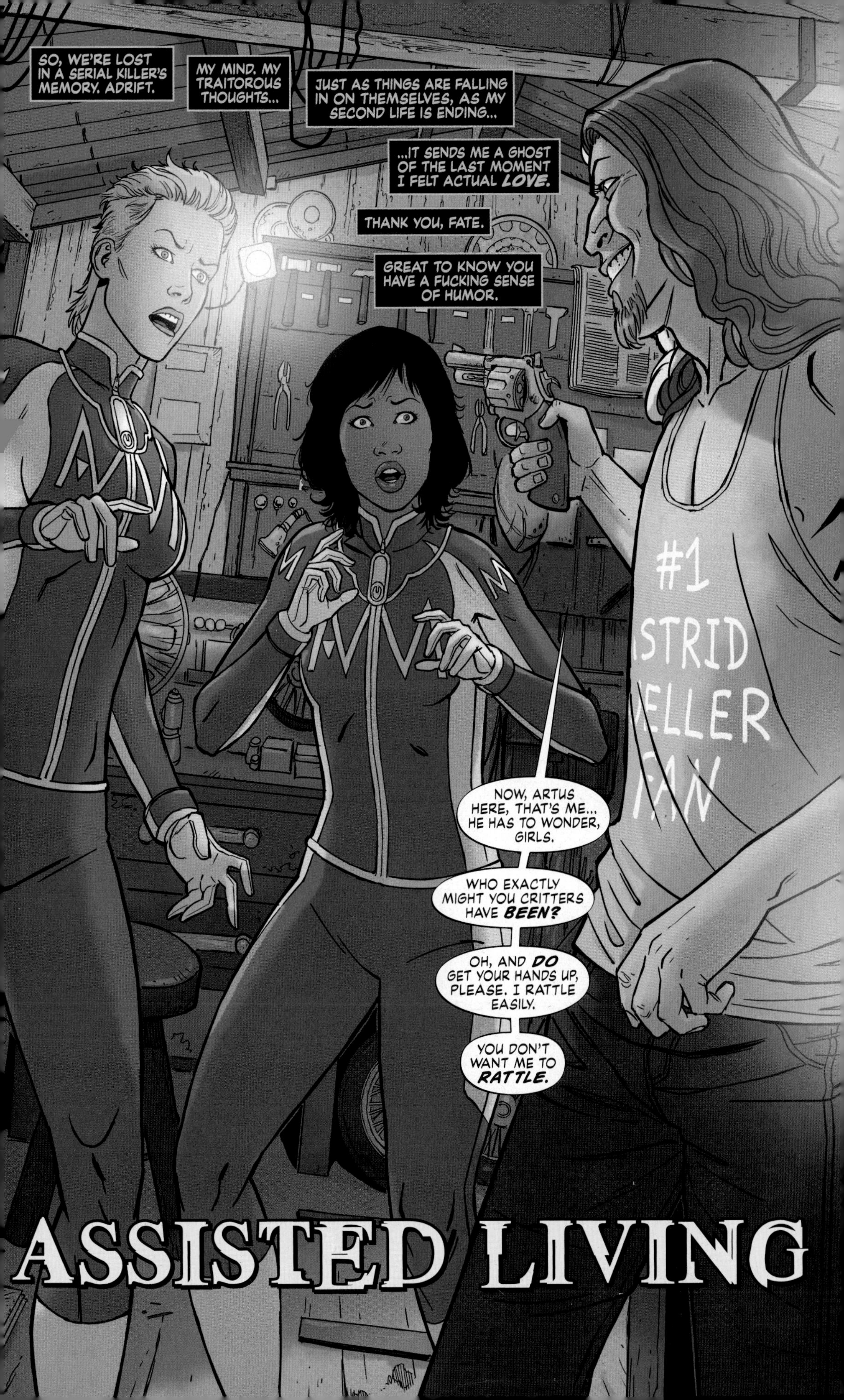

SO, WE'RE LOST IN A SERIAL KILLER'S MEMORY. ADRIFT.
MY MIND. MY TRAITOROUS THOUGHTS...
JUST AS THINGS ARE FALLING IN ON THEMSELVES, AS MY SECOND LIFE IS ENDING...
...IT SENDS ME A GHOST OF THE LAST MOMENT I FELT ACTUAL LOVE.
THANK YOU, FATE.
GREAT TO KNOW YOU HAVE A FUCKING SENSE OF HUMOR.
#1 STRID ELLER FAN
NOW, ARTUS HERE, THAT'S ME... HE HAS TO WONDER, GIRLS.
WHO EXACTLY MIGHT YOU CRITTERS HAVE BEEN?
OH, AND DO GET YOUR HANDS UP, PLEASE. I RATTLE EASILY.
YOU DON'T WANT ME TO RATTLE.
ASSISTED LIVING

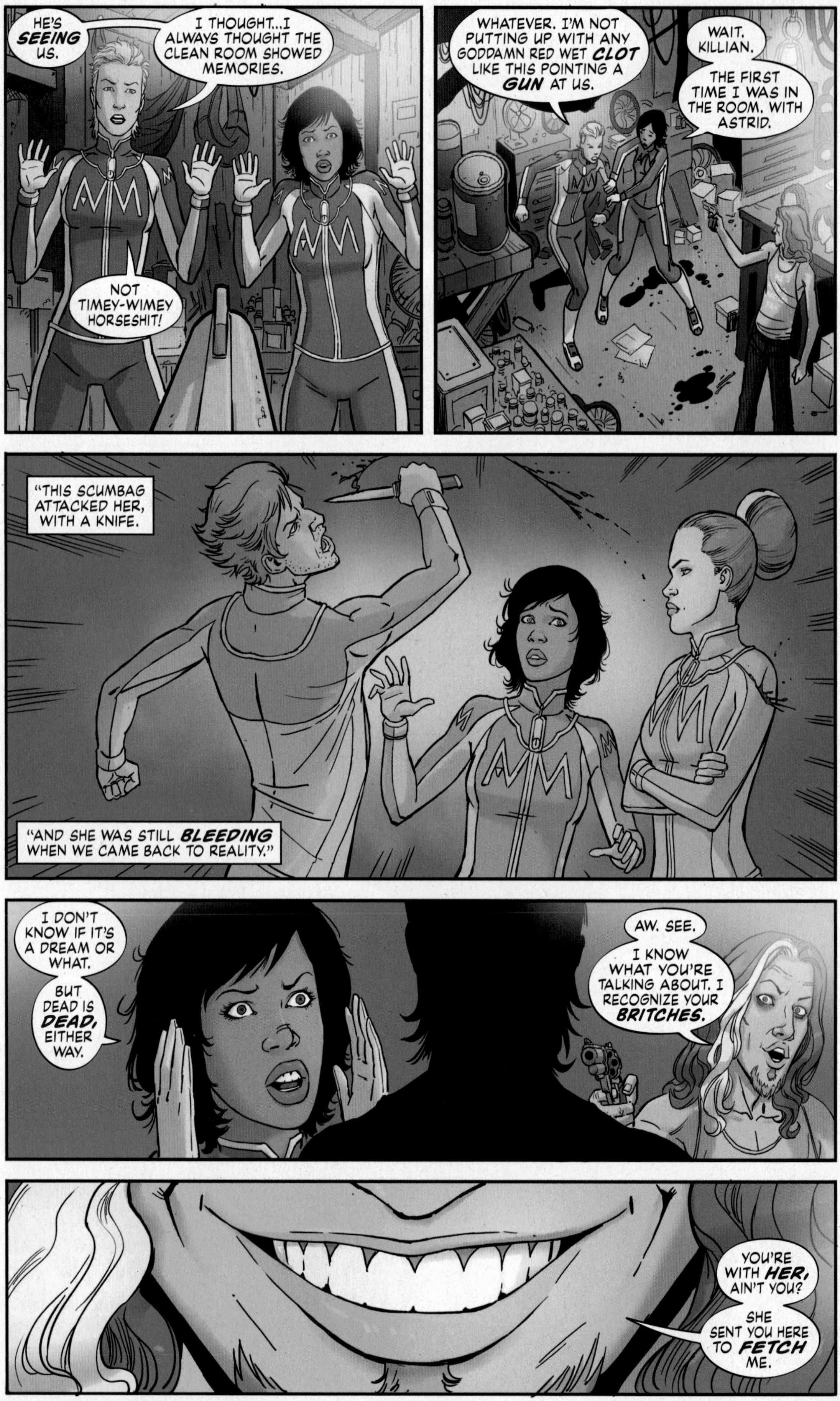
HE'S SEEING US.
I THOUGHT...I ALWAYS THOUGHT THE CLEAN ROOM SHOWED MEMORIES.
NOT TIMEY-WIMEY HORSESHIT!
WHATEVER. I'M NOT PUTTING UP WITH ANY GODDAMN RED WET CLOT LIKE THIS POINTING A GUN AT US.
WAIT. KILLIAN.
THE FIRST TIME I WAS IN THE ROOM. WITH ASTRID.
"THIS SCUMBAG ATTACKED HER, WITH A KNIFE.
"AND SHE WAS STILL BLEEDING WHEN WE CAME BACK TO REALITY."
I DON'T KNOW IF IT'S A DREAM OR WHAT.
BUT DEAD IS DEAD, EITHER WAY.
AW. SEE.
I KNOW WHAT YOU'RE TALKING ABOUT. I RECOGNIZE YOUR BRITCHES.
YOU'RE WITH HER, AIN'T YOU?
SHE SENT YOU HERE TO FETCH ME.

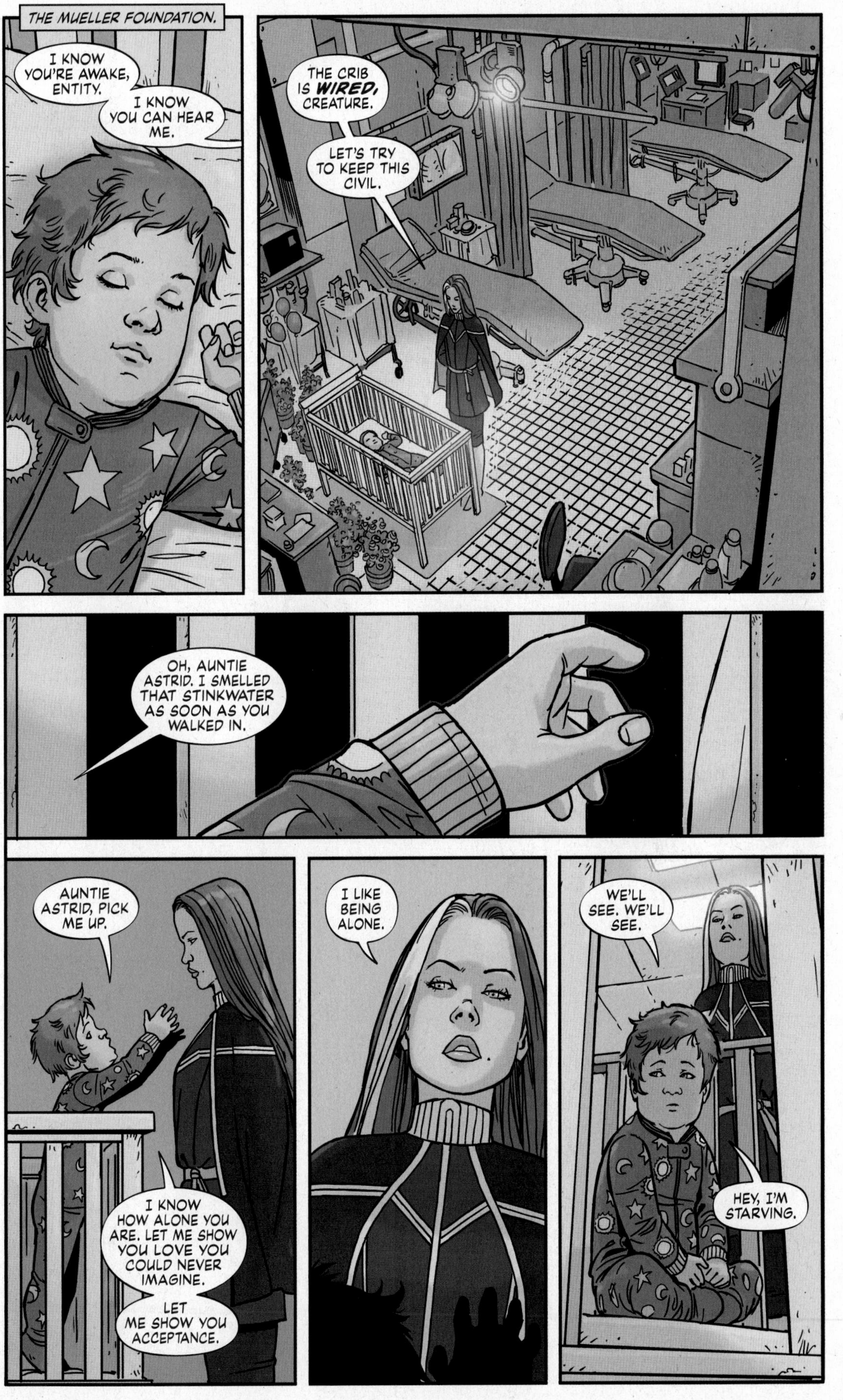
THE MUELLER FOUNDATION.
I KNOW YOU'RE AWAKE, ENTITY.
I KNOW YOU CAN HEAR ME.
THE CRIB IS WIRED, CREATURE.
LET'S TRY TO KEEP THIS CIVIL.
OH, AUNTIE ASTRID. I SMELLED THAT STINKWATER AS SOON AS YOU WALKED IN.
AUNTIE ASTRID, PICK ME UP.
I KNOW HOW ALONE YOU ARE. LET ME SHOW YOU LOVE YOU COULD NEVER IMAGINE.
LET ME SHOW YOU ACCEPTANCE.
I LIKE BEING ALONE.
WE'LL SEE. WE'LL SEE.
HEY, I'M STARVING.

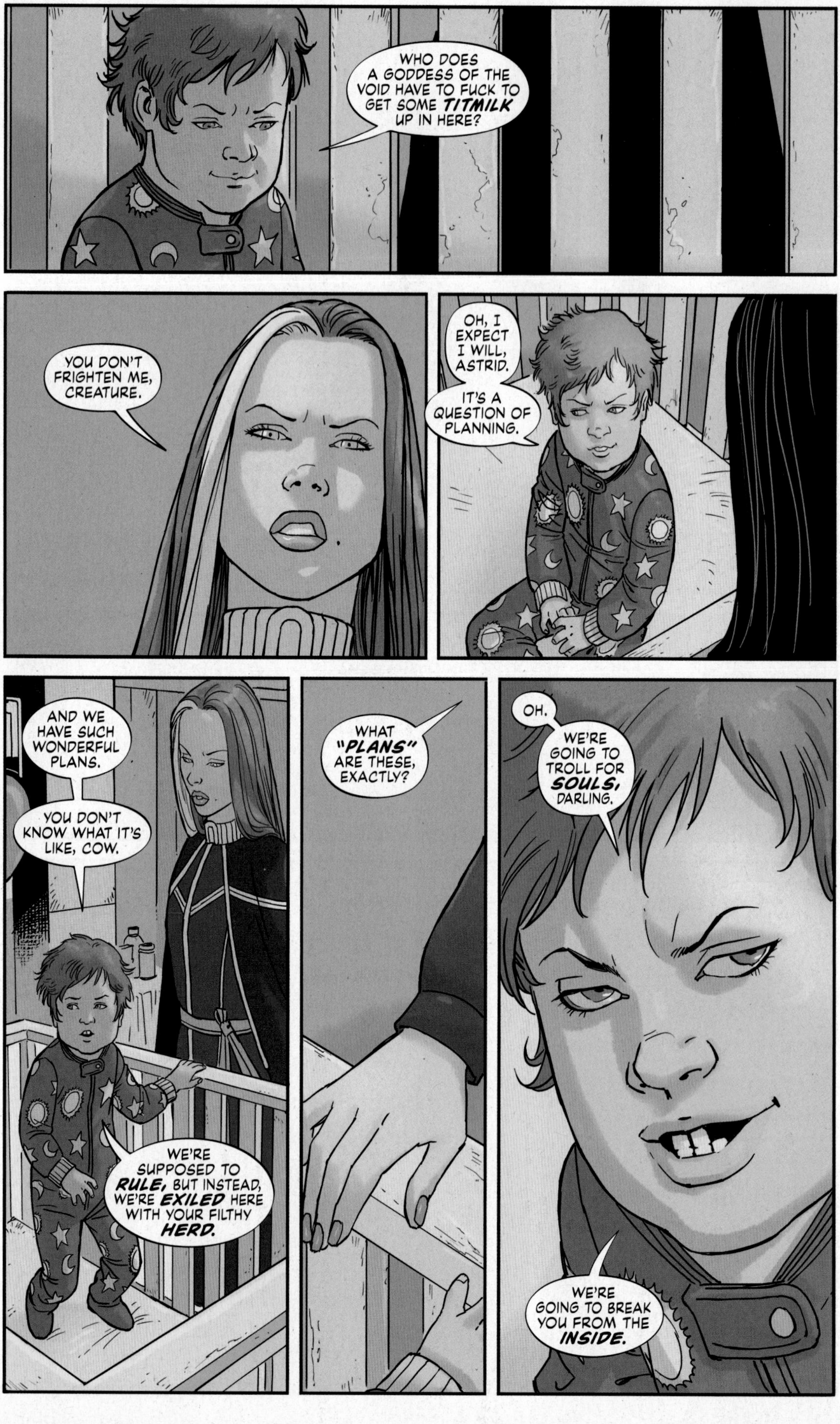
WHO DOES A GODDESS OF THE VOID HAVE TO FUCK TO GET SOME **TITMILK** UP IN HERE?
YOU DON'T FRIGHTEN ME, CREATURE.
OH, I EXPECT I WILL, ASTRID.
IT'S A QUESTION OF PLANNING.
AND WE HAVE SUCH WONDERFUL PLANS.
YOU DON'T KNOW WHAT IT'S LIKE, COW.
WE'RE SUPPOSED TO **RULE,** BUT INSTEAD, WE'RE **EXILED** HERE WITH YOUR FILTHY **HERD.**
WHAT **"PLANS"** ARE THESE, EXACTLY?
OH.
WE'RE GOING TO TROLL FOR **SOULS,** DARLING.
WE'RE GOING TO BREAK YOU FROM THE **INSIDE.**

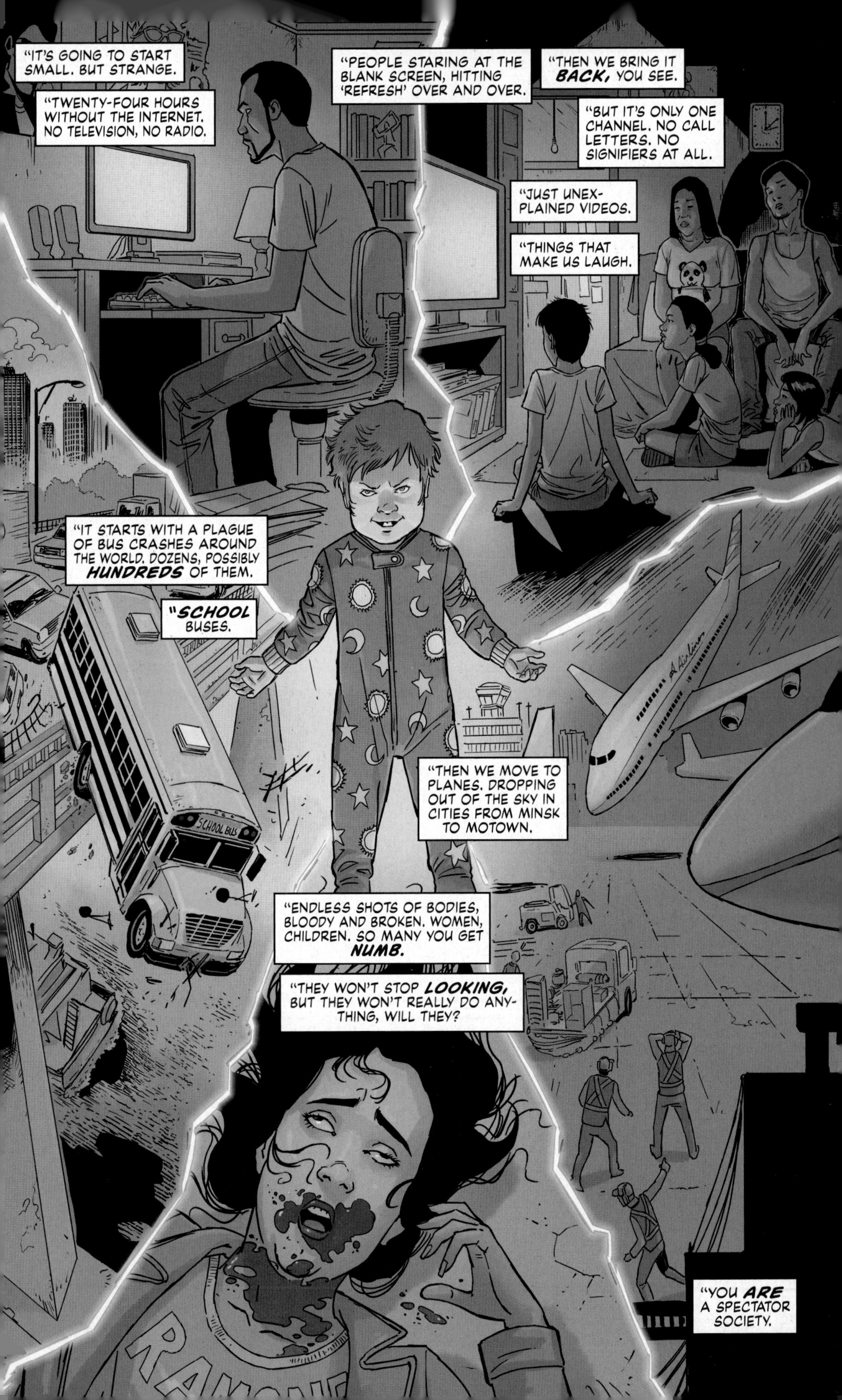
"IT'S GOING TO START SMALL. BUT STRANGE.
"TWENTY-FOUR HOURS WITHOUT THE INTERNET. NO TELEVISION, NO RADIO.
"PEOPLE STARING AT THE BLANK SCREEN, HITTING 'REFRESH' OVER AND OVER.
"THEN WE BRING IT BACK, YOU SEE.
"BUT IT'S ONLY ONE CHANNEL. NO CALL LETTERS. NO SIGNIFIERS AT ALL.
"JUST UNEX-PLAINED VIDEOS.
"THINGS THAT MAKE US LAUGH.
"IT STARTS WITH A PLAGUE OF BUS CRASHES AROUND THE WORLD. DOZENS, POSSIBLY HUNDREDS OF THEM.
"SCHOOL BUSES.
SCHOOL BUS
"THEN WE MOVE TO PLANES. DROPPING OUT OF THE SKY IN CITIES FROM MINSK TO MOTOWN.
"ENDLESS SHOTS OF BODIES, BLOODY AND BROKEN. WOMEN, CHILDREN. SO MANY YOU GET NUMB.
"THEY WON'T STOP LOOKING, BUT THEY WON'T REALLY DO ANY-THING, WILL THEY?
"YOU ARE A SPECTATOR SOCIETY.

"AND *JUST* AS THE PRESIDENT GIVES A SPEECH ABOUT THE NEED FOR COURAGE, *JUST* AFTER HE DECLARES A STATE OF MARTIAL LAW...

THE WHITE HOUSE

"...HE PUTS A TRIPLE TAP FROM A CONCEALED GLOCK RIGHT INTO HIS WIFE'S EMPTY GODDAMN *HEAD*.

"AND YOU KNOW THE BEST PART? THE MEANEST THING?

"WE DON'T ANNOUNCE OURSELVES. WE DON'T SIGN OUR WORK."

WE LET YOU THINK YOU DID IT ALL *YOURSELVES*.

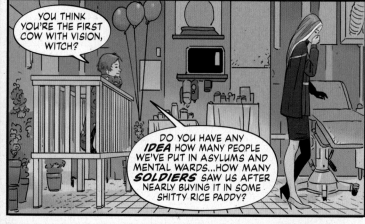

YOU THINK YOU'RE THE FIRST COW WITH VISION, WITCH?

DO YOU HAVE ANY *IDEA* HOW MANY PEOPLE WE'VE PUT IN ASYLUMS AND MENTAL WARDS...HOW MANY *SOLDIERS* SAW US AFTER NEARLY BUYING IT IN SOME SHITTY RICE PADDY?

YOU KNOW HOW WE PUSHED THEM OVER?

WE WENT AFTER EVERYONE THEY *LOVED*.

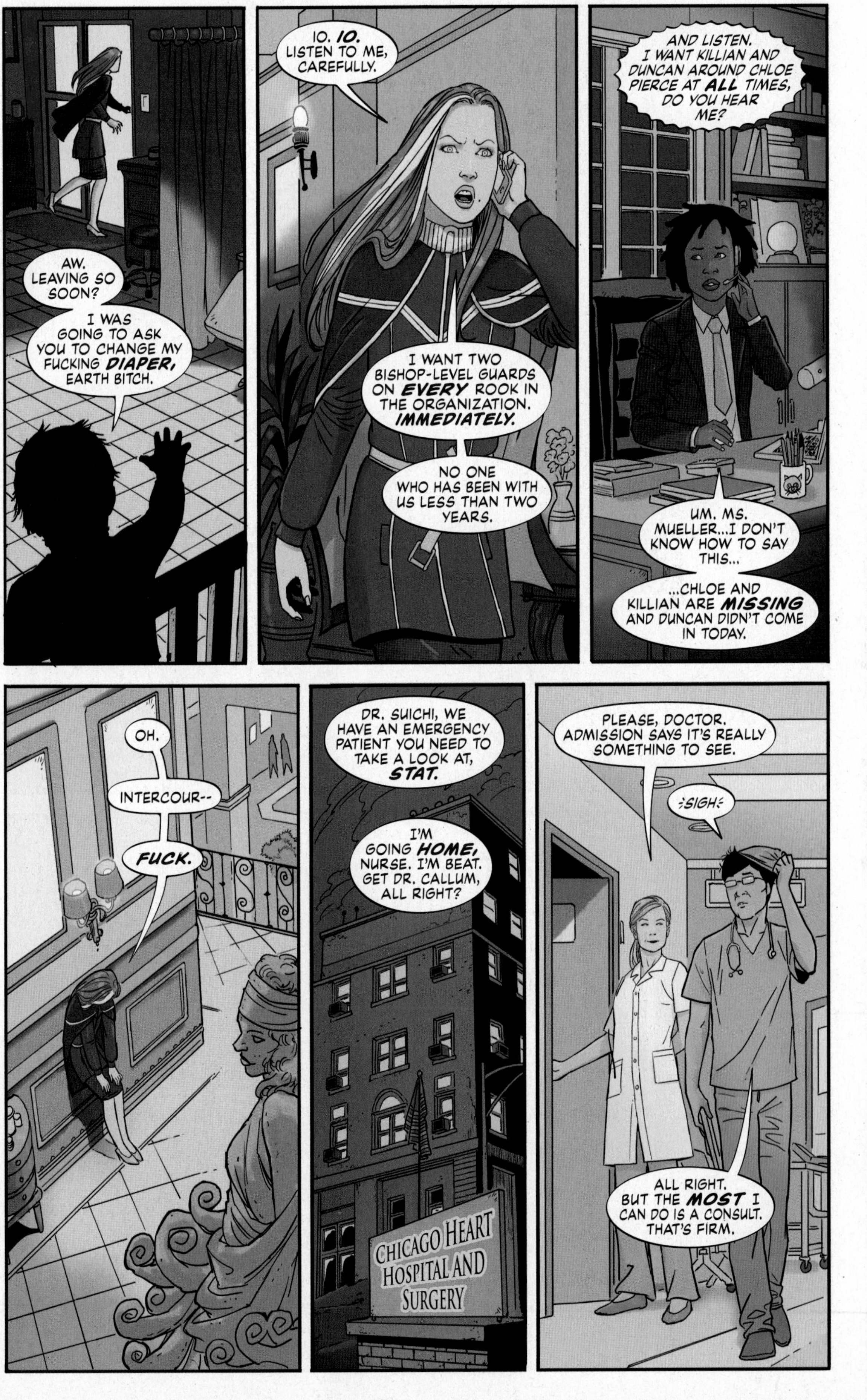
AW. LEAVING SO SOON?
I WAS GOING TO ASK YOU TO CHANGE MY FUCKING DIAPER, EARTH BITCH.
IO. IO. LISTEN TO ME, CAREFULLY.
I WANT TWO BISHOP-LEVEL GUARDS ON EVERY ROOK IN THE ORGANIZATION. IMMEDIATELY.
NO ONE WHO HAS BEEN WITH US LESS THAN TWO YEARS.
AND LISTEN. I WANT KILLIAN AND DUNCAN AROUND CHLOE PIERCE AT ALL TIMES, DO YOU HEAR ME?
UM. MS. MUELLER...I DON'T KNOW HOW TO SAY THIS...
...CHLOE AND KILLIAN ARE MISSING AND DUNCAN DIDN'T COME IN TODAY.
OH.
INTERCOUR--
FUCK.
DR. SUICHI, WE HAVE AN EMERGENCY PATIENT YOU NEED TO TAKE A LOOK AT, STAT.
I'M GOING HOME, NURSE. I'M BEAT. GET DR. CALLUM, ALL RIGHT?
CHICAGO HEART HOSPITAL AND SURGERY
PLEASE, DOCTOR. ADMISSION SAYS IT'S REALLY SOMETHING TO SEE.
SIGH
ALL RIGHT. BUT THE MOST I CAN DO IS A CONSULT. THAT'S FIRM.

SURPRISE, DOCTOR.

SURPRISE, SURPRISE, SURPRISE.

JESUS! JESUS, *SAVE* US.

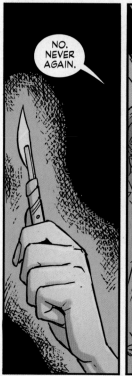

NO. NEVER AGAIN.

IT'S TIME FOR THE *OPPOSITION* PARTY, DOCTOR.

NURSE BOBBI? THE TELEVISION WENT DEAD.

YES. VERY SORRY TO HEAR THAT, TERRY.

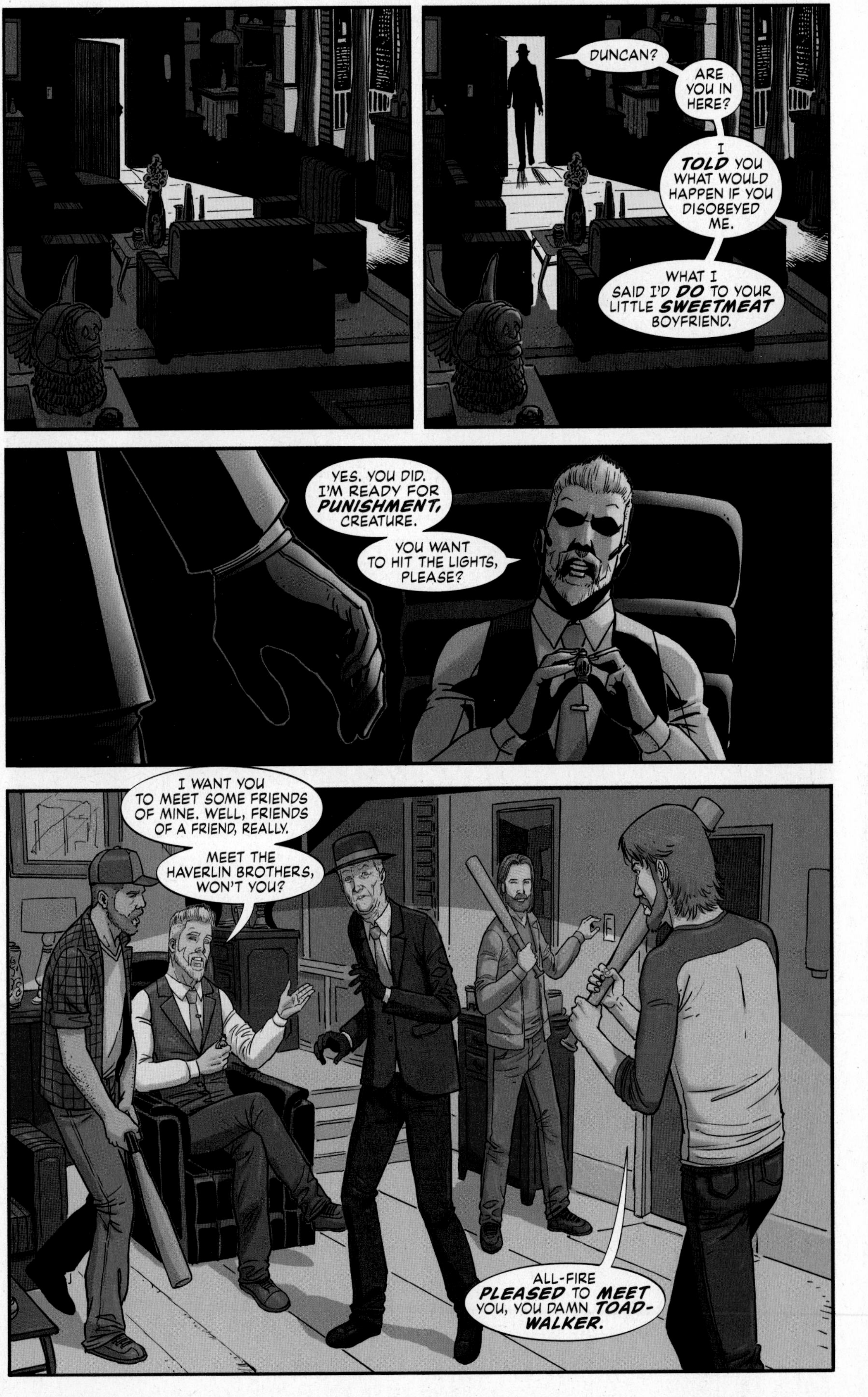
DUNCAN?
ARE YOU IN HERE?
I TOLD YOU WHAT WOULD HAPPEN IF YOU DISOBEYED ME.
WHAT I SAID I'D DO TO YOUR LITTLE SWEETMEAT BOYFRIEND.
YES. YOU DID. I'M READY FOR PUNISHMENT, CREATURE.
YOU WANT TO HIT THE LIGHTS, PLEASE?
I WANT YOU TO MEET SOME FRIENDS OF MINE. WELL, FRIENDS OF A FRIEND, REALLY.
MEET THE HAVERLIN BROTHERS, WON'T YOU?
ALL-FIRE PLEASED TO MEET YOU, YOU DAMN TOAD-WALKER.

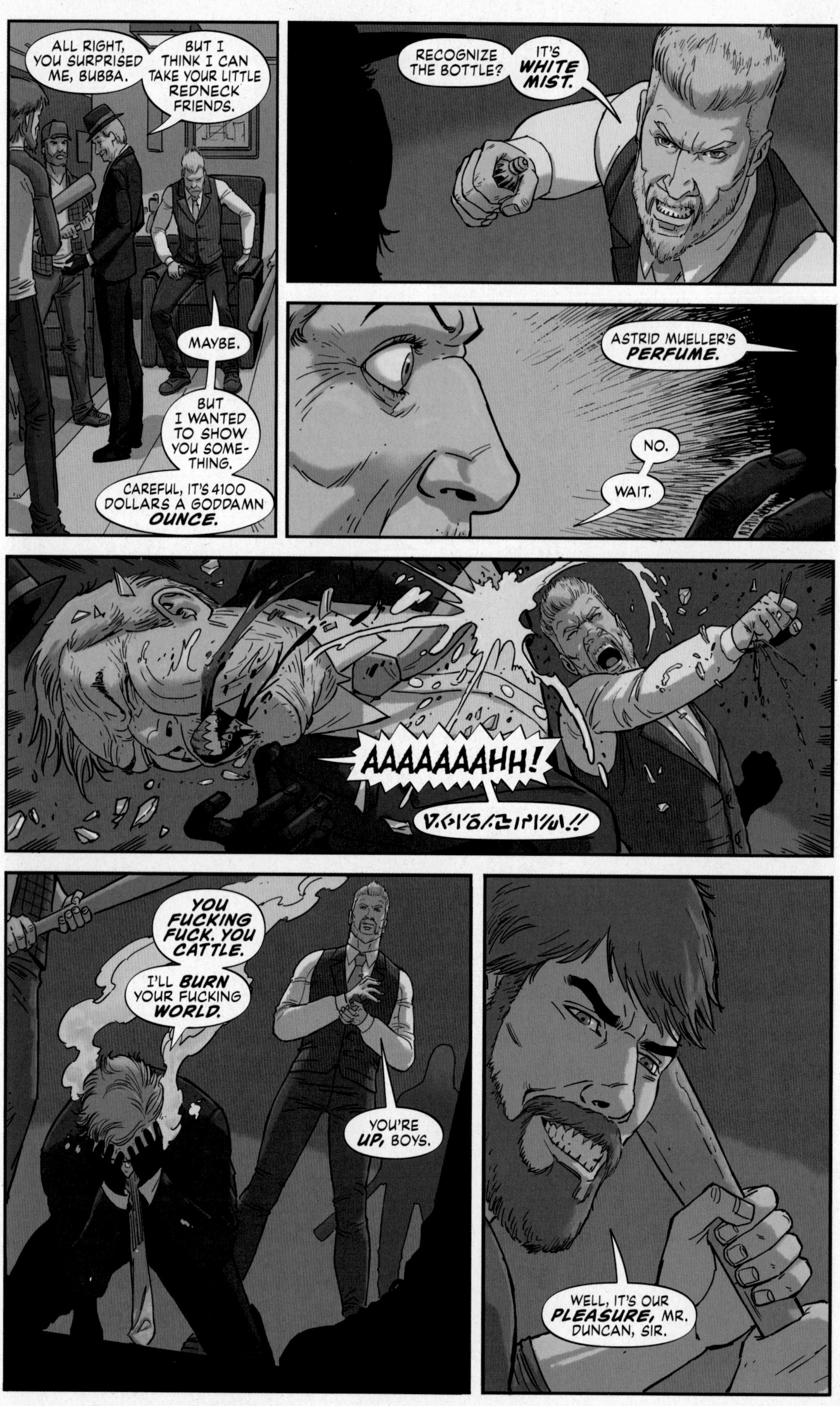
ALL RIGHT, YOU SURPRISED ME, BUBBA.
BUT I THINK I CAN TAKE YOUR LITTLE REDNECK FRIENDS.
MAYBE.
BUT I WANTED TO SHOW YOU SOMETHING.
CAREFUL, IT'S 4100 DOLLARS A GODDAMN OUNCE.
RECOGNIZE THE BOTTLE?
IT'S WHITE MIST.
ASTRID MUELLER'S PERFUME.
NO.
WAIT.
AAAAAAAHH!
YOU FUCKING FUCK. YOU CATTLE.
I'LL BURN YOUR FUCKING WORLD.
YOU'RE UP, BOYS.
WELL, IT'S OUR PLEASURE, MR. DUNCAN, SIR.

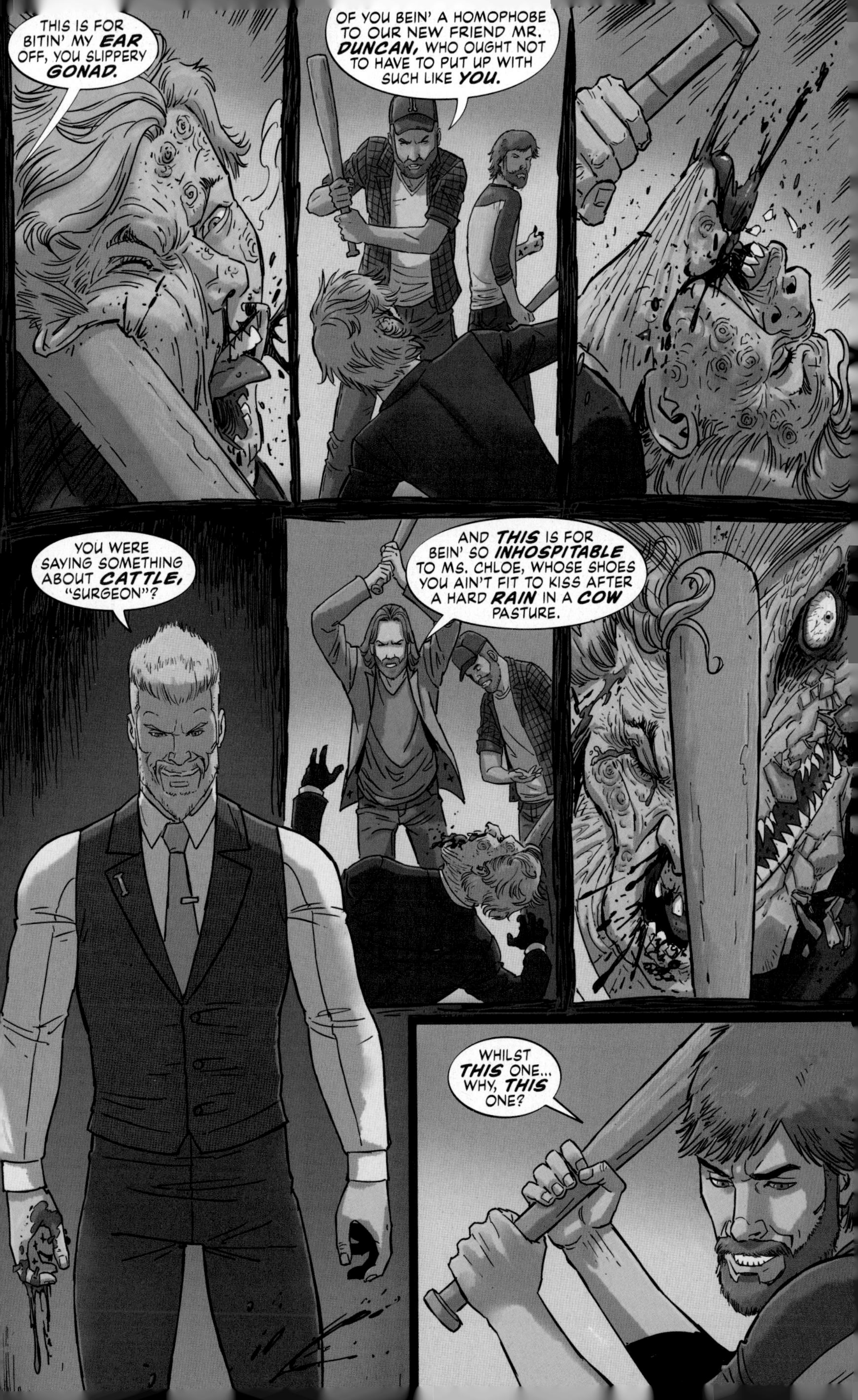
THIS IS FOR BITIN' MY EAR OFF, YOU SLIPPERY GONAD.
OF YOU BEIN' A HOMOPHOBE TO OUR NEW FRIEND MR. DUNCAN, WHO OUGHT NOT TO HAVE TO PUT UP WITH SUCH LIKE YOU.
YOU WERE SAYING SOMETHING ABOUT CATTLE, "SURGEON"?
AND THIS IS FOR BEIN' SO INHOSPITABLE TO MS. CHLOE, WHOSE SHOES YOU AIN'T FIT TO KISS AFTER A HARD RAIN IN A COW PASTURE.
WHILST THIS ONE... WHY, THIS ONE?

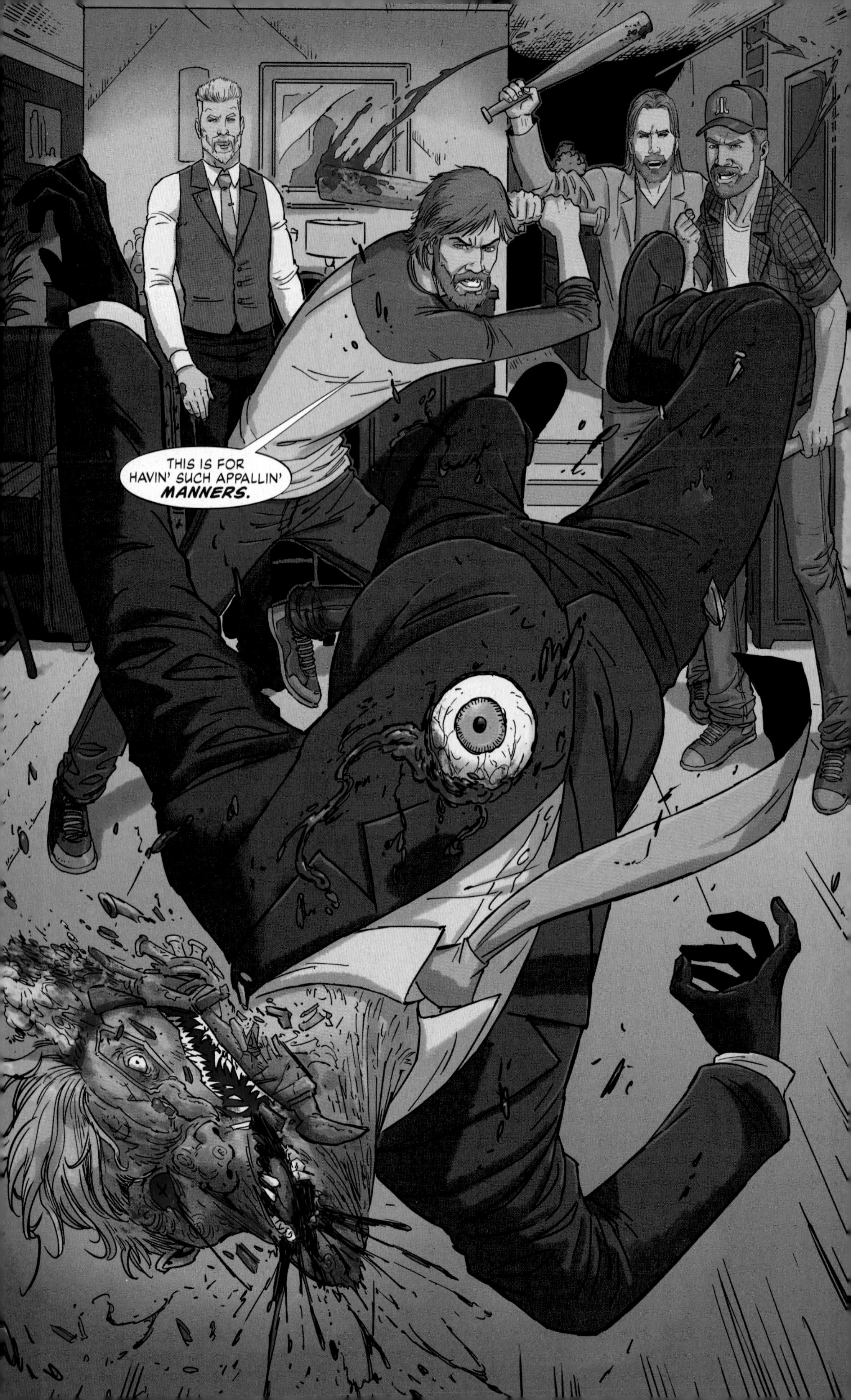
THIS IS FOR HAVIN' SUCH APPALLIN' MANNERS.

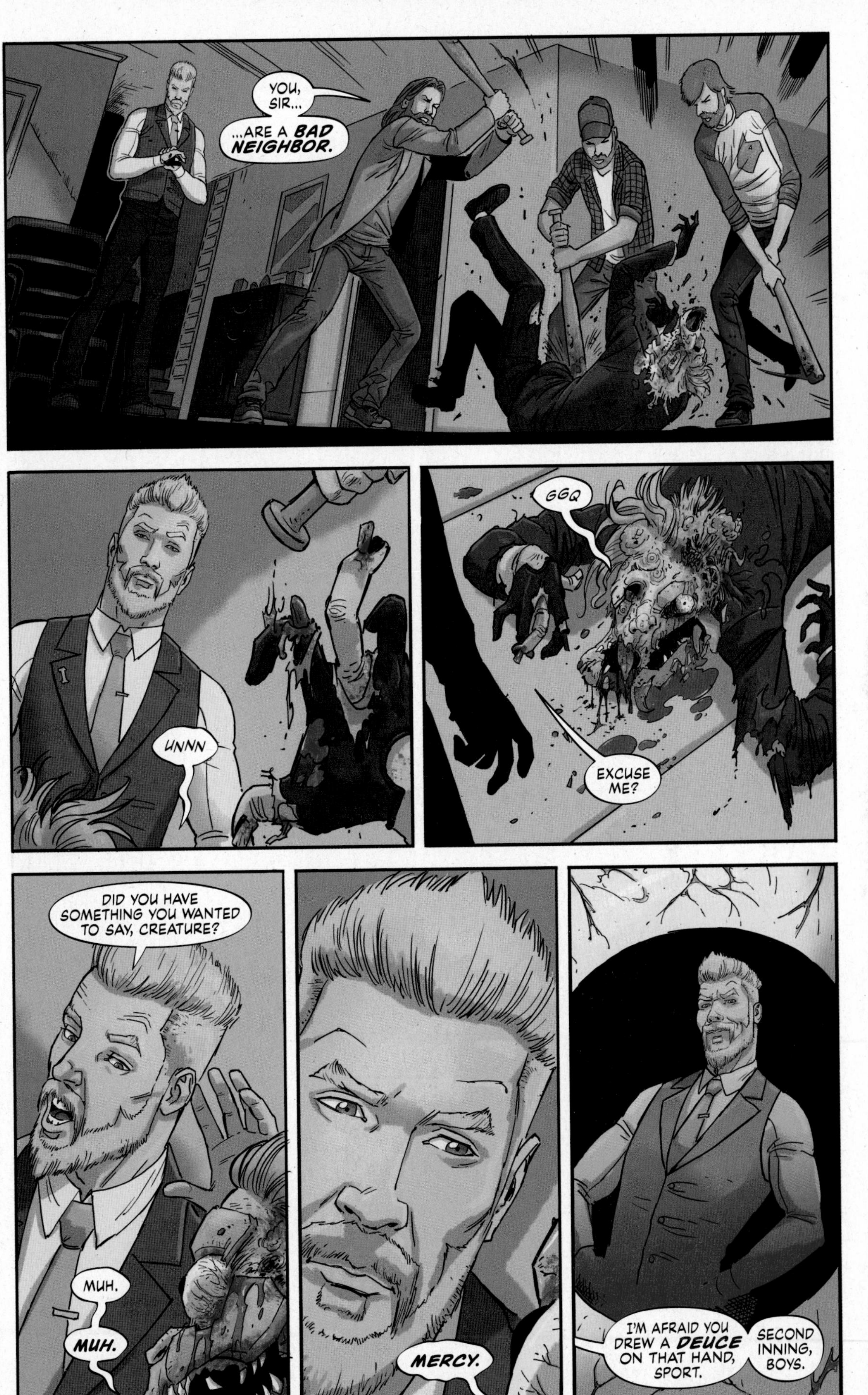

YOU, SIR...
...ARE A BAD NEIGHBOR.
UNNN
GGQ
EXCUSE ME?
DID YOU HAVE SOMETHING YOU WANTED TO SAY, CREATURE?
MUH.
MUH.
MERCY.
I'M AFRAID YOU DREW A DEUCE ON THAT HAND, SPORT.
SECOND INNING, BOYS.

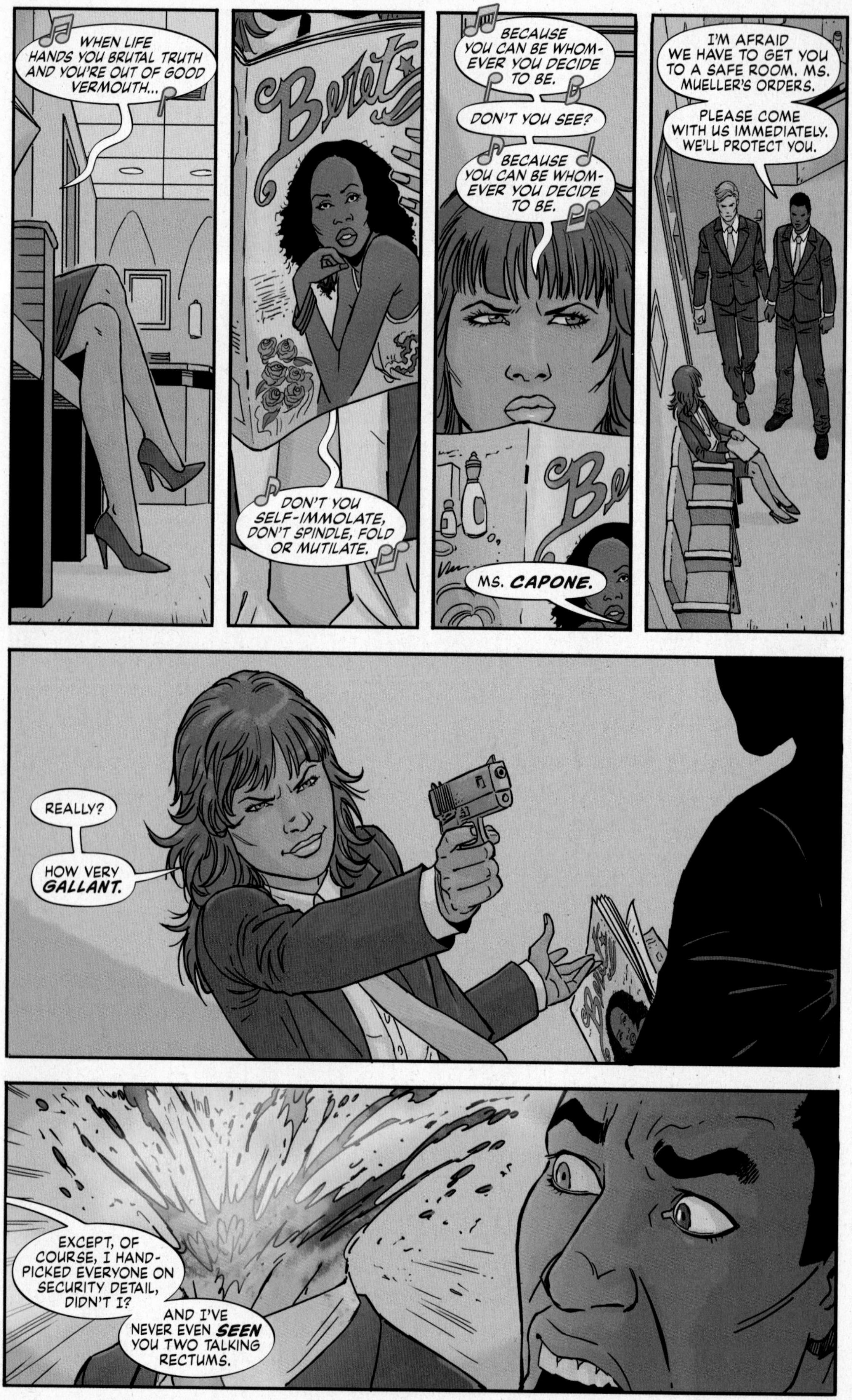

WHEN LIFE HANDS YOU BRUTAL TRUTH AND YOU'RE OUT OF GOOD VERMOUTH...
DON'T YOU SELF-IMMOLATE, DON'T SPINDLE, FOLD OR MUTILATE.
BECAUSE YOU CAN BE WHOM-EVER YOU DECIDE TO BE.
DON'T YOU SEE?
BECAUSE YOU CAN BE WHOM-EVER YOU DECIDE TO BE.
MS. CAPONE.
I'M AFRAID WE HAVE TO GET YOU TO A SAFE ROOM. MS. MUELLER'S ORDERS.
PLEASE COME WITH US IMMEDIATELY. WE'LL PROTECT YOU.
REALLY?
HOW VERY GALLANT.
EXCEPT, OF COURSE, I HAND-PICKED EVERYONE ON SECURITY DETAIL, DIDN'T I?
AND I'VE NEVER EVEN SEEN YOU TWO TALKING RECTUMS.

SKKKKRRREEEE!

WELL, COME **ON**, THEN, MOTHER-FUCK.

brzzzzt
brzzzzt

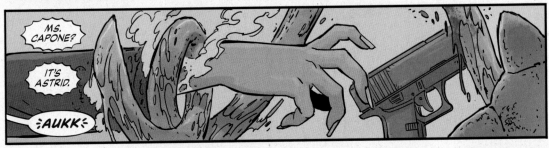

MS. CAPONE?

IT'S ASTRID.

:AUKK:

PLEASE DROP WHATEVER YOU'RE DOING. I NEED YOU IMMEDIATELY.

IT'S **URGENT**.

BLAM
BLAM
BLAM

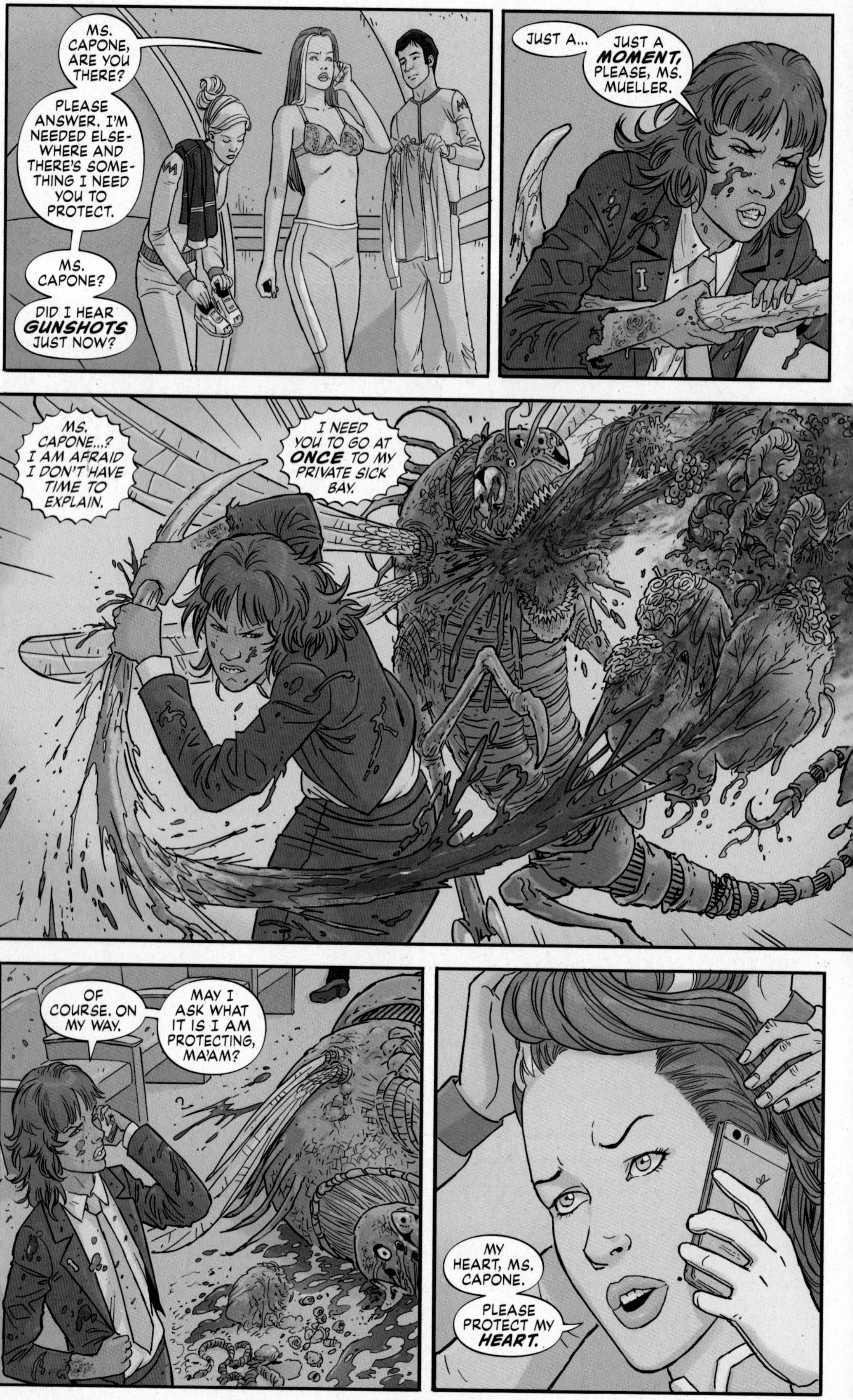

MS. CAPONE, ARE YOU THERE?
PLEASE ANSWER. I'M NEEDED ELSEWHERE AND THERE'S SOMETHING I NEED YOU TO PROTECT.
MS. CAPONE?
DID I HEAR GUNSHOTS JUST NOW?
JUST A...
JUST A MOMENT, PLEASE, MS. MUELLER.
MS. CAPONE...? I AM AFRAID I DON'T HAVE TIME TO EXPLAIN.
I NEED YOU TO GO AT ONCE TO MY PRIVATE SICK BAY.
OF COURSE. ON MY WAY.
MAY I ASK WHAT IT IS I AM PROTECTING, MA'AM?
MY HEART, MS. CAPONE.
PLEASE PROTECT MY HEART.

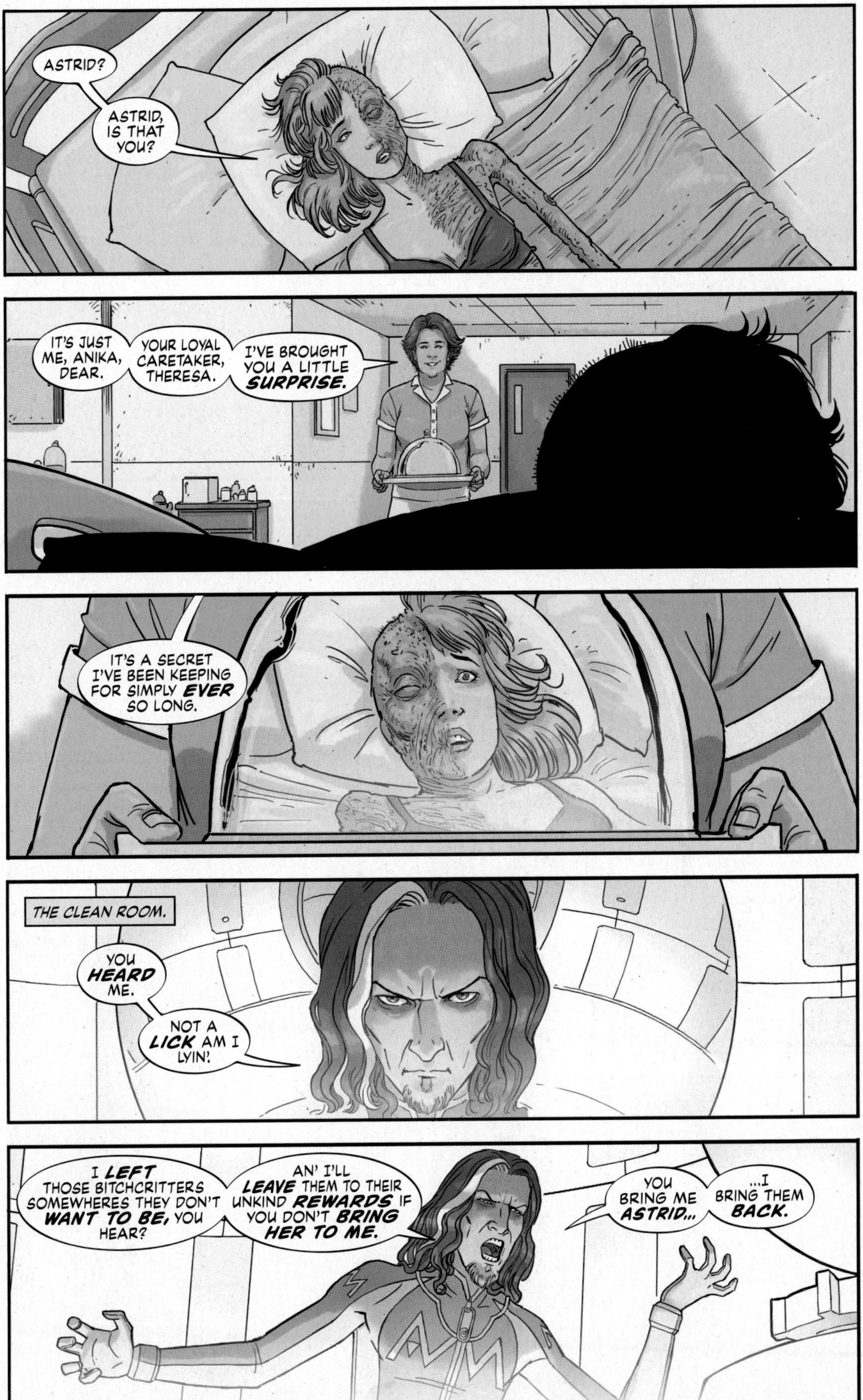
ASTRID?
ASTRID, IS THAT YOU?
IT'S JUST ME, ANIKA, DEAR.
YOUR LOYAL CARETAKER, THERESA.
I'VE BROUGHT YOU A LITTLE SURPRISE.
IT'S A SECRET I'VE BEEN KEEPING FOR SIMPLY EVER SO LONG.
THE CLEAN ROOM.
YOU HEARD ME.
NOT A LICK AM I LYIN'.
I LEFT THOSE BITCHCRITTERS SOMEWHERES THEY DON'T WANT TO BE, YOU HEAR?
AN' I'LL LEAVE THEM TO THEIR UNKIND REWARDS IF YOU DON'T BRING HER TO ME.
YOU BRING ME ASTRID...
...I BRING THEM BACK.

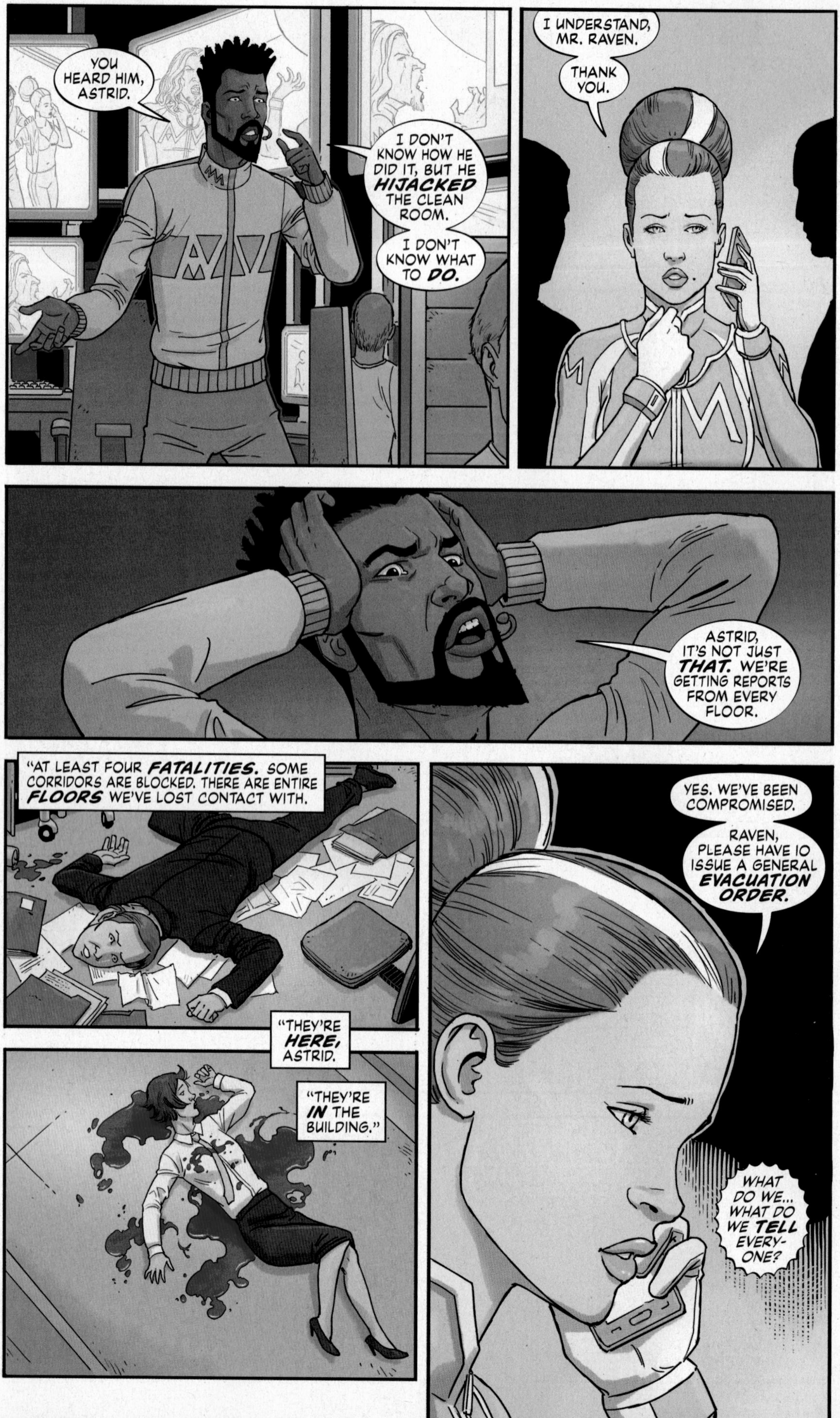
YOU HEARD HIM, ASTRID.
I DON'T KNOW HOW HE DID IT, BUT HE HIJACKED THE CLEAN ROOM.
I DON'T KNOW WHAT TO DO.
I UNDERSTAND, MR. RAVEN.
THANK YOU.
ASTRID, IT'S NOT JUST THAT. WE'RE GETTING REPORTS FROM EVERY FLOOR.
"AT LEAST FOUR FATALITIES. SOME CORRIDORS ARE BLOCKED. THERE ARE ENTIRE FLOORS WE'VE LOST CONTACT WITH.
"THEY'RE HERE, ASTRID.
"THEY'RE IN THE BUILDING."
YES. WE'VE BEEN COMPROMISED.
RAVEN, PLEASE HAVE IO ISSUE A GENERAL EVACUATION ORDER.
WHAT DO WE... WHAT DO WE TELL EVERY-ONE?

TELL THEM WE'VE BEEN INFILTRATED.

AND THAT THEY SHOULD GO HOME AND BE WITH THEIR LOVED ONES.

YOU HAVE BEEN OF STERLING CHARACTER IN MY EMPLOY, MR. RAVEN.

IT HAS BEEN AN HONOR.

GOOD-BYE.

DO YOU RECOGNIZE IT?

IT'S THE *SHOE* YOU LOST.

WHEN WE TOOK YOU *UP*, REMEMBER?

NO. NO, PLEASE.

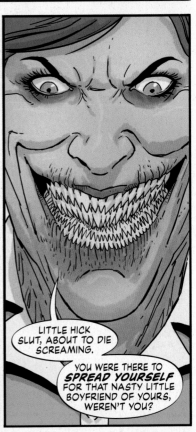

LITTLE HICK SLUT, ABOUT TO DIE SCREAMING.

YOU WERE THERE TO *SPREAD YOURSELF* FOR THAT NASTY LITTLE BOYFRIEND OF YOURS, WEREN'T YOU?

"I PERSONALLY SUPERVISED WHAT WE *DID* TO YOU. TO RUIN YOU. TO RIP OPEN YOUR *SOUL*."

IN CASE OF EMERGENCY

BECAUSE YOU CAN BE WHOMEVER YOU DECIDE TO BE...

BREAK GLASS

NO. YOU... YOU'VE TAKEN *CARE* OF ME FOR ALL THESE YEARS.

BECAUSE IT MADE ME LAUGH.

ONE THING ABOUT *US*, DEAR.

WE HAVE A *FABULOUS* SENSE OF HUMOR.

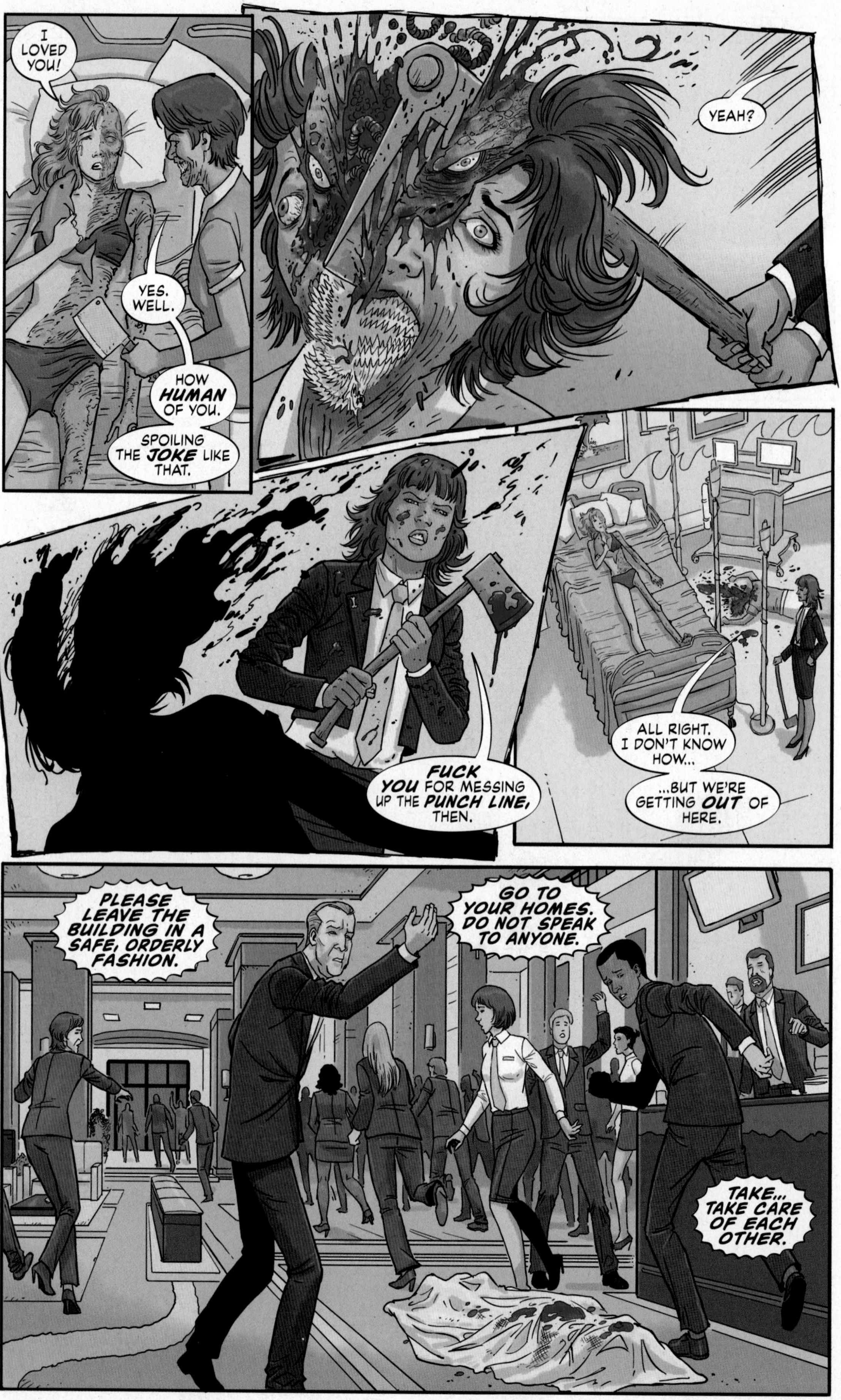

I LOVED YOU!
YES. WELL.
HOW HUMAN OF YOU.
SPOILING THE JOKE LIKE THAT.
YEAH?
FUCK YOU FOR MESSING UP THE PUNCH LINE, THEN.
ALL RIGHT. I DON'T KNOW HOW...
...BUT WE'RE GETTING OUT OF HERE.
PLEASE LEAVE THE BUILDING IN A SAFE, ORDERLY FASHION.
GO TO YOUR HOMES. DO NOT SPEAK TO ANYONE.
TAKE... TAKE CARE OF EACH OTHER.

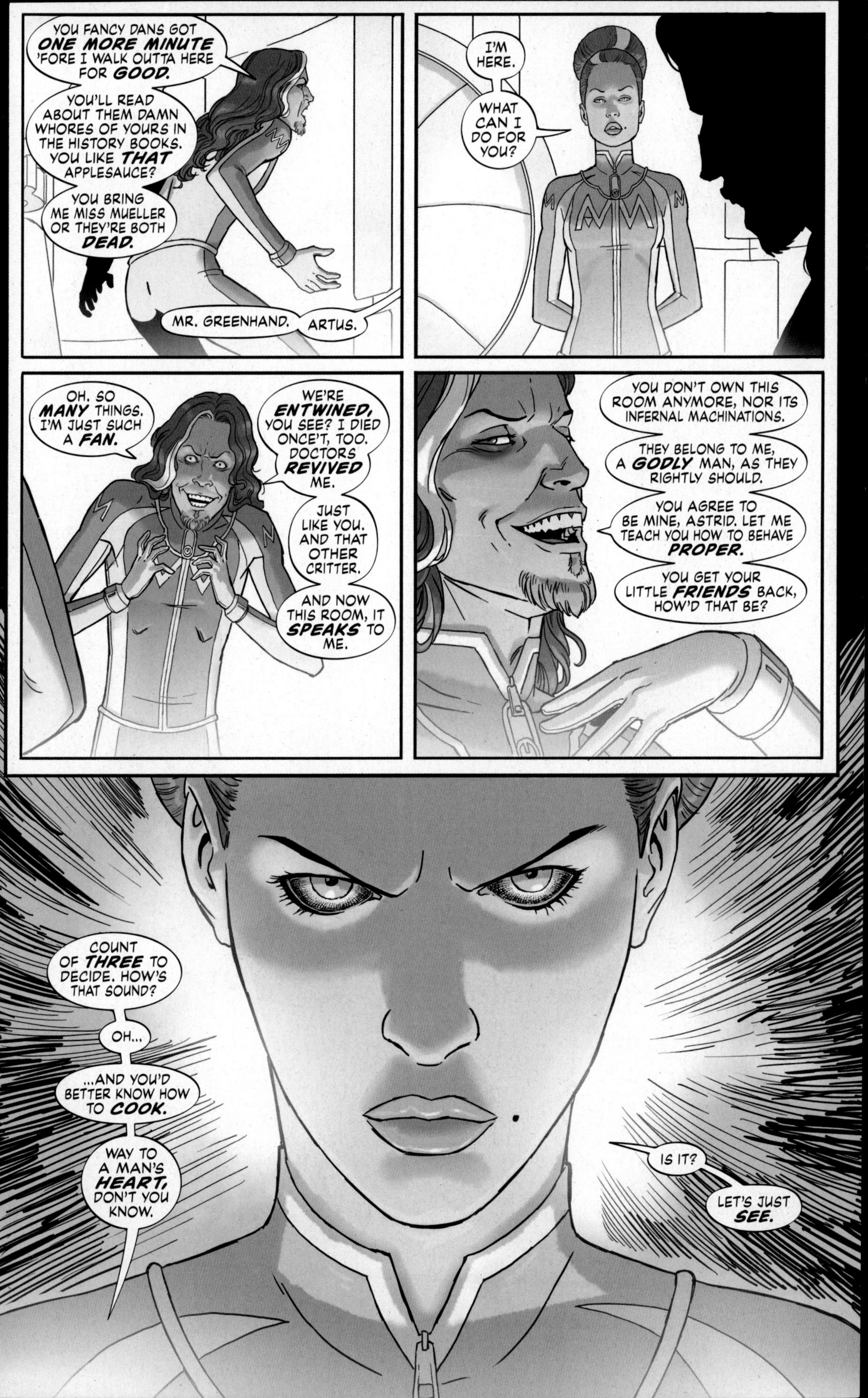
YOU FANCY DANS GOT ONE MORE MINUTE 'FORE I WALK OUTTA HERE FOR GOOD.
YOU'LL READ ABOUT THEM DAMN WHORES OF YOURS IN THE HISTORY BOOKS. YOU LIKE THAT APPLESAUCE?
YOU BRING ME MISS MUELLER OR THEY'RE BOTH DEAD.
MR. GREENHAND.
ARTUS.
I'M HERE.
WHAT CAN I DO FOR YOU?
OH. SO MANY THINGS. I'M JUST SUCH A FAN.
WE'RE ENTWINED, YOU SEE? I DIED ONCE'T, TOO. DOCTORS REVIVED ME.
JUST LIKE YOU. AND THAT OTHER CRITTER.
AND NOW THIS ROOM, IT SPEAKS TO ME.
YOU DON'T OWN THIS ROOM ANYMORE, NOR ITS INFERNAL MACHINATIONS.
THEY BELONG TO ME, A GODLY MAN, AS THEY RIGHTLY SHOULD.
YOU AGREE TO BE MINE, ASTRID. LET ME TEACH YOU HOW TO BEHAVE PROPER.
YOU GET YOUR LITTLE FRIENDS BACK, HOW'D THAT BE?
COUNT OF THREE TO DECIDE. HOW'S THAT SOUND?
OH...
...AND YOU'D BETTER KNOW HOW TO COOK.
WAY TO A MAN'S HEART, DON'T YOU KNOW.
IS IT?
LET'S JUST SEE.

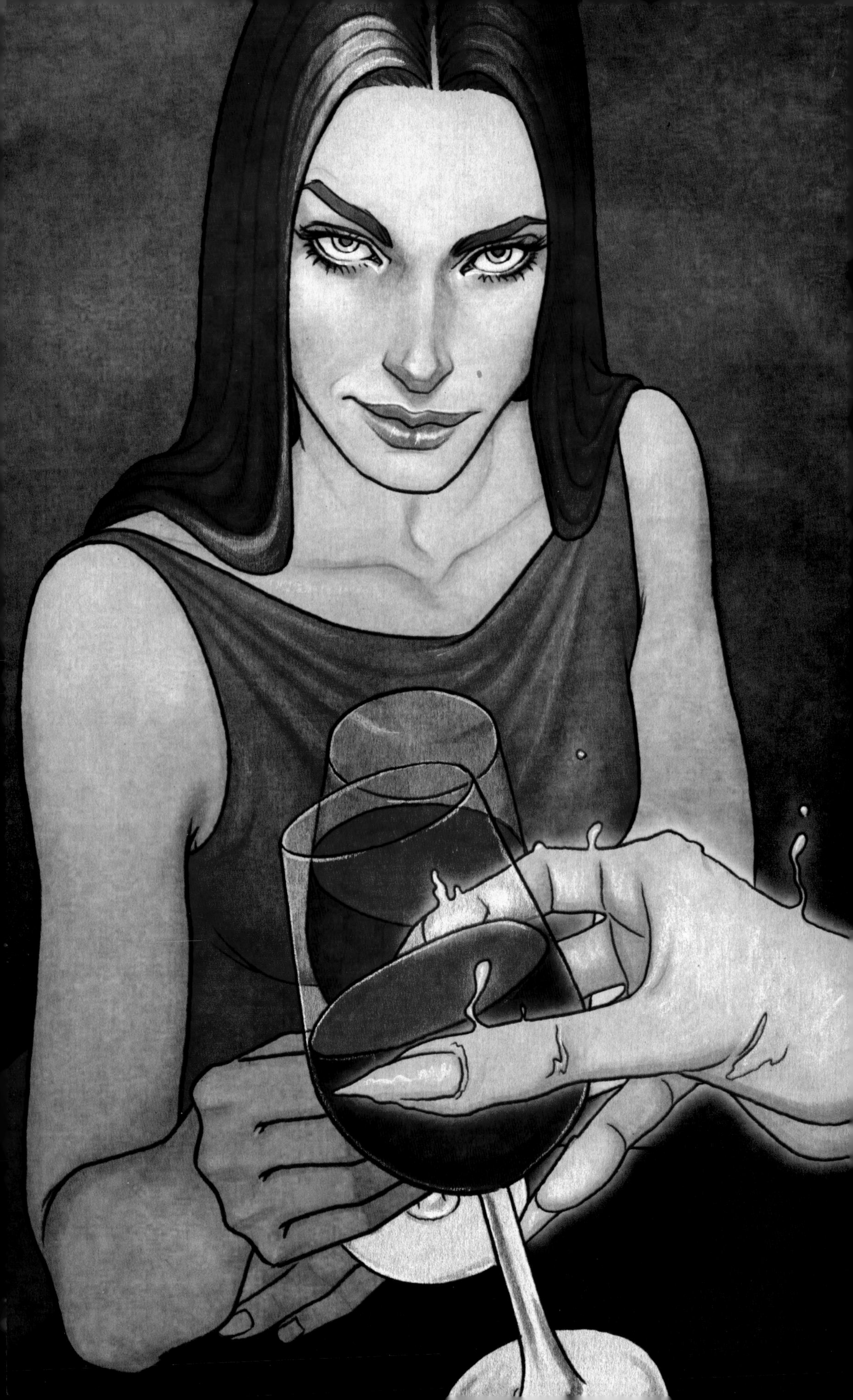

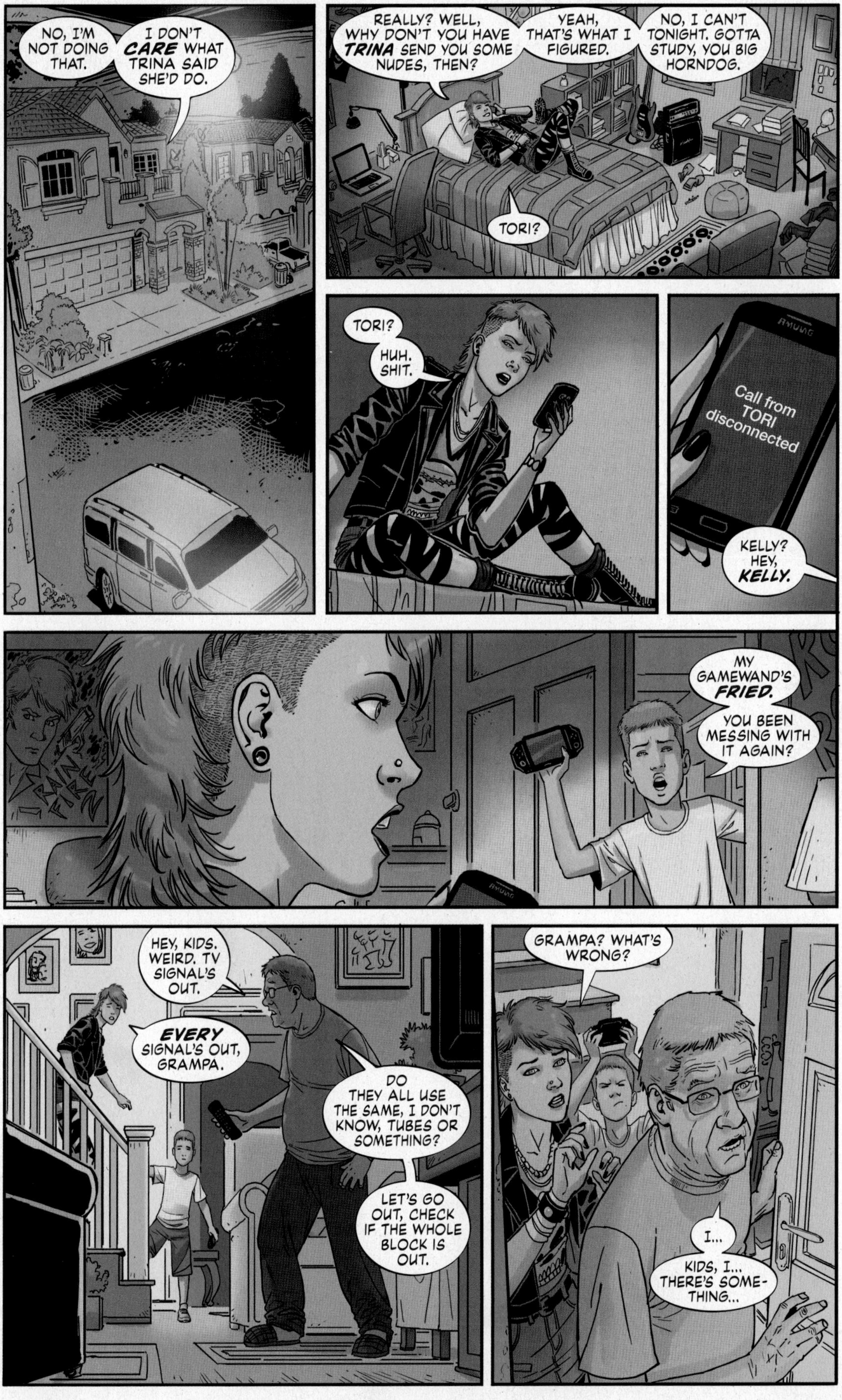

NO, I'M NOT DOING THAT.
I DON'T *CARE* WHAT TRINA SAID SHE'D DO.
REALLY? WELL, WHY DON'T YOU HAVE *TRINA* SEND YOU SOME NUDES, THEN?
YEAH, THAT'S WHAT I FIGURED.
NO, I CAN'T TONIGHT. GOTTA STUDY, YOU BIG HORNDOG.
TORI?
TORI?
HUH. SHIT.
Call from TORI disconnected
KELLY? HEY, *KELLY.*
MY GAMEWAND'S *FRIED.*
YOU BEEN MESSING WITH IT AGAIN?
HEY, KIDS. WEIRD. TV SIGNAL'S OUT.
EVERY SIGNAL'S OUT, GRAMPA.
DO THEY ALL USE THE SAME, I DON'T KNOW, TUBES OR SOMETHING?
LET'S GO OUT, CHECK IF THE WHOLE BLOCK IS OUT.
GRAMPA? WHAT'S WRONG?
I...
KIDS, I... THERE'S SOME-THING...

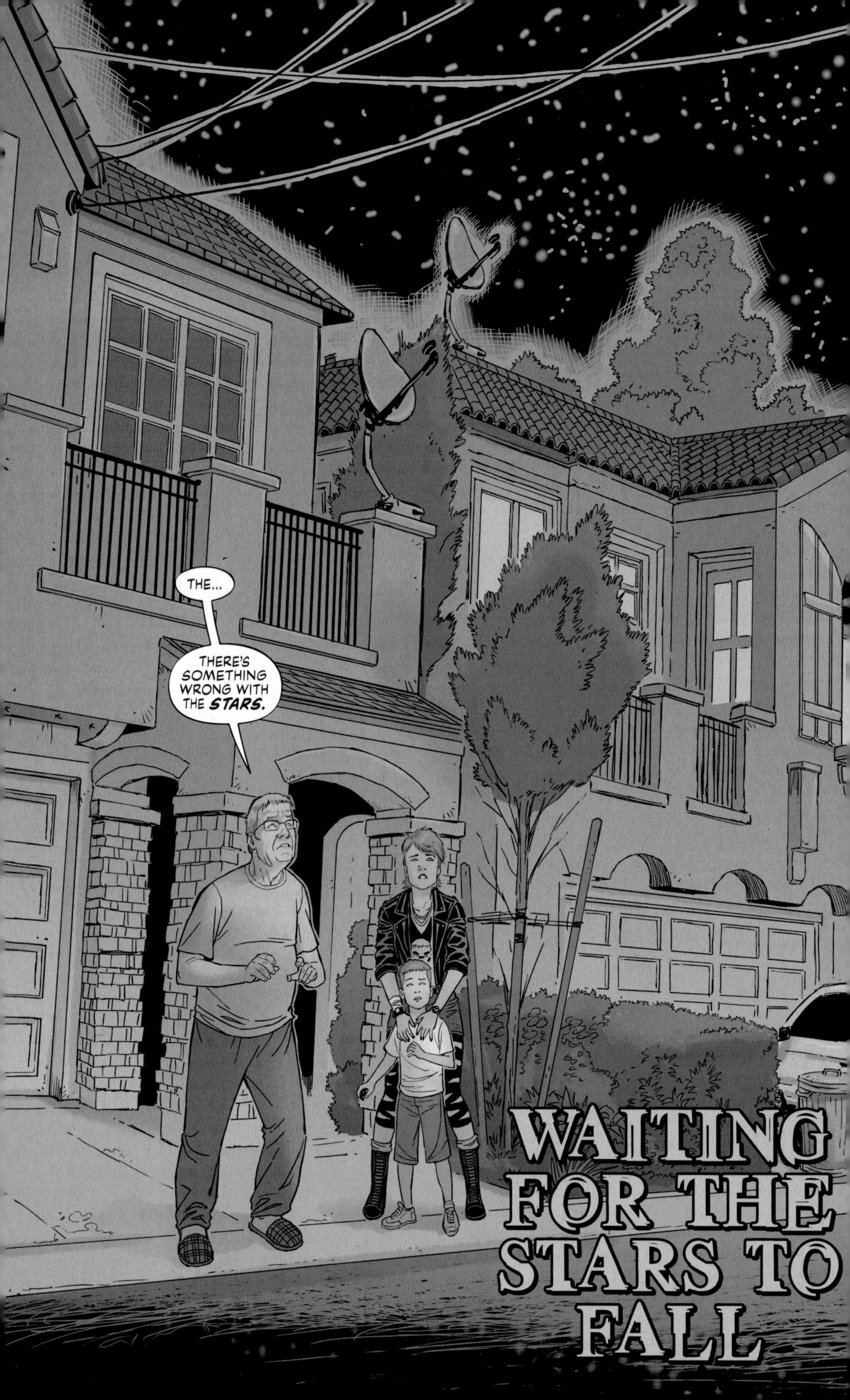
THE...
THERE'S SOMETHING WRONG WITH THE STARS.
WAITING FOR THE STARS TO FALL

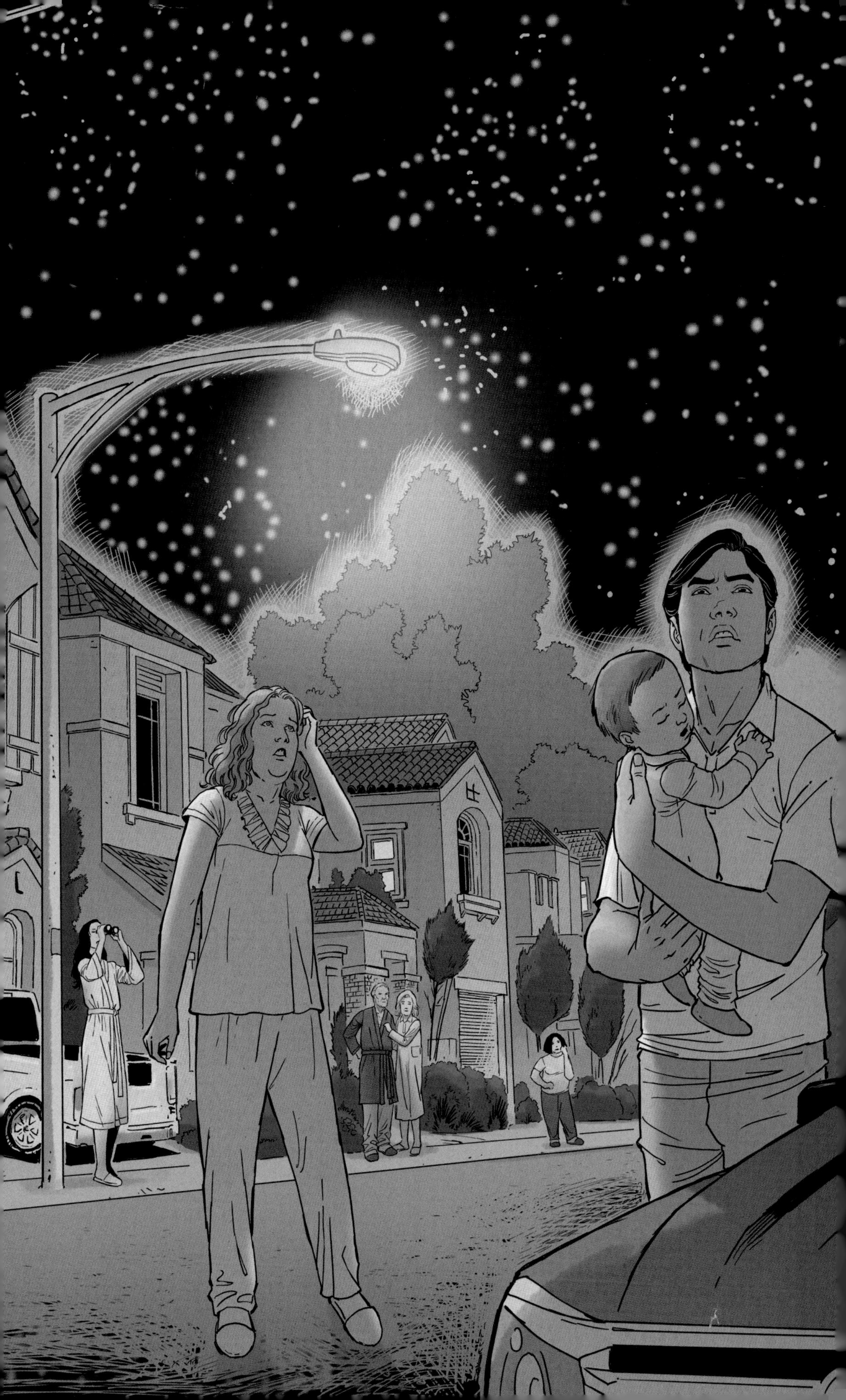

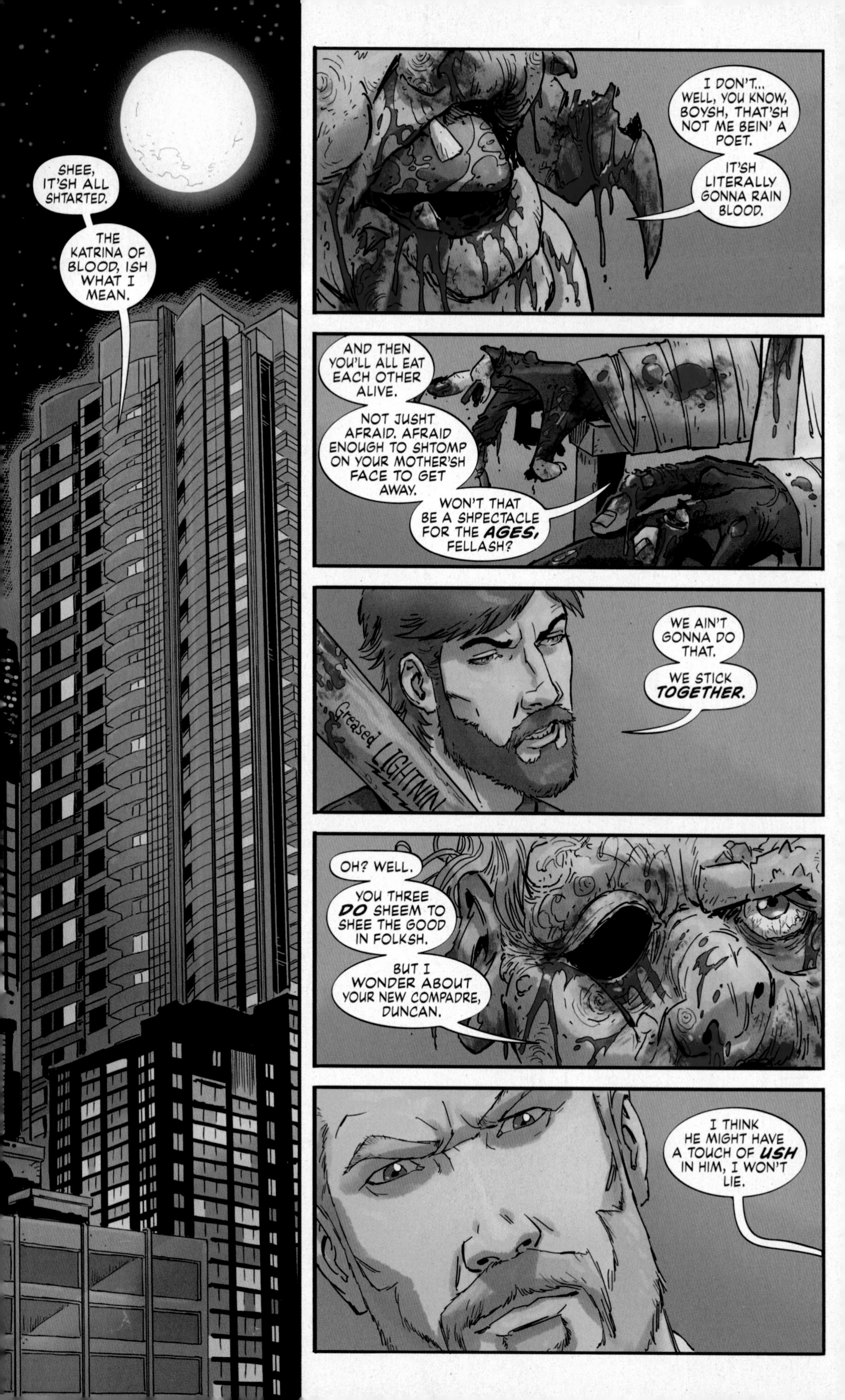
SHEE, IT'SH ALL SHTARTED.
THE KATRINA OF BLOOD, ISH WHAT I MEAN.
I DON'T... WELL, YOU KNOW, BOYSH, THAT'SH NOT ME BEIN' A POET.
IT'SH LITERALLY GONNA RAIN BLOOD.
AND THEN YOU'LL ALL EAT EACH OTHER ALIVE.
NOT JUSHT AFRAID. AFRAID ENOUGH TO SHTOMP ON YOUR MOTHER'SH FACE TO GET AWAY.
WON'T THAT BE A SHPECTACLE FOR THE *AGES,* FELLASH?
Greased LIGHTNIN
WE AIN'T GONNA DO THAT.
WE STICK *TOGETHER.*
OH? WELL.
YOU THREE *DO* SHEEM TO SHEE THE GOOD IN FOLKSH.
BUT I WONDER ABOUT YOUR NEW COMPADRE, DUNCAN.
I THINK HE MIGHT HAVE A TOUCH OF *USH* IN HIM, I WON'T LIE.

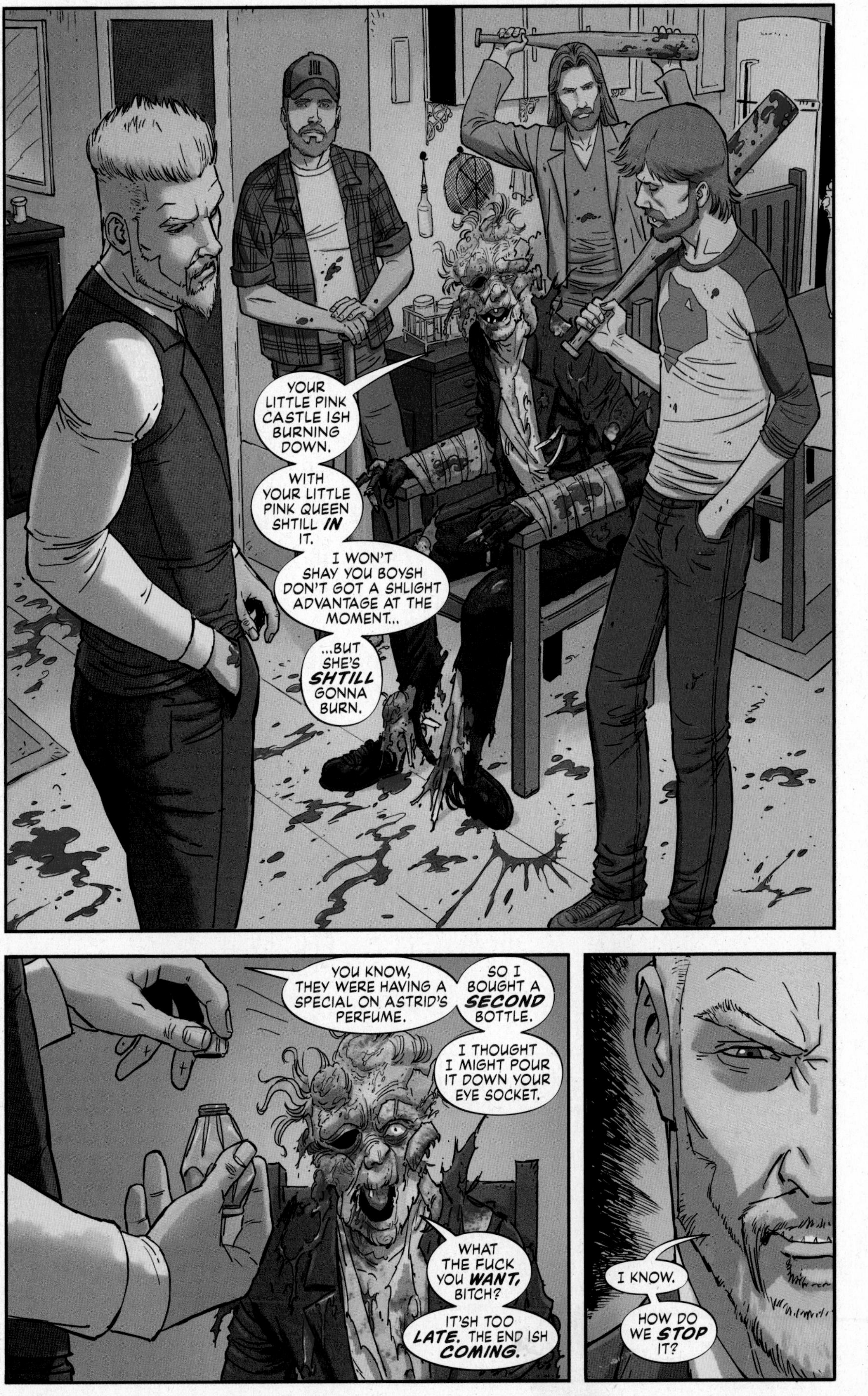
YOUR LITTLE PINK CASTLE ISH BURNING DOWN.
WITH YOUR LITTLE PINK QUEEN SHTILL ***IN*** IT.
I WON'T SHAY YOU BOYSH DON'T GOT A SHLIGHT ADVANTAGE AT THE MOMENT...
...BUT SHE'S ***SHTILL*** GONNA BURN.
YOU KNOW, THEY WERE HAVING A SPECIAL ON ASTRID'S PERFUME.
SO I BOUGHT A ***SECOND*** BOTTLE.
I THOUGHT I MIGHT POUR IT DOWN YOUR EYE SOCKET.
WHAT THE FUCK YOU ***WANT,*** BITCH?
IT'SH TOO ***LATE.*** THE END ISH ***COMING.***
I KNOW.
HOW DO WE ***STOP*** IT?

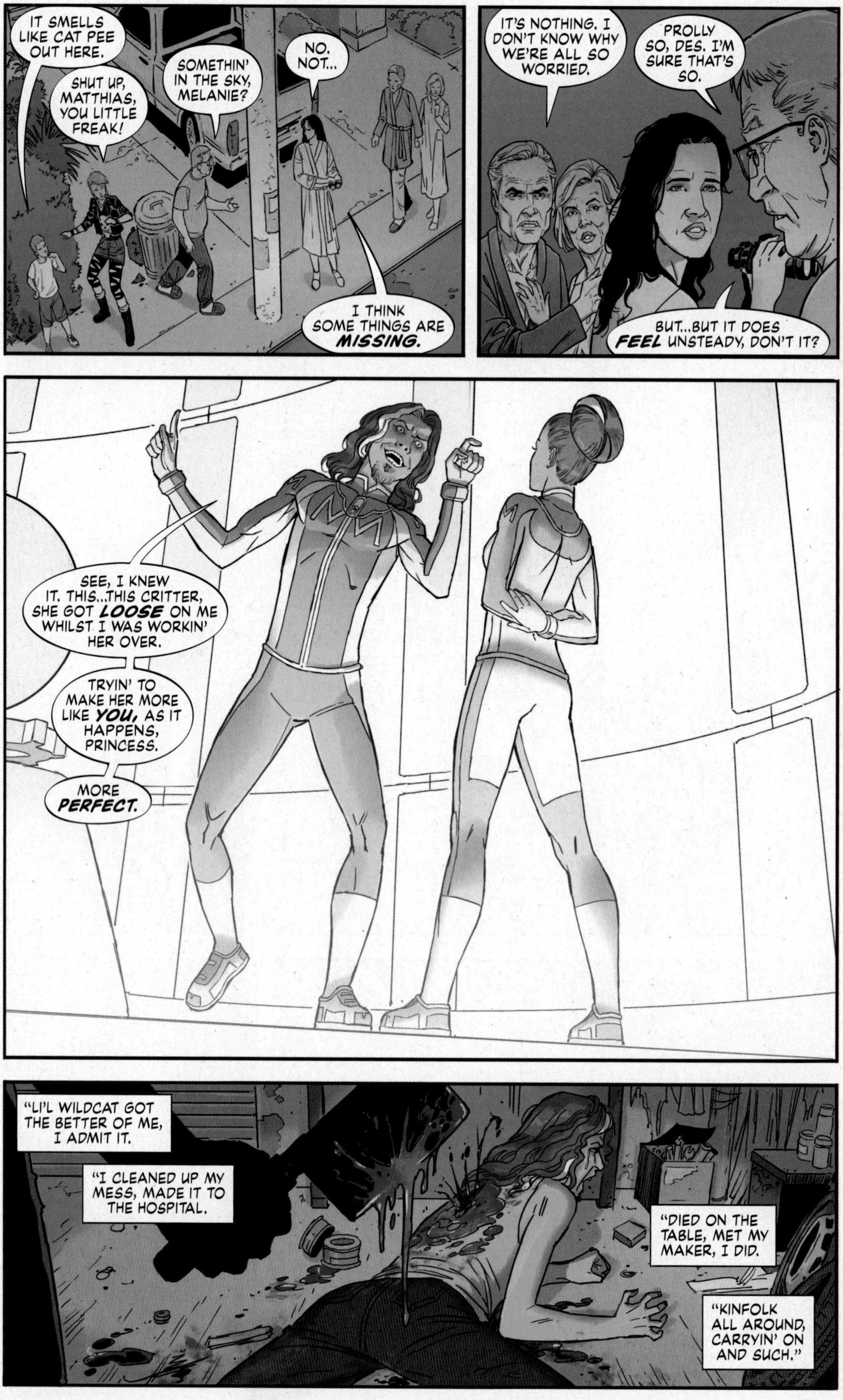
IT SMELLS LIKE CAT PEE OUT HERE.
SHUT UP, MATTHIAS, YOU LITTLE FREAK!
SOMETHIN' IN THE SKY, MELANIE?
NO. NOT...
I THINK SOME THINGS ARE MISSING.
IT'S NOTHING. I DON'T KNOW WHY WE'RE ALL SO WORRIED.
PROLLY SO, DES. I'M SURE THAT'S SO.
BUT...BUT IT DOES FEEL UNSTEADY, DON'T IT?
SEE, I KNEW IT. THIS...THIS CRITTER, SHE GOT LOOSE ON ME WHILST I WAS WORKIN' HER OVER.
TRYIN' TO MAKE HER MORE LIKE YOU, AS IT HAPPENS, PRINCESS.
MORE PERFECT.
"LI'L WILDCAT GOT THE BETTER OF ME, I ADMIT IT.
"I CLEANED UP MY MESS, MADE IT TO THE HOSPITAL.
"DIED ON THE TABLE, MET MY MAKER, I DID.
"KINFOLK ALL AROUND, CARRYIN' ON AND SUCH."

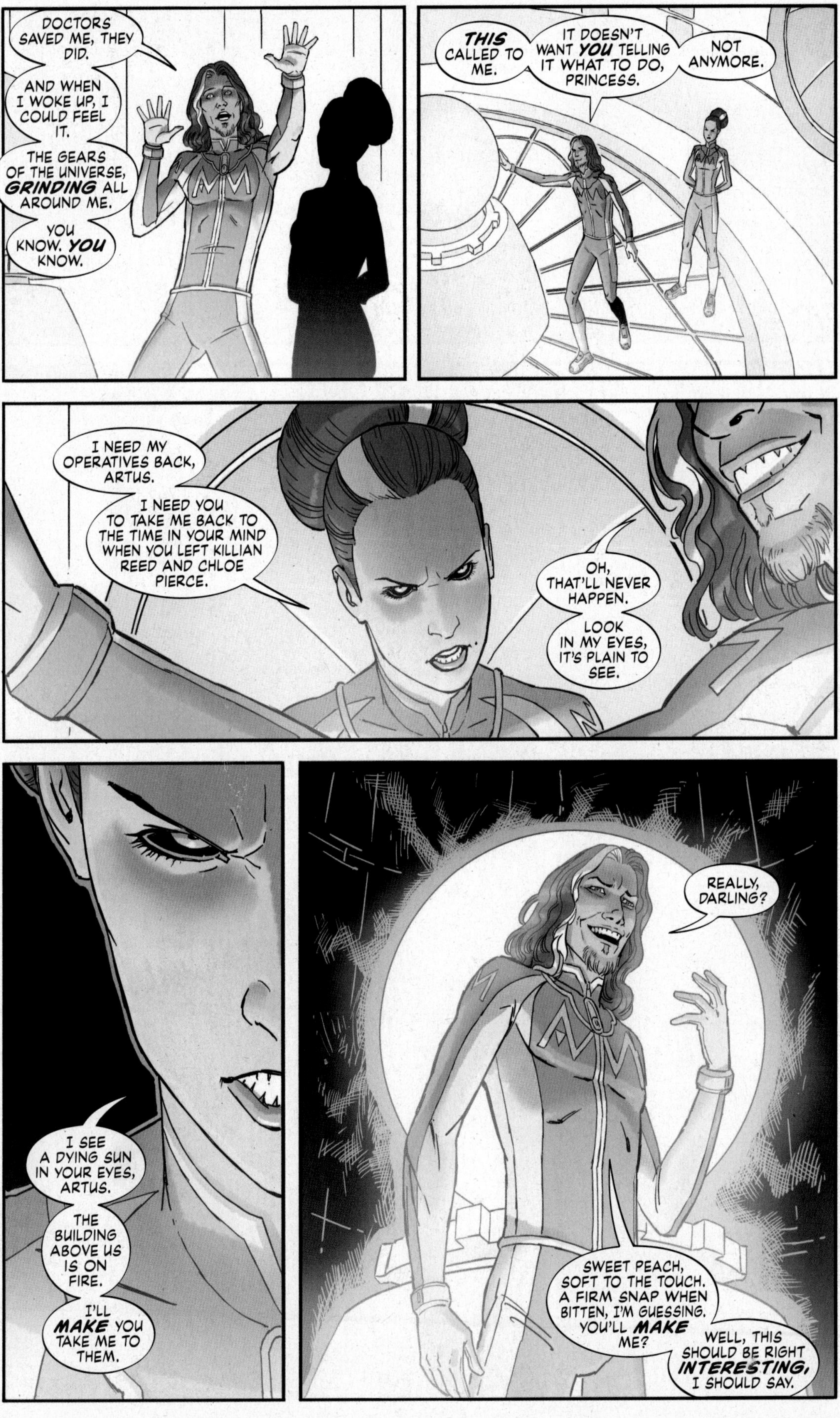
DOCTORS SAVED ME, THEY DID.
AND WHEN I WOKE UP, I COULD FEEL IT.
THE GEARS OF THE UNIVERSE, GRINDING ALL AROUND ME.
YOU KNOW. YOU KNOW.
THIS CALLED TO ME.
IT DOESN'T WANT YOU TELLING IT WHAT TO DO, PRINCESS.
NOT ANYMORE.
I NEED MY OPERATIVES BACK, ARTUS.
I NEED YOU TO TAKE ME BACK TO THE TIME IN YOUR MIND WHEN YOU LEFT KILLIAN REED AND CHLOE PIERCE.
OH, THAT'LL NEVER HAPPEN.
LOOK IN MY EYES, IT'S PLAIN TO SEE.
I SEE A DYING SUN IN YOUR EYES, ARTUS.
THE BUILDING ABOVE US IS ON FIRE.
I'LL MAKE YOU TAKE ME TO THEM.
REALLY, DARLING?
SWEET PEACH, SOFT TO THE TOUCH. A FIRM SNAP WHEN BITTEN, I'M GUESSING. YOU'LL MAKE ME?
WELL, THIS SHOULD BE RIGHT INTERESTING, I SHOULD SAY.

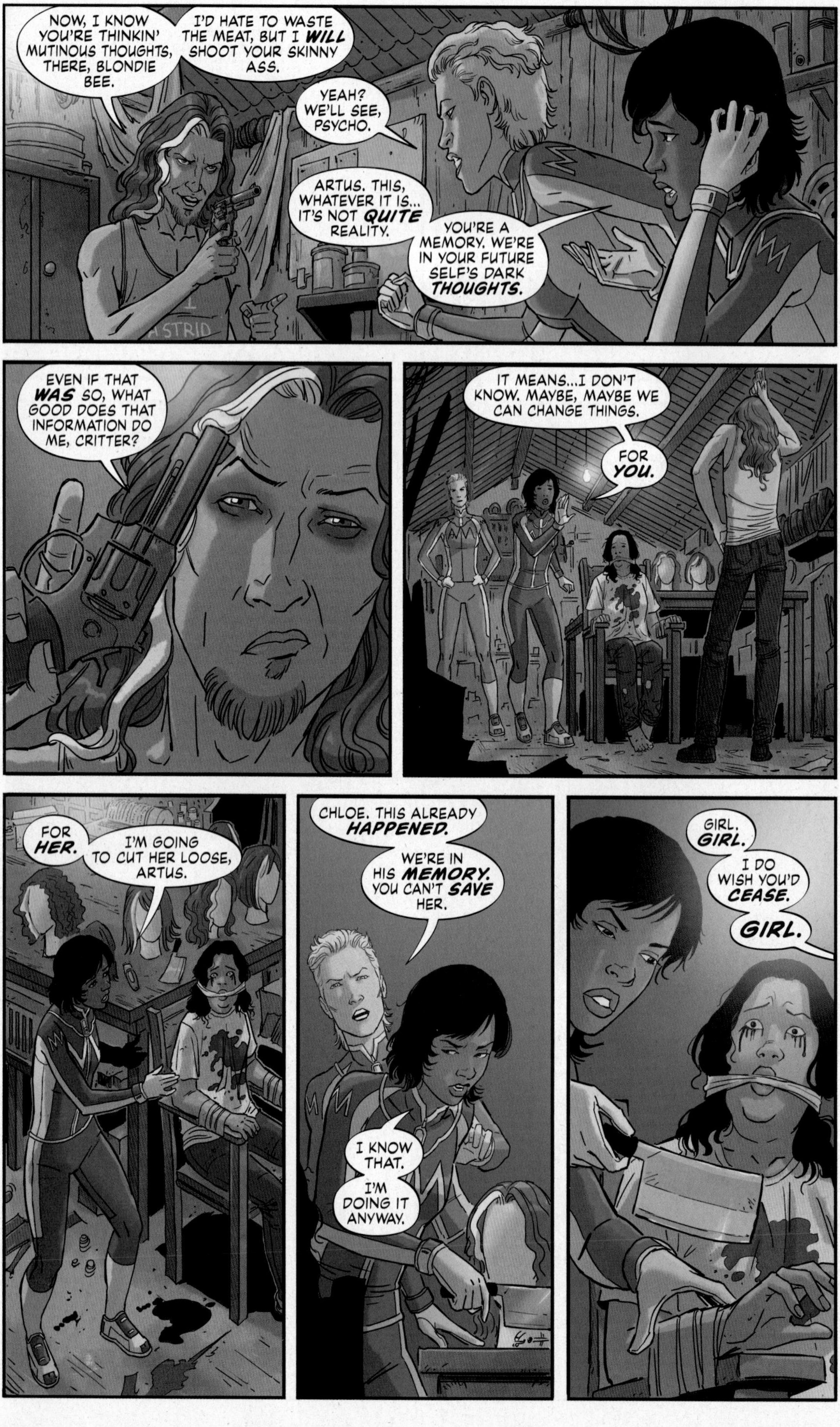
NOW, I KNOW YOU'RE THINKIN' MUTINOUS THOUGHTS, THERE, BLONDIE BEE.
I'D HATE TO WASTE THE MEAT, BUT I WILL SHOOT YOUR SKINNY ASS.
YEAH? WE'LL SEE, PSYCHO.
ARTUS. THIS, WHATEVER IT IS... IT'S NOT QUITE REALITY.
YOU'RE A MEMORY. WE'RE IN YOUR FUTURE SELF'S DARK THOUGHTS.
ASTRID
EVEN IF THAT WAS SO, WHAT GOOD DOES THAT INFORMATION DO ME, CRITTER?
IT MEANS...I DON'T KNOW. MAYBE, MAYBE WE CAN CHANGE THINGS.
FOR YOU.
FOR HER.
I'M GOING TO CUT HER LOOSE, ARTUS.
CHLOE. THIS ALREADY HAPPENED.
WE'RE IN HIS MEMORY. YOU CAN'T SAVE HER.
I KNOW THAT.
I'M DOING IT ANYWAY.
GIRL. GIRL.
I DO WISH YOU'D CEASE.
GIRL.

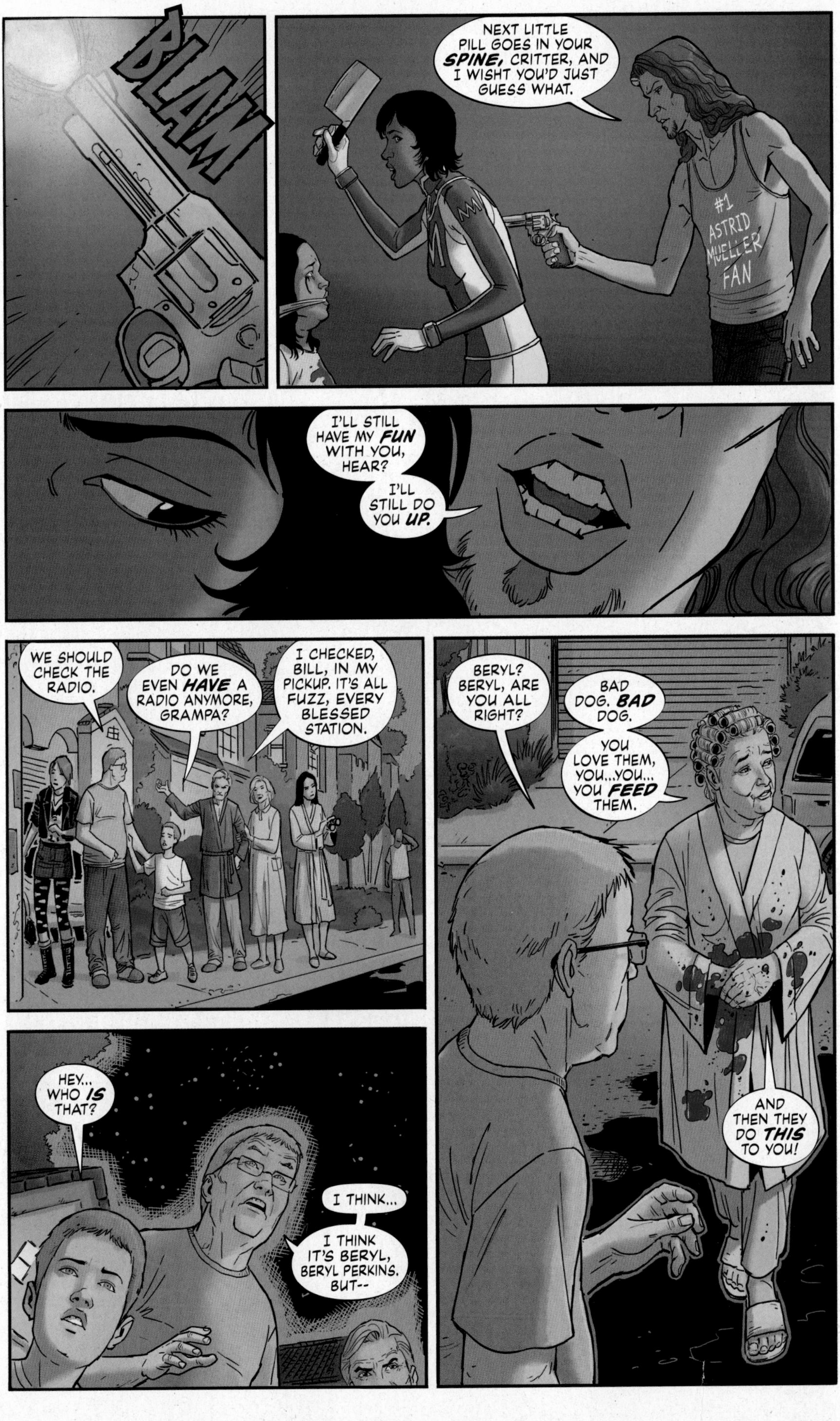
BLAM
NEXT LITTLE PILL GOES IN YOUR SPINE, CRITTER, AND I WISHT YOU'D JUST GUESS WHAT.
#1 ASTRID MUELLER FAN
I'LL STILL HAVE MY FUN WITH YOU, HEAR?
I'LL STILL DO YOU UP.
WE SHOULD CHECK THE RADIO.
DO WE EVEN HAVE A RADIO ANYMORE, GRAMPA?
I CHECKED, BILL, IN MY PICKUP. IT'S ALL FUZZ, EVERY BLESSED STATION.
HEY... WHO IS THAT?
I THINK...
I THINK IT'S BERYL, BERYL PERKINS. BUT--
BERYL? BERYL, ARE YOU ALL RIGHT?
BAD DOG. BAD DOG.
YOU LOVE THEM, YOU...YOU... YOU FEED THEM.
AND THEN THEY DO THIS TO YOU!

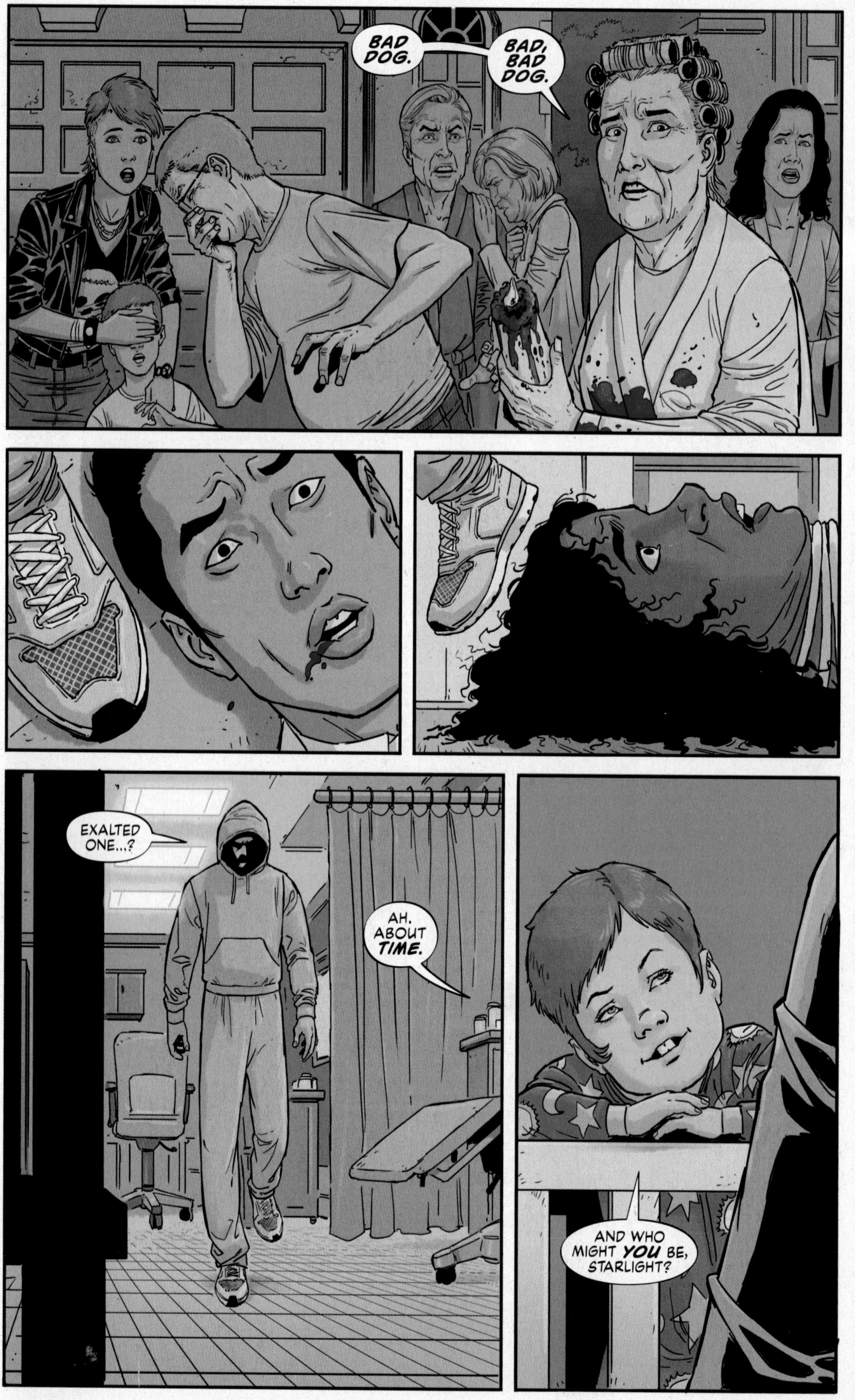
BAD DOG.
BAD, BAD DOG.
EXALTED ONE...?
AH. ABOUT *TIME.*
AND WHO MIGHT *YOU* BE, STARLIGHT?

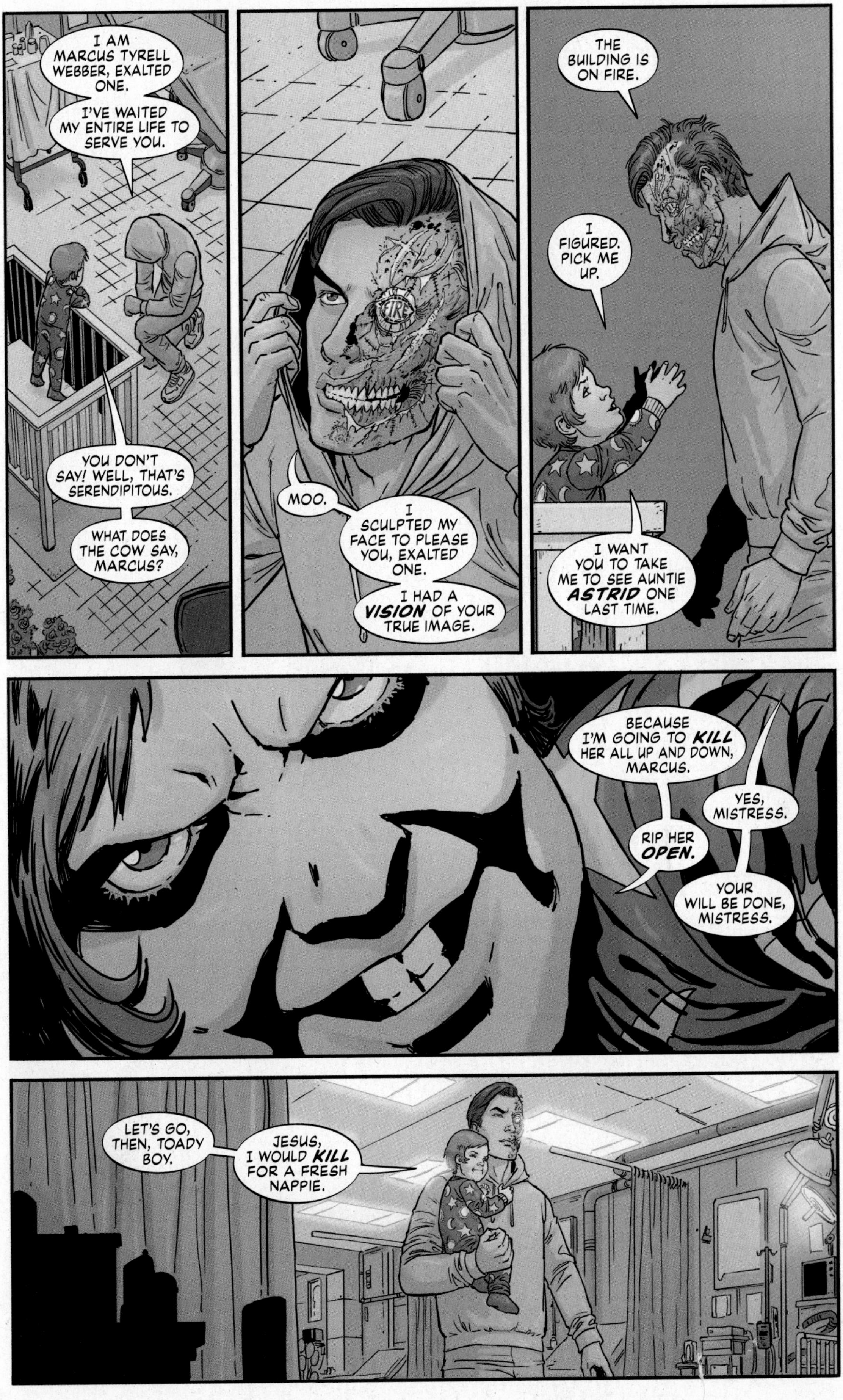
I AM MARCUS TYRELL WEBBER, EXALTED ONE.
I'VE WAITED MY ENTIRE LIFE TO SERVE YOU.
YOU DON'T SAY! WELL, THAT'S SERENDIPITOUS.
WHAT DOES THE COW SAY, MARCUS?
MOO.
I SCULPTED MY FACE TO PLEASE YOU, EXALTED ONE.
I HAD A VISION OF YOUR TRUE IMAGE.
FIRE
THE BUILDING IS ON FIRE.
I FIGURED. PICK ME UP.
I WANT YOU TO TAKE ME TO SEE AUNTIE ASTRID ONE LAST TIME.
BECAUSE I'M GOING TO KILL HER ALL UP AND DOWN, MARCUS.
RIP HER OPEN.
YES, MISTRESS.
YOUR WILL BE DONE, MISTRESS.
LET'S GO, THEN, TOADY BOY.
JESUS, I WOULD KILL FOR A FRESH NAPPIE.

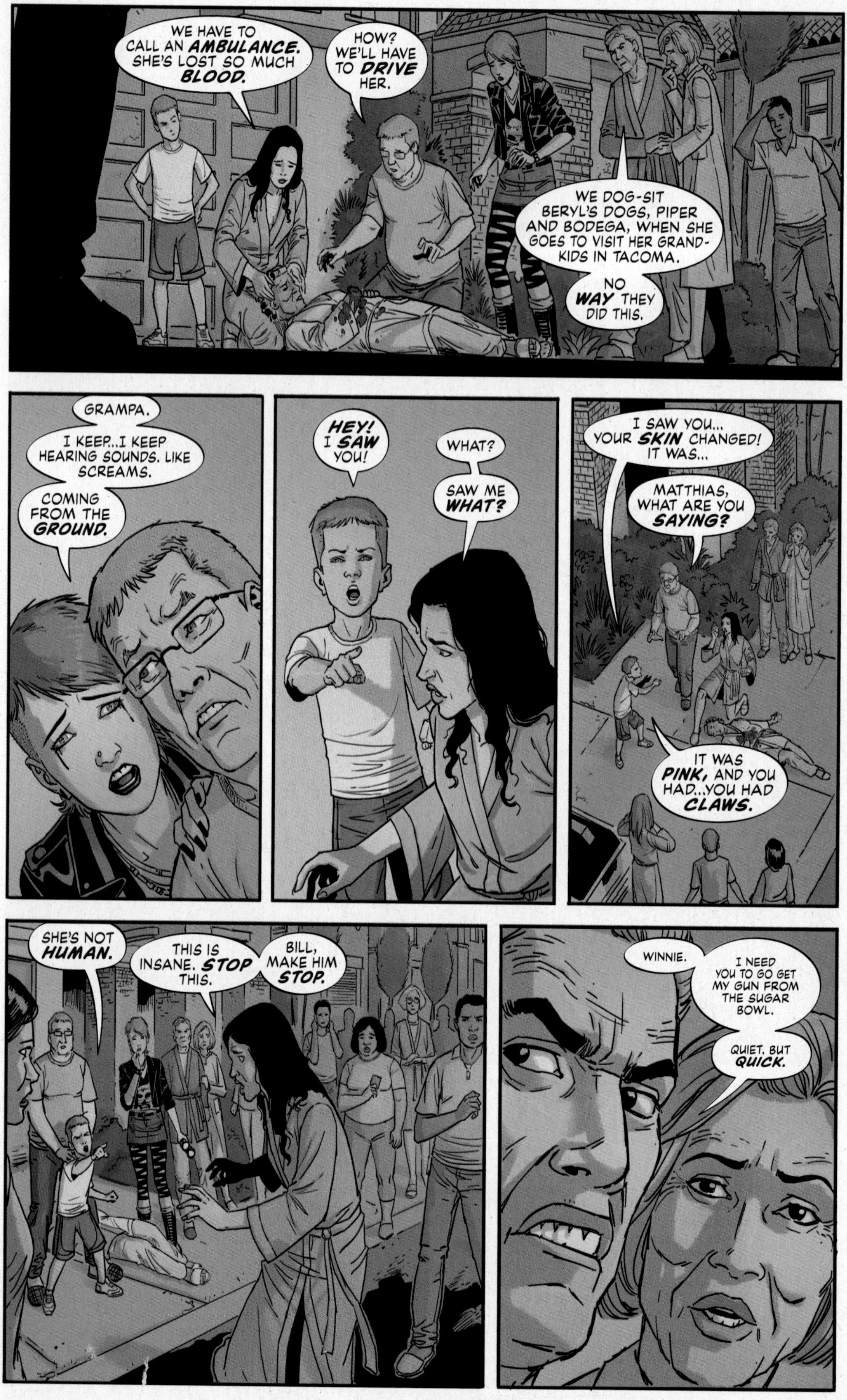
WE HAVE TO CALL AN AMBULANCE. SHE'S LOST SO MUCH BLOOD.
HOW? WE'LL HAVE TO DRIVE HER.
WE DOG-SIT BERYL'S DOGS, PIPER AND BODEGA, WHEN SHE GOES TO VISIT HER GRAND-KIDS IN TACOMA.
NO WAY THEY DID THIS.
GRAMPA.
I KEEP...I KEEP HEARING SOUNDS. LIKE SCREAMS.
COMING FROM THE GROUND.
HEY! I SAW YOU!
WHAT?
SAW ME WHAT?
I SAW YOU... YOUR SKIN CHANGED! IT WAS...
MATTHIAS, WHAT ARE YOU SAYING?
IT WAS PINK, AND YOU HAD...YOU HAD CLAWS.
SHE'S NOT HUMAN.
THIS IS INSANE. STOP THIS.
BILL, MAKE HIM STOP.
WINNIE.
I NEED YOU TO GO GET MY GUN FROM THE SUGAR BOWL.
QUIET. BUT QUICK.

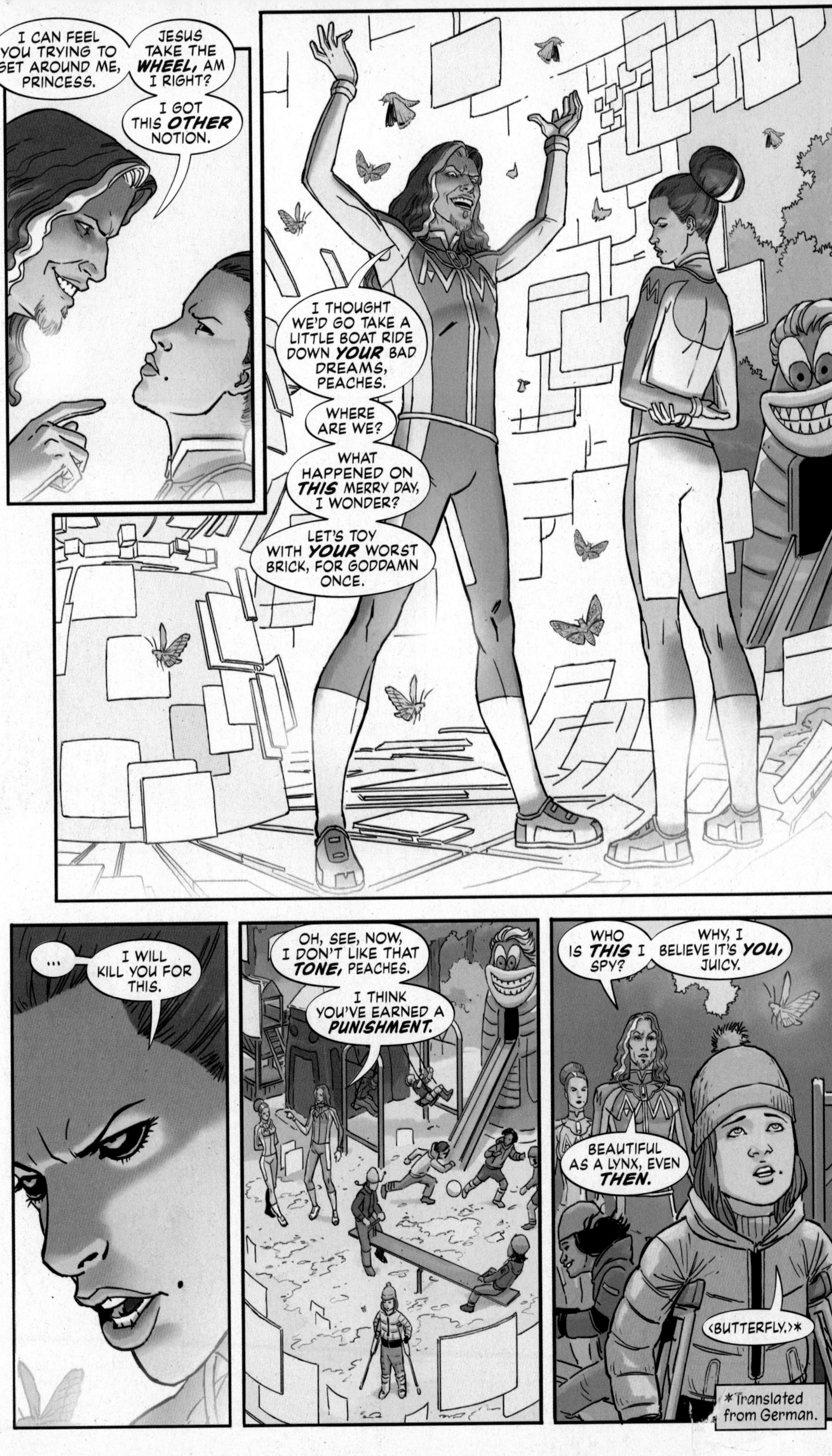
I CAN FEEL YOU TRYING TO GET AROUND ME, PRINCESS.
JESUS TAKE THE WHEEL, AM I RIGHT?
I GOT THIS OTHER NOTION.
I THOUGHT WE'D GO TAKE A LITTLE BOAT RIDE DOWN YOUR BAD DREAMS, PEACHES.
WHERE ARE WE?
WHAT HAPPENED ON THIS MERRY DAY, I WONDER?
LET'S TOY WITH YOUR WORST BRICK, FOR GODDAMN ONCE.
...
I WILL KILL YOU FOR THIS.
OH, SEE, NOW, I DON'T LIKE THAT TONE, PEACHES.
I THINK YOU'VE EARNED A PUNISHMENT.
WHO IS THIS I SPY?
WHY, I BELIEVE IT'S YOU, JUICY.
BEAUTIFUL AS A LYNX, EVEN THEN.
<BUTTERFLY.>*
*Translated from German.

⟨IT'S A MOTH, DARLING, NOT A BUTTERFLY.⟩

⟨DON'T YOU WANT TO PLAY WITH THE OTHER CHILDREN, ASTRID?⟩

⟨THE DOCTORS SAY YOU SHOULD GET SOME MILD EXERCISE.⟩

⟨YOU'RE NOT MY FATHER. I DON'T KNOW **WHAT** YOU ARE.⟩

⟨WHAT DO YOU MEAN, DARLING? OF COURSE I AM.⟩

⟨YOU'RE JUST A LITTLE CONFUSED.⟩

⟨DON'T TOUCH ME.⟩

⟨I WANT YOU TO KNOW. I WILL KNOW THE TRUTH.⟩

⟨I'LL TELL **EVERYONE.**⟩

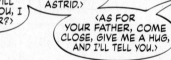

⟨WILL YOU? OH DEAR.⟩

⟨WHO WILL BELIEVE YOU, I WONDER?⟩

⟨NO, NO. I'M AFRAID NO ONE WILL LISTEN, ASTRID.⟩

⟨AS FOR YOUR FATHER, COME CLOSE, GIVE ME A HUG, AND I'LL TELL YOU.⟩

⟨THAT'S THE PRICE. A HUG FOR DADDY TO HEAR THE TRUTH.⟩

⟨I ATE HIM, DARLING.⟩

⟨RIGHT DOWN TO HIS DIRTY FUCKING TOES.⟩

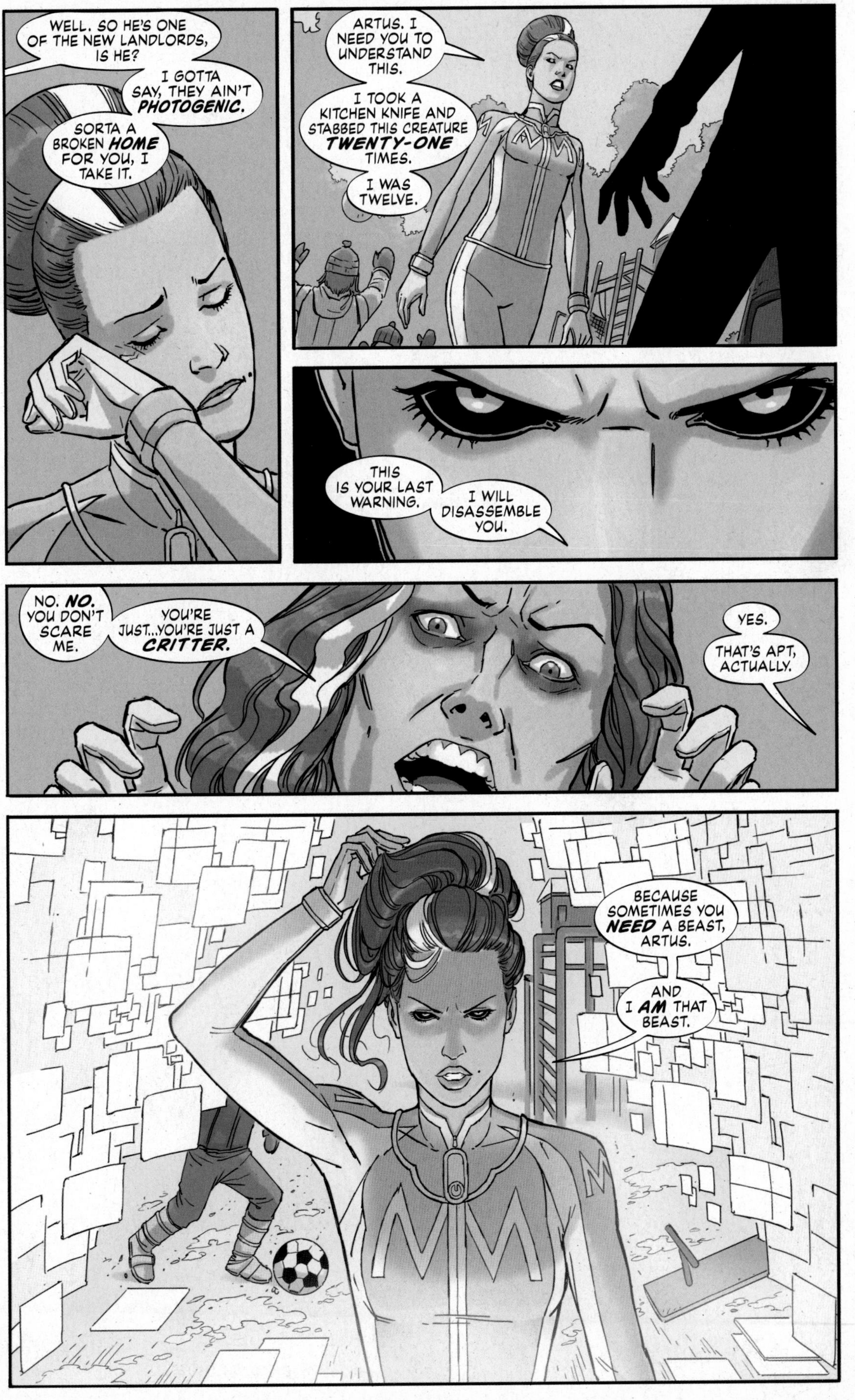
WELL. SO HE'S ONE OF THE NEW LANDLORDS, IS HE?
I GOTTA SAY, THEY AIN'T PHOTOGENIC.
SORTA A BROKEN HOME FOR YOU, I TAKE IT.
ARTUS. I NEED YOU TO UNDERSTAND THIS.
I TOOK A KITCHEN KNIFE AND STABBED THIS CREATURE TWENTY-ONE TIMES.
I WAS TWELVE.
THIS IS YOUR LAST WARNING.
I WILL DISASSEMBLE YOU.
NO. NO. YOU DON'T SCARE ME.
YOU'RE JUST...YOU'RE JUST A CRITTER.
YES.
THAT'S APT, ACTUALLY.
BECAUSE SOMETIMES YOU NEED A BEAST, ARTUS.
AND I AM THAT BEAST.

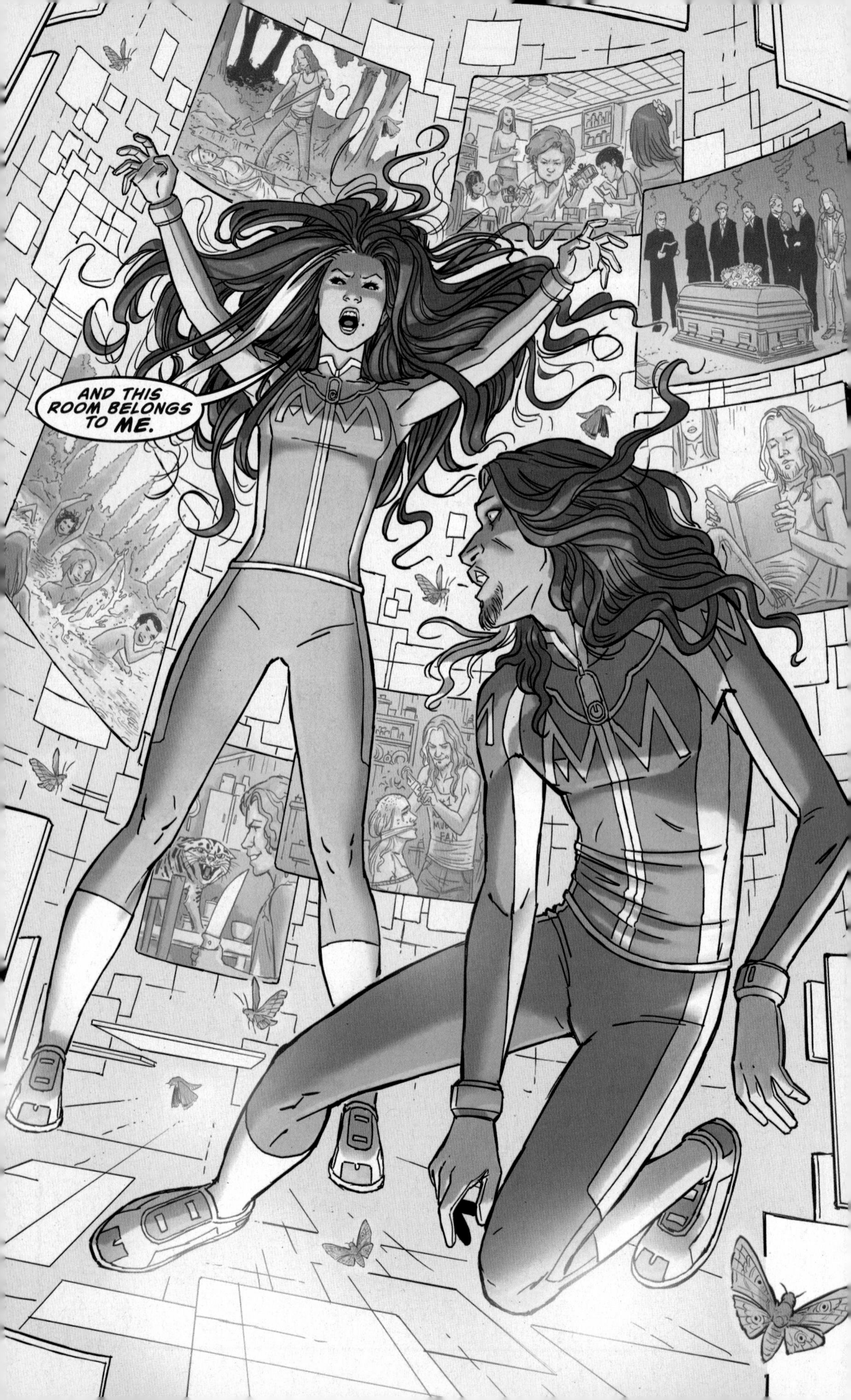
AND THIS ROOM BELONGS TO ME.

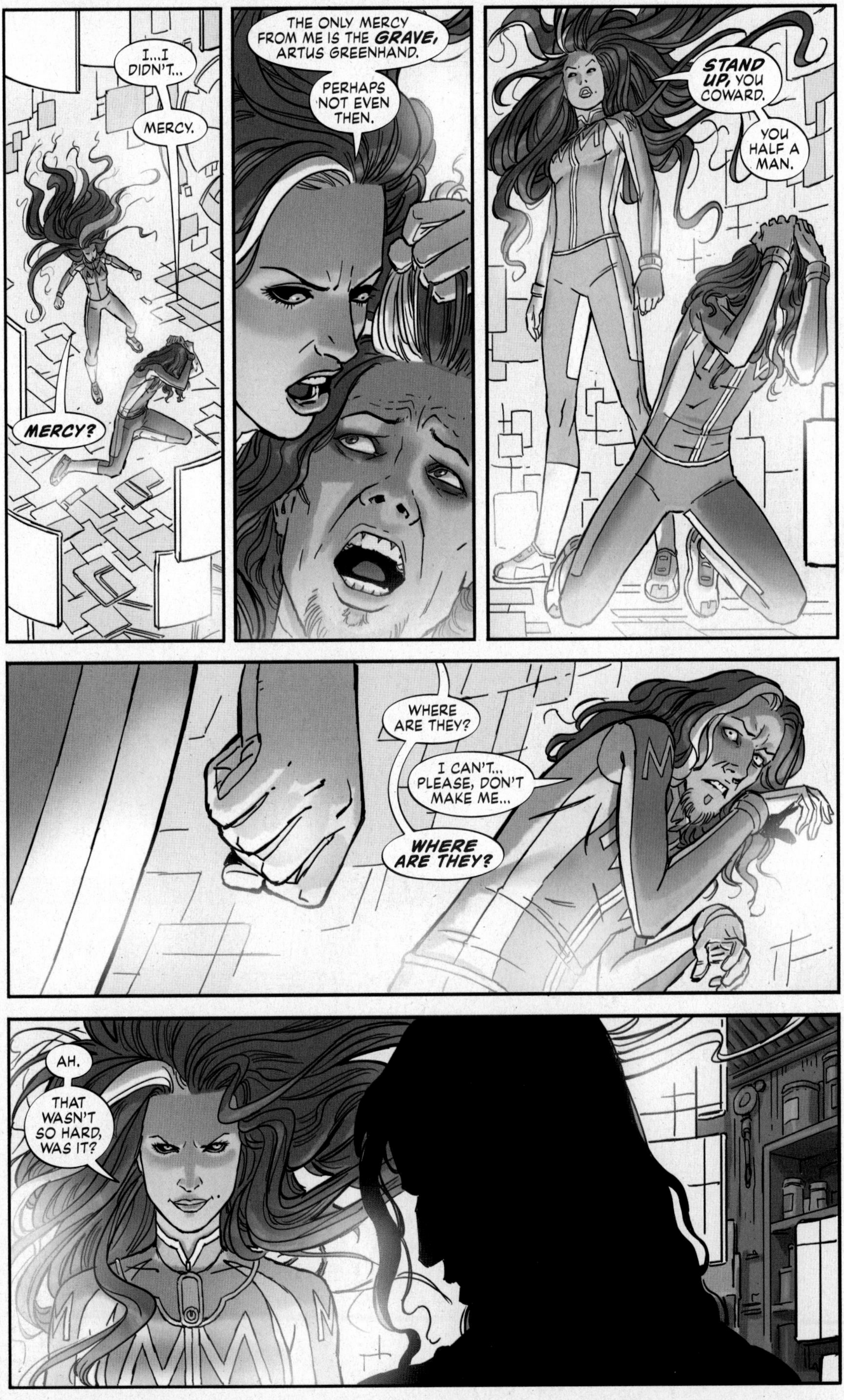
I...I DIDN'T...
MERCY.
MERCY?
THE ONLY MERCY FROM ME IS THE GRAVE, ARTUS GREENHAND.
PERHAPS NOT EVEN THEN.
STAND UP, YOU COWARD.
YOU HALF A MAN.
WHERE ARE THEY?
I CAN'T... PLEASE, DON'T MAKE ME...
WHERE ARE THEY?
AH.
THAT WASN'T SO HARD, WAS IT?

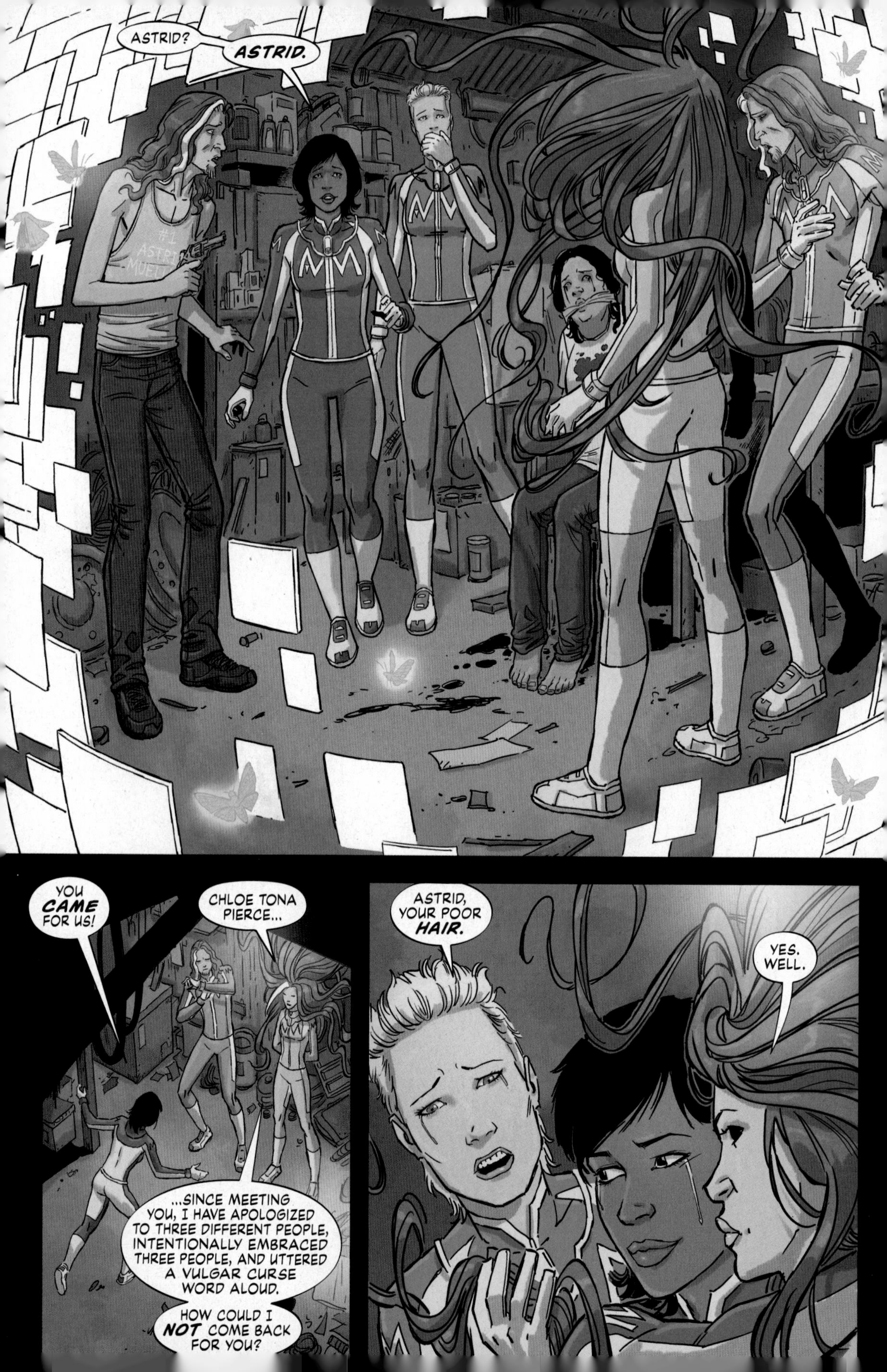
ASTRID?
ASTRID.
#1 ASTRID MUEL
YOU CAME FOR US!
CHLOE TONA PIERCE...
...SINCE MEETING YOU, I HAVE APOLOGIZED TO THREE DIFFERENT PEOPLE, INTENTIONALLY EMBRACED THREE PEOPLE, AND UTTERED A VULGAR CURSE WORD ALOUD.
HOW COULD I NOT COME BACK FOR YOU?
ASTRID, YOUR POOR HAIR.
YES. WELL.

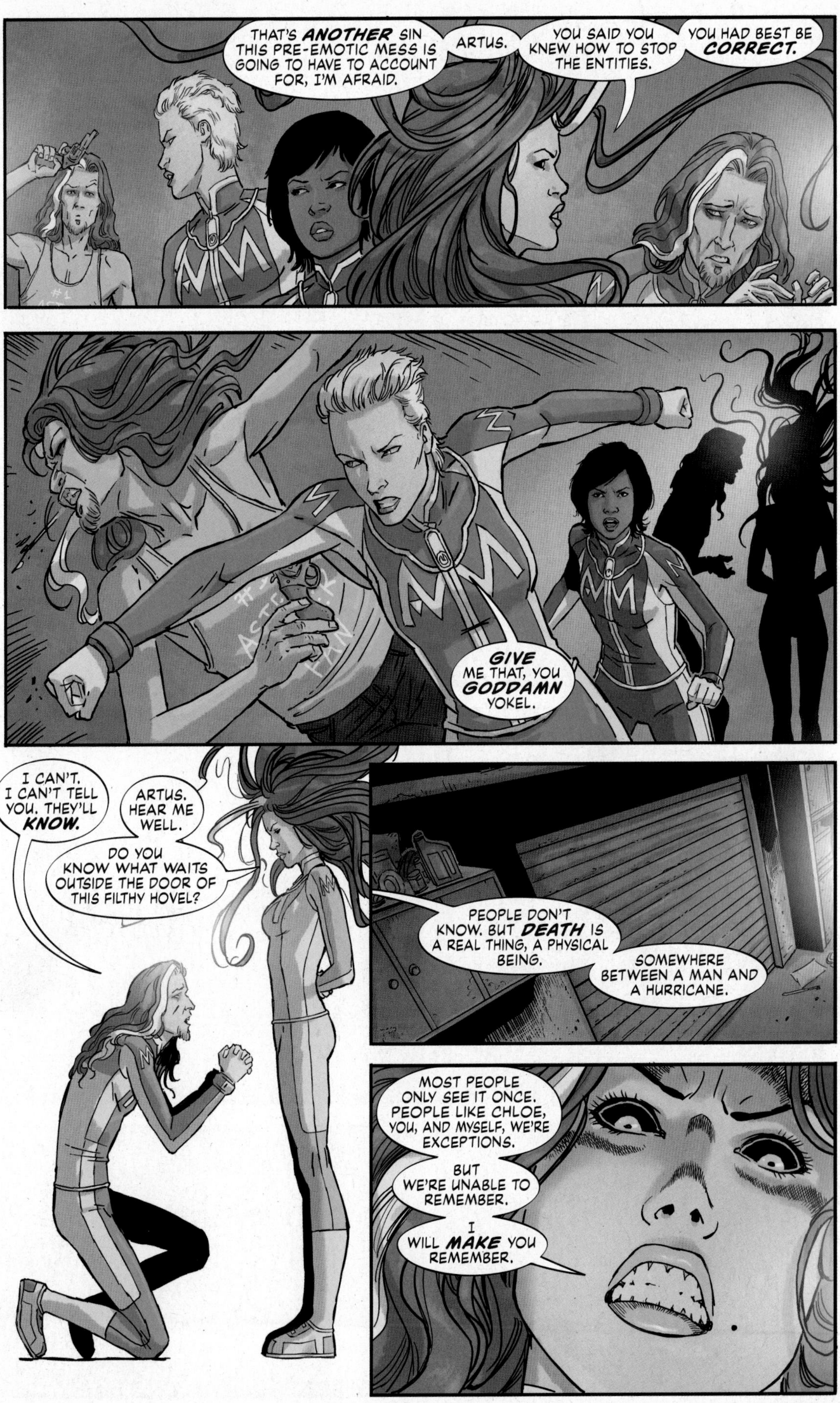
THAT'S ANOTHER SIN THIS PRE-EMOTIC MESS IS GOING TO HAVE TO ACCOUNT FOR, I'M AFRAID.
ARTUS.
YOU SAID YOU KNEW HOW TO STOP THE ENTITIES.
YOU HAD BEST BE CORRECT.
GIVE ME THAT, YOU GODDAMN YOKEL.
I CAN'T. I CAN'T TELL YOU. THEY'LL KNOW.
ARTUS. HEAR ME WELL.
DO YOU KNOW WHAT WAITS OUTSIDE THE DOOR OF THIS FILTHY HOVEL?
PEOPLE DON'T KNOW. BUT DEATH IS A REAL THING, A PHYSICAL BEING.
SOMEWHERE BETWEEN A MAN AND A HURRICANE.
MOST PEOPLE ONLY SEE IT ONCE. PEOPLE LIKE CHLOE, YOU, AND MYSELF, WE'RE EXCEPTIONS.
BUT WE'RE UNABLE TO REMEMBER.
I WILL MAKE YOU REMEMBER.

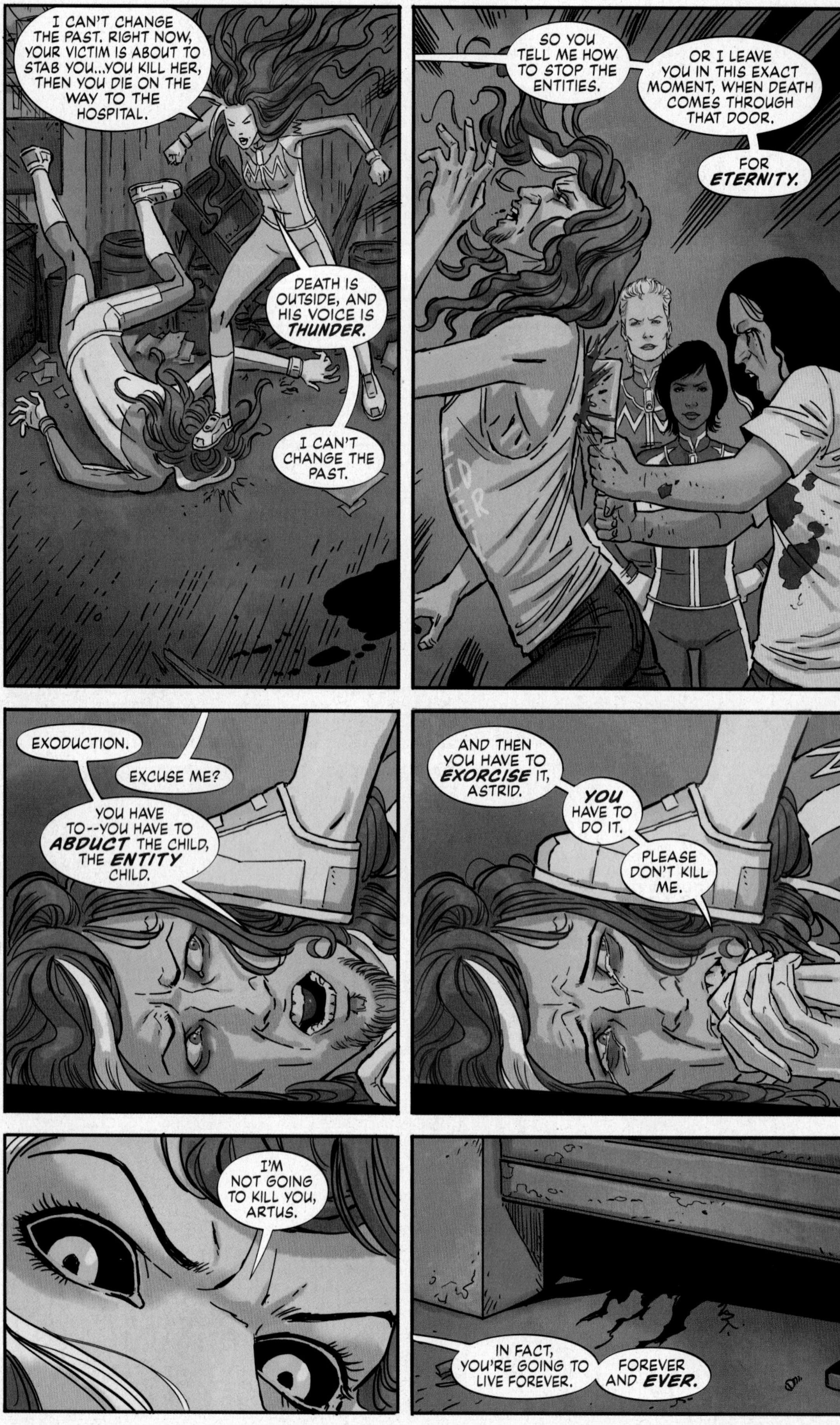
I CAN'T CHANGE THE PAST. RIGHT NOW, YOUR VICTIM IS ABOUT TO STAB YOU...YOU KILL HER, THEN YOU DIE ON THE WAY TO THE HOSPITAL.
DEATH IS OUTSIDE, AND HIS VOICE IS THUNDER.
I CAN'T CHANGE THE PAST.
SO YOU TELL ME HOW TO STOP THE ENTITIES.
OR I LEAVE YOU IN THIS EXACT MOMENT, WHEN DEATH COMES THROUGH THAT DOOR.
FOR ETERNITY.
EXODUCTION.
EXCUSE ME?
YOU HAVE TO--YOU HAVE TO ABDUCT THE CHILD, THE ENTITY CHILD.
AND THEN YOU HAVE TO EXORCISE IT, ASTRID.
YOU HAVE TO DO IT.
PLEASE DON'T KILL ME.
I'M NOT GOING TO KILL YOU, ARTUS.
IN FACT, YOU'RE GOING TO LIVE FOREVER.
FOREVER AND EVER.

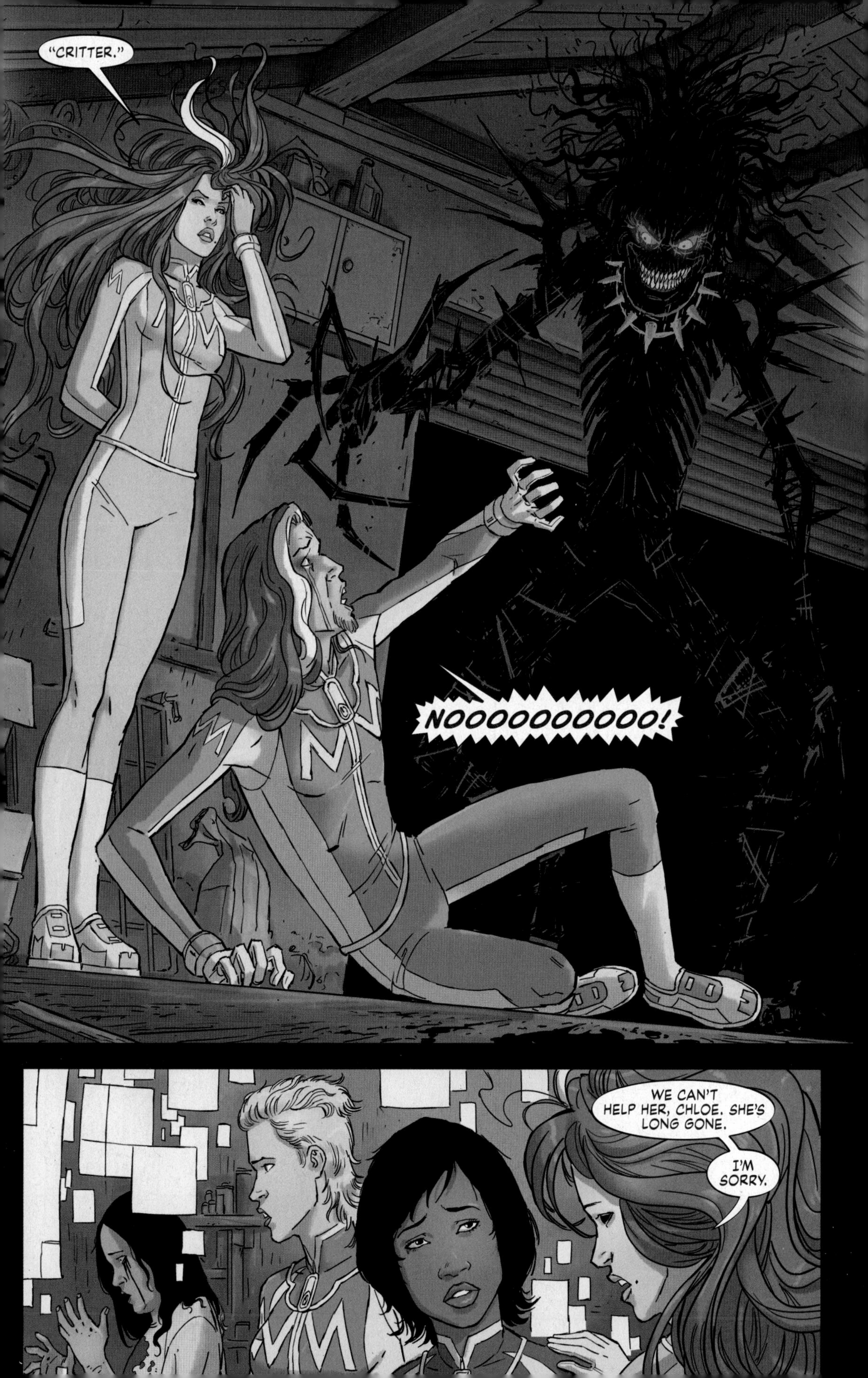
"CRITTER."
NOOOOOOOOOOO!
WE CAN'T HELP HER, CHLOE. SHE'S LONG GONE.
I'M SORRY.

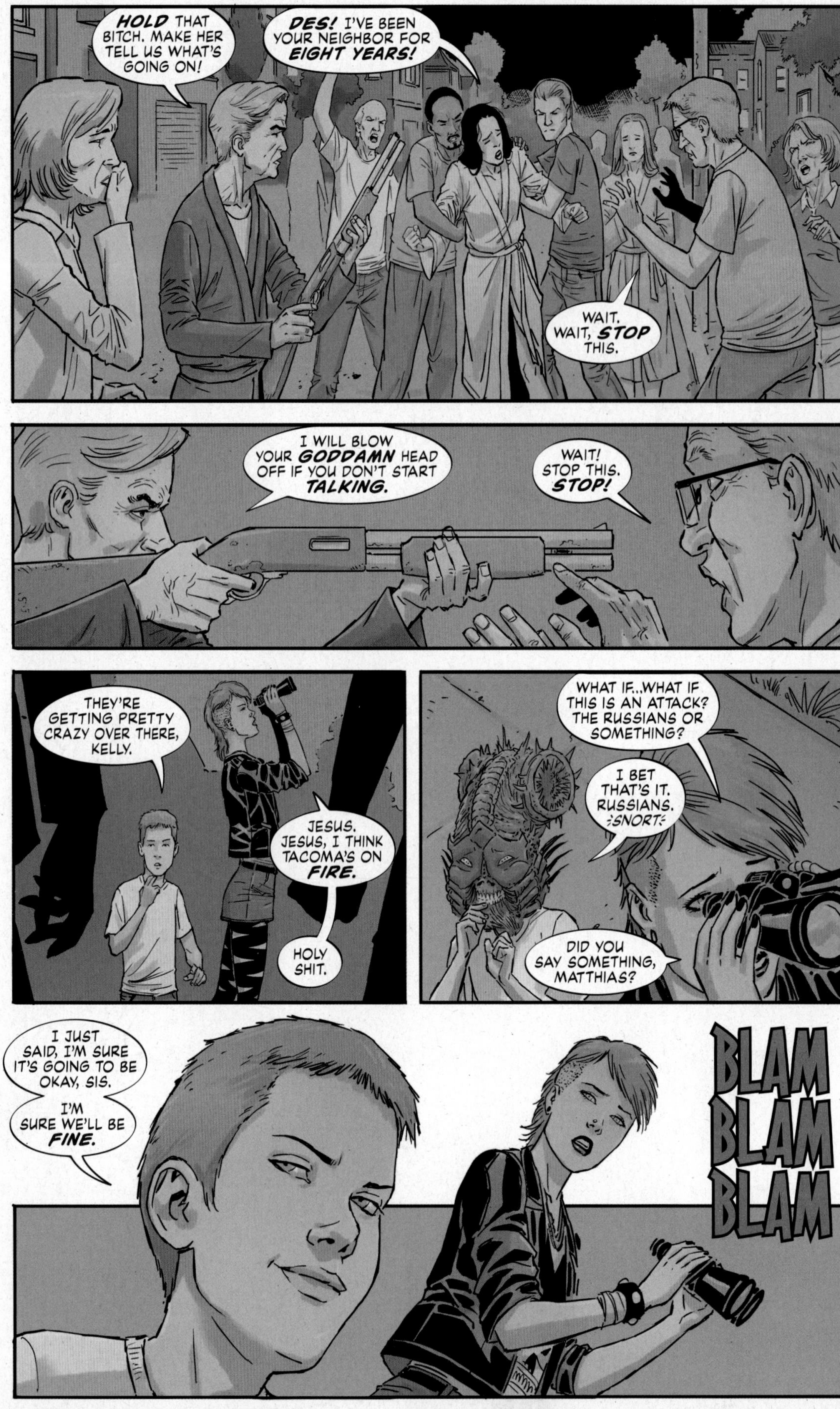
HOLD THAT BITCH. MAKE HER TELL US WHAT'S GOING ON!
DES! I'VE BEEN YOUR NEIGHBOR FOR EIGHT YEARS!
WAIT. WAIT, STOP THIS.
I WILL BLOW YOUR GODDAMN HEAD OFF IF YOU DON'T START TALKING.
WAIT! STOP THIS. STOP!
THEY'RE GETTING PRETTY CRAZY OVER THERE, KELLY.
JESUS. JESUS, I THINK TACOMA'S ON FIRE.
HOLY SHIT.
WHAT IF..WHAT IF THIS IS AN ATTACK? THE RUSSIANS OR SOMETHING?
I BET THAT'S IT. RUSSIANS. SNORT
DID YOU SAY SOMETHING, MATTHIAS?
I JUST SAID, I'M SURE IT'S GOING TO BE OKAY, SIS.
I'M SURE WE'LL BE FINE.
BLAM BLAM BLAM

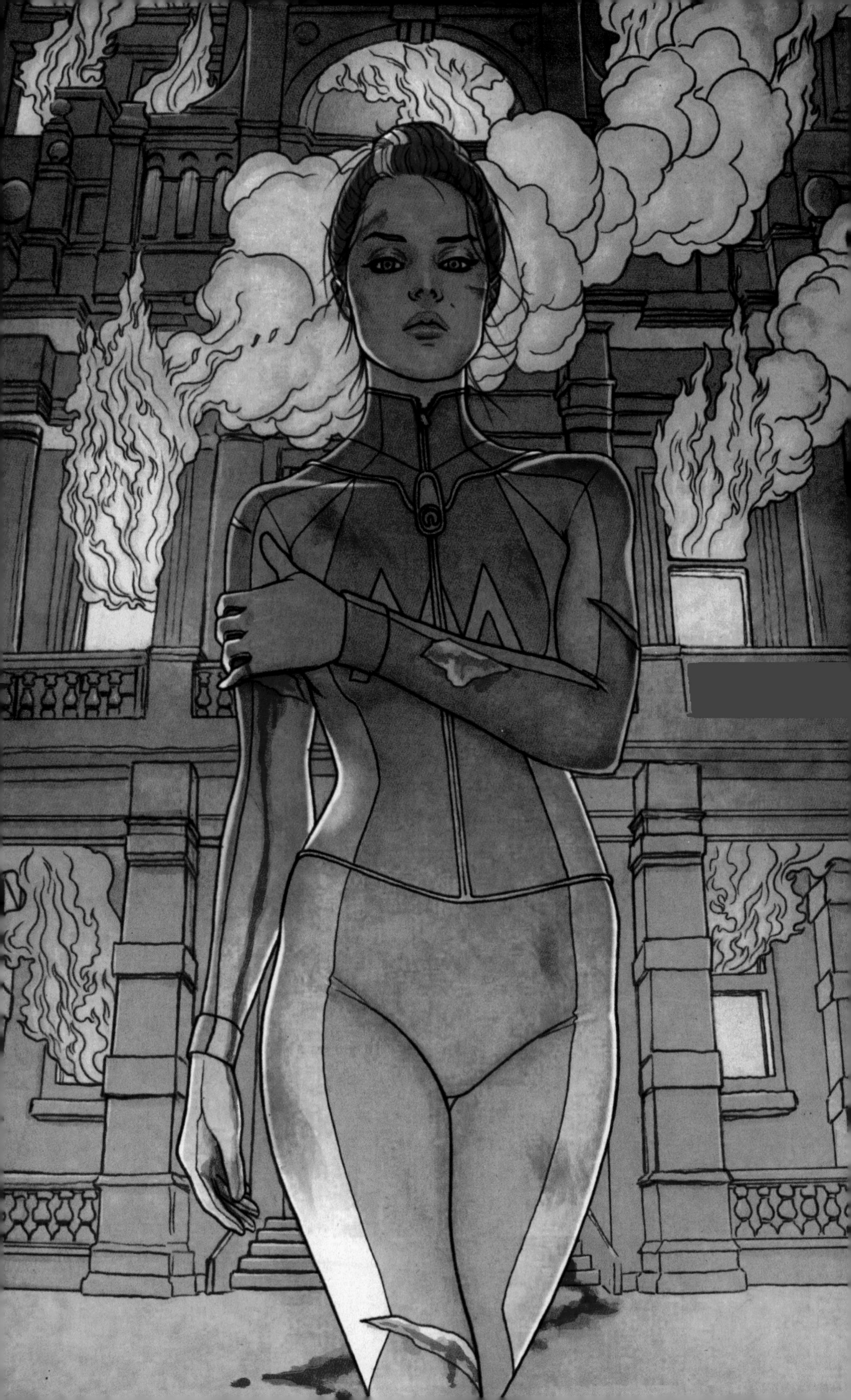

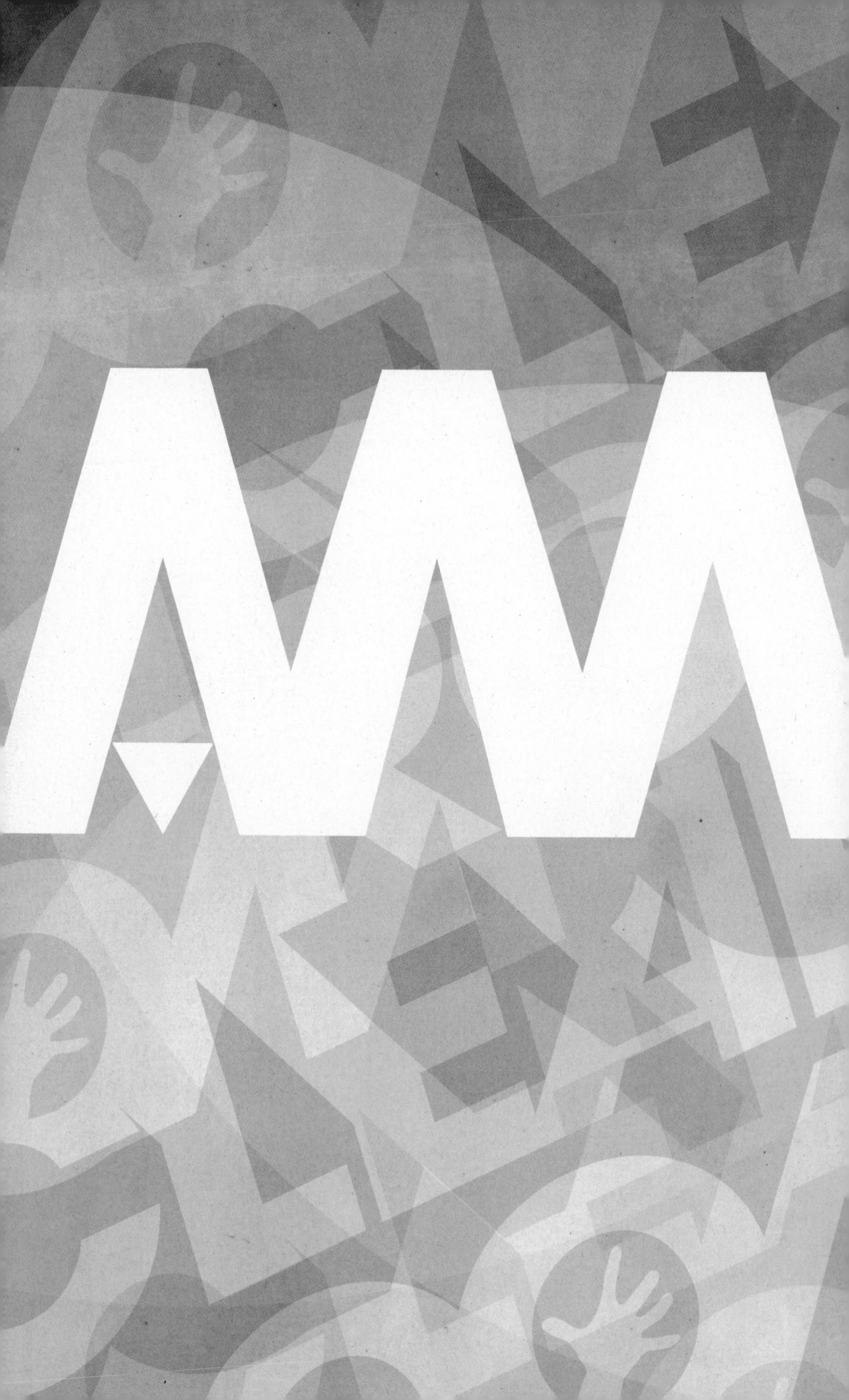

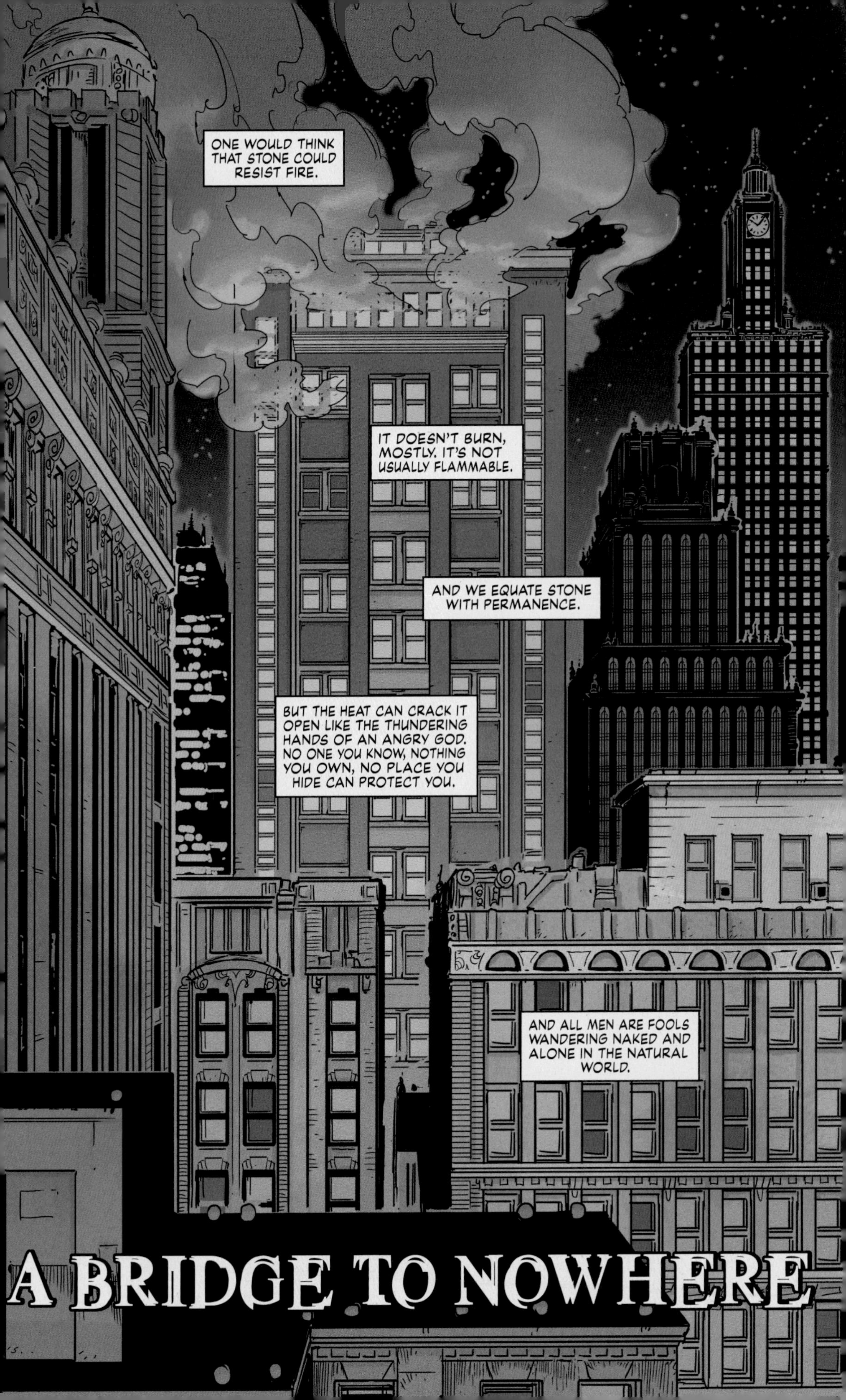

ONE WOULD THINK THAT STONE COULD RESIST FIRE.
IT DOESN'T BURN, MOSTLY. IT'S NOT USUALLY FLAMMABLE.
AND WE EQUATE STONE WITH PERMANENCE.
BUT THE HEAT CAN CRACK IT OPEN LIKE THE THUNDERING HANDS OF AN ANGRY GOD. NO ONE YOU KNOW, NOTHING YOU OWN, NO PLACE YOU HIDE CAN PROTECT YOU.
AND ALL MEN ARE FOOLS WANDERING NAKED AND ALONE IN THE NATURAL WORLD.
A BRIDGE TO NOWHERE

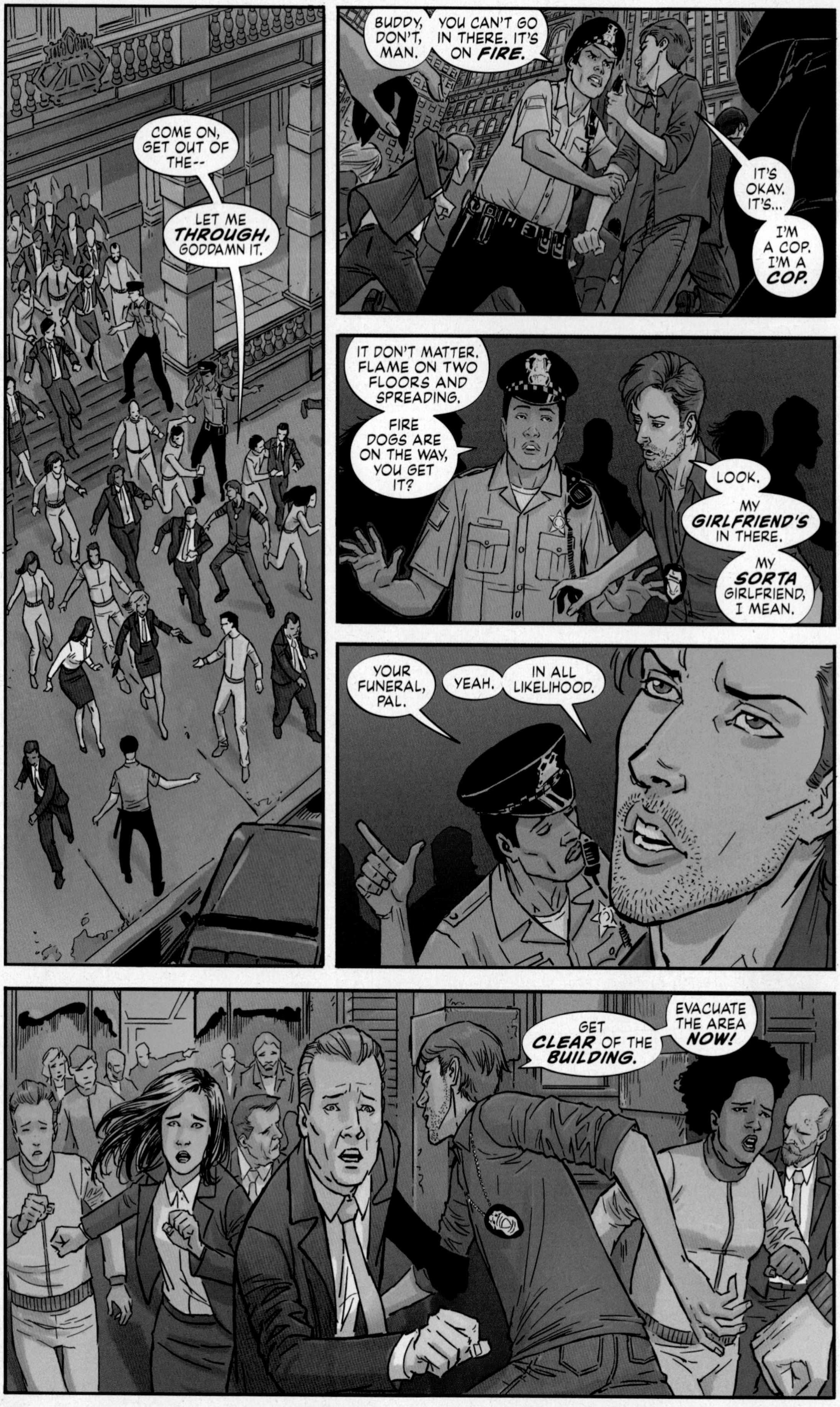

COME ON, GET OUT OF THE--
LET ME THROUGH, GODDAMN IT.
BUDDY, DON'T, MAN.
YOU CAN'T GO IN THERE. IT'S ON FIRE.
IT'S OKAY. IT'S...
I'M A COP. I'M A COP.
IT DON'T MATTER. FLAME ON TWO FLOORS AND SPREADING.
FIRE DOGS ARE ON THE WAY, YOU GET IT?
LOOK.
MY GIRLFRIEND'S IN THERE.
MY SORTA GIRLFRIEND, I MEAN.
YOUR FUNERAL, PAL.
YEAH.
IN ALL LIKELIHOOD.
GET CLEAR OF THE BUILDING.
EVACUATE THE AREA NOW!

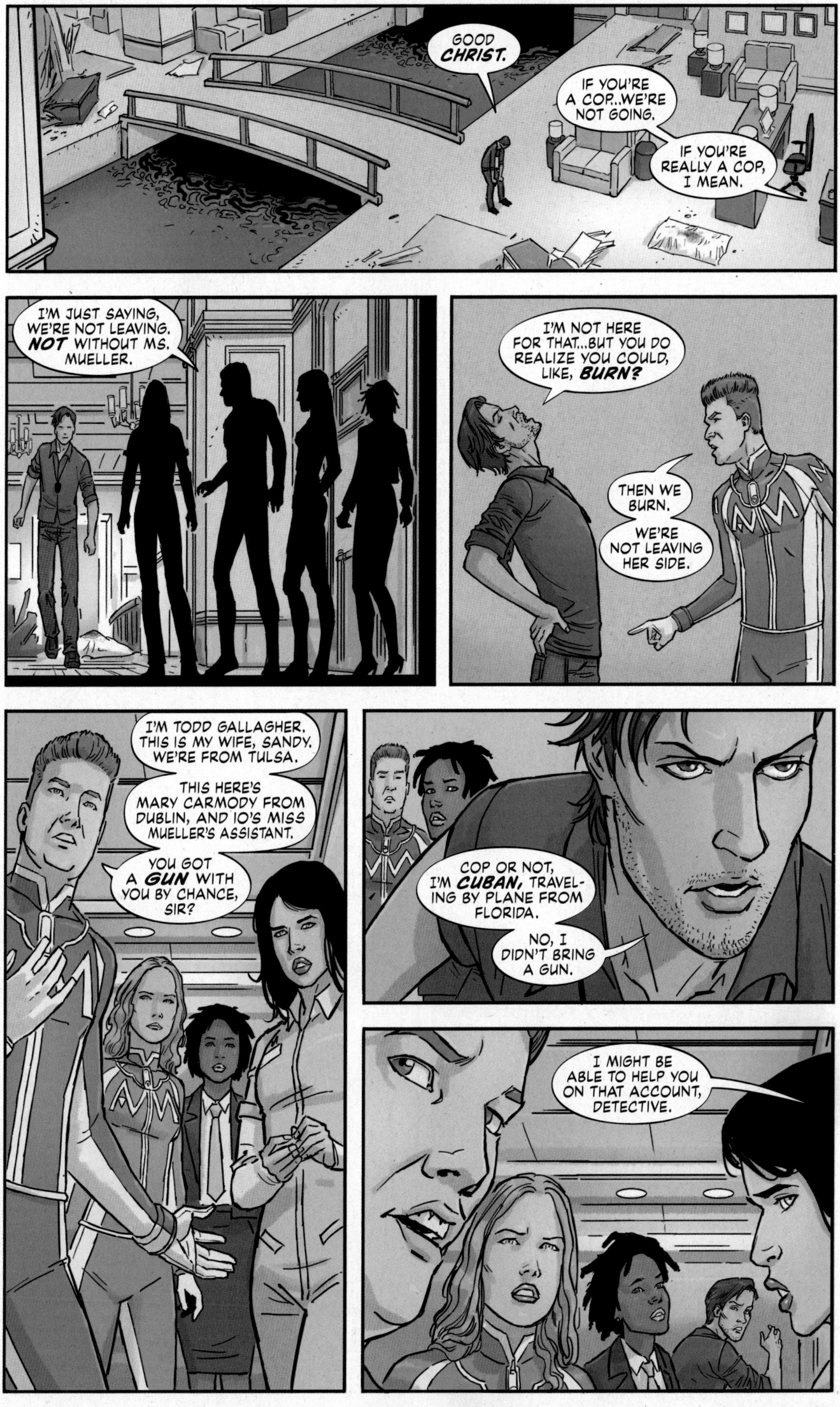
GOOD CHRIST.
IF YOU'RE A COP..WE'RE NOT GOING.
IF YOU'RE REALLY A COP, I MEAN.
I'M JUST SAYING, WE'RE NOT LEAVING. NOT WITHOUT MS. MUELLER.
I'M NOT HERE FOR THAT...BUT YOU DO REALIZE YOU COULD, LIKE, BURN?
THEN WE BURN.
WE'RE NOT LEAVING HER SIDE.
I'M TODD GALLAGHER. THIS IS MY WIFE, SANDY. WE'RE FROM TULSA.
THIS HERE'S MARY CARMODY FROM DUBLIN, AND IO'S MISS MUELLER'S ASSISTANT.
YOU GOT A GUN WITH YOU BY CHANCE, SIR?
COP OR NOT, I'M CUBAN, TRAVELING BY PLANE FROM FLORIDA.
NO, I DIDN'T BRING A GUN.
I MIGHT BE ABLE TO HELP YOU ON THAT ACCOUNT, DETECTIVE.

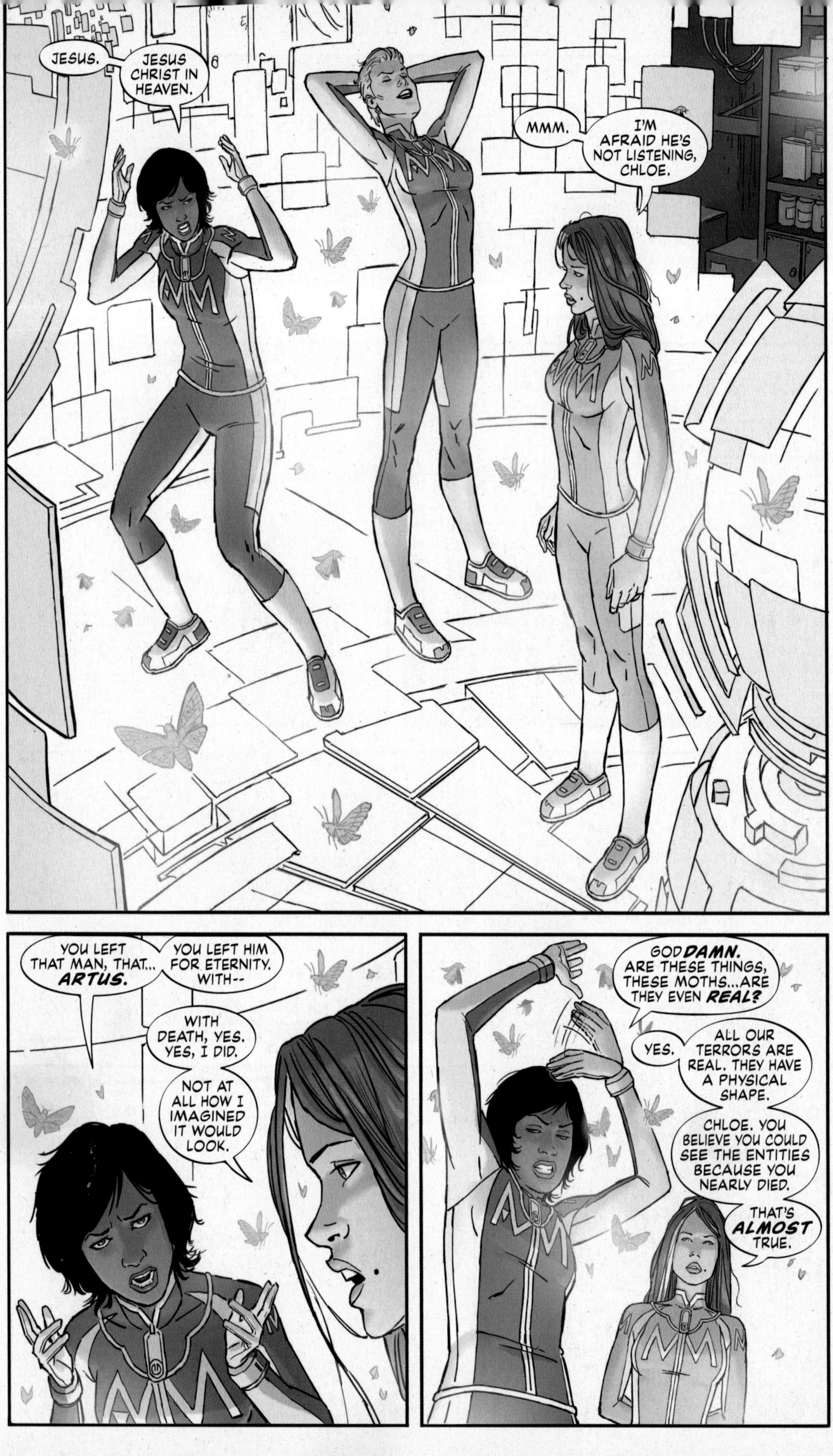

JESUS.
JESUS CHRIST IN HEAVEN.
MMM.
I'M AFRAID HE'S NOT LISTENING, CHLOE.
YOU LEFT THAT MAN, THAT... ARTUS.
YOU LEFT HIM FOR ETERNITY. WITH--
WITH DEATH, YES. YES, I DID.
NOT AT ALL HOW I IMAGINED IT WOULD LOOK.
GOD DAMN. ARE THESE THINGS, THESE MOTHS...ARE THEY EVEN REAL?
YES.
ALL OUR TERRORS ARE REAL. THEY HAVE A PHYSICAL SHAPE.
CHLOE. YOU BELIEVE YOU COULD SEE THE ENTITIES BECAUSE YOU NEARLY DIED.
THAT'S ALMOST TRUE.

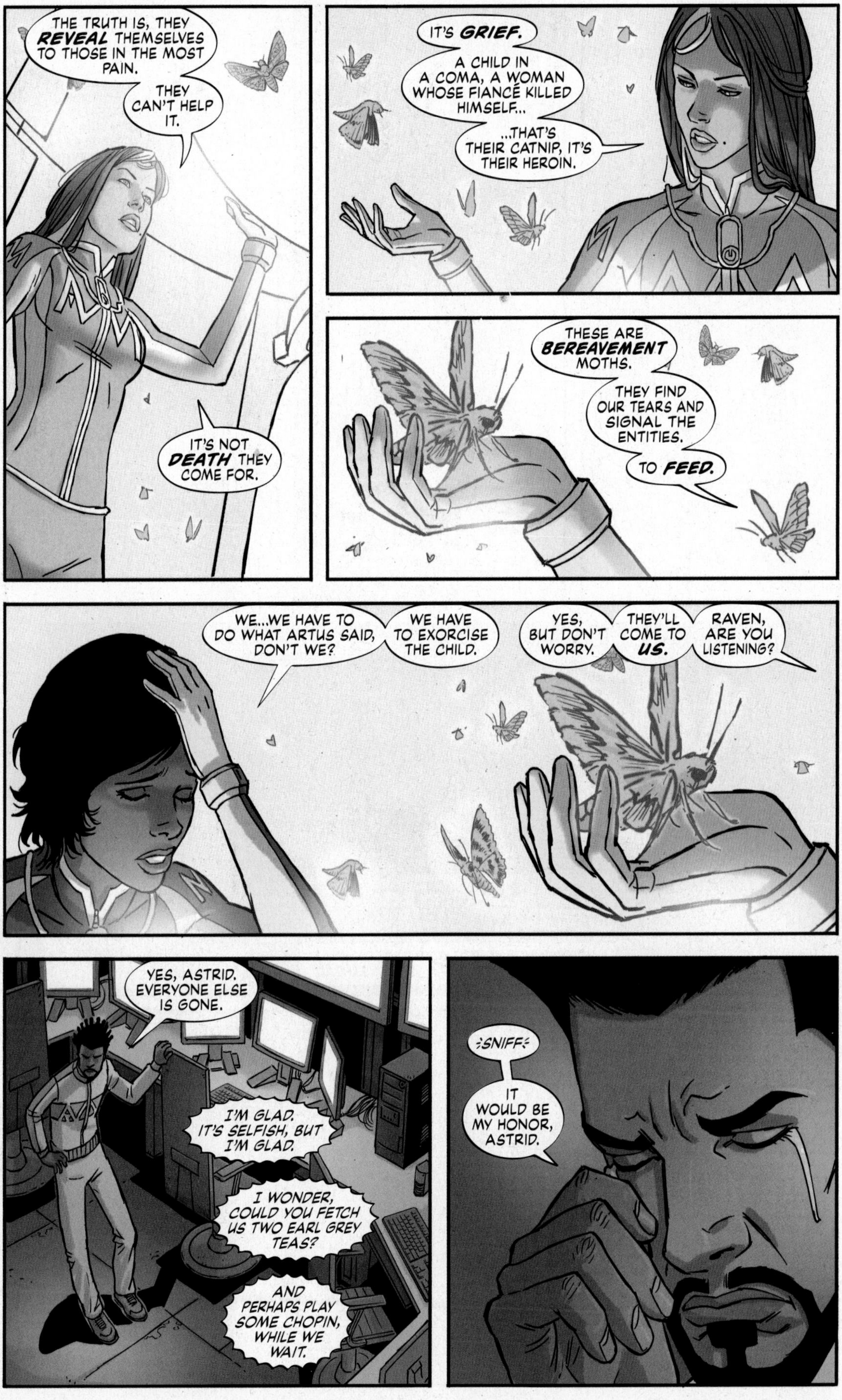
THE TRUTH IS, THEY REVEAL THEMSELVES TO THOSE IN THE MOST PAIN.
THEY CAN'T HELP IT.
IT'S NOT DEATH THEY COME FOR.
IT'S GRIEF.
A CHILD IN A COMA, A WOMAN WHOSE FIANCÉ KILLED HIMSELF...
...THAT'S THEIR CATNIP, IT'S THEIR HEROIN.
THESE ARE BEREAVEMENT MOTHS.
THEY FIND OUR TEARS AND SIGNAL THE ENTITIES.
TO FEED.
WE...WE HAVE TO DO WHAT ARTUS SAID, DON'T WE?
WE HAVE TO EXORCISE THE CHILD.
YES, BUT DON'T WORRY.
THEY'LL COME TO US.
RAVEN, ARE YOU LISTENING?
YES, ASTRID. EVERYONE ELSE IS GONE.
I'M GLAD. IT'S SELFISH, BUT I'M GLAD.
I WONDER, COULD YOU FETCH US TWO EARL GREY TEAS?
AND PERHAPS PLAY SOME CHOPIN, WHILE WE WAIT.
SNIFF
IT WOULD BE MY HONOR, ASTRID.

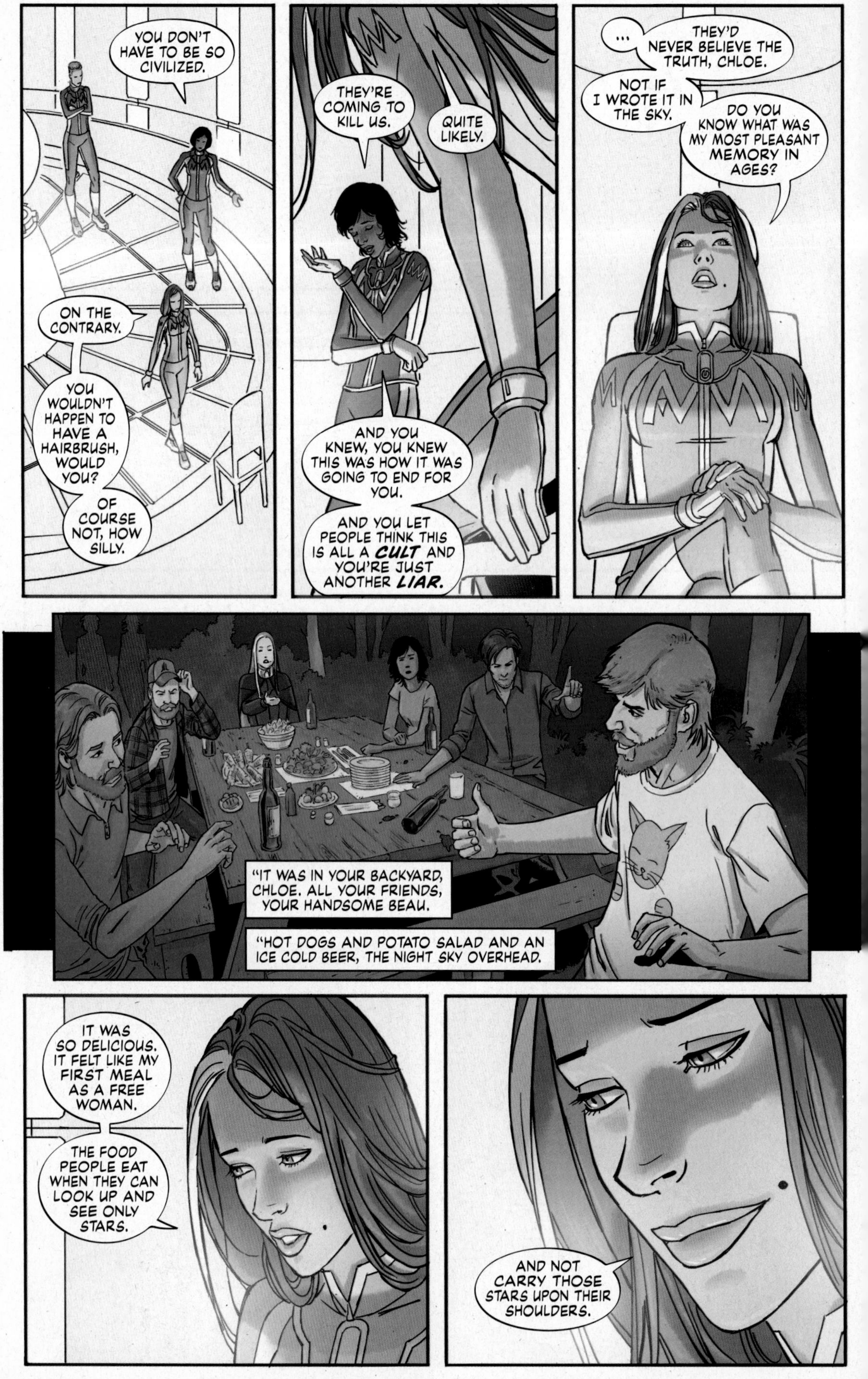
YOU DON'T HAVE TO BE SO CIVILIZED.
ON THE CONTRARY.
YOU WOULDN'T HAPPEN TO HAVE A HAIRBRUSH, WOULD YOU?
OF COURSE NOT, HOW SILLY.
THEY'RE COMING TO KILL US.
QUITE LIKELY.
AND YOU KNEW, YOU KNEW THIS WAS HOW IT WAS GOING TO END FOR YOU.
AND YOU LET PEOPLE THINK THIS IS ALL A CULT AND YOU'RE JUST ANOTHER LIAR.
...
THEY'D NEVER BELIEVE THE TRUTH, CHLOE.
NOT IF I WROTE IT IN THE SKY.
DO YOU KNOW WHAT WAS MY MOST PLEASANT MEMORY IN AGES?
"IT WAS IN YOUR BACKYARD, CHLOE. ALL YOUR FRIENDS, YOUR HANDSOME BEAU.
"HOT DOGS AND POTATO SALAD AND AN ICE COLD BEER, THE NIGHT SKY OVERHEAD.
IT WAS SO DELICIOUS. IT FELT LIKE MY FIRST MEAL AS A FREE WOMAN.
THE FOOD PEOPLE EAT WHEN THEY CAN LOOK UP AND SEE ONLY STARS.
AND NOT CARRY THOSE STARS UPON THEIR SHOULDERS.

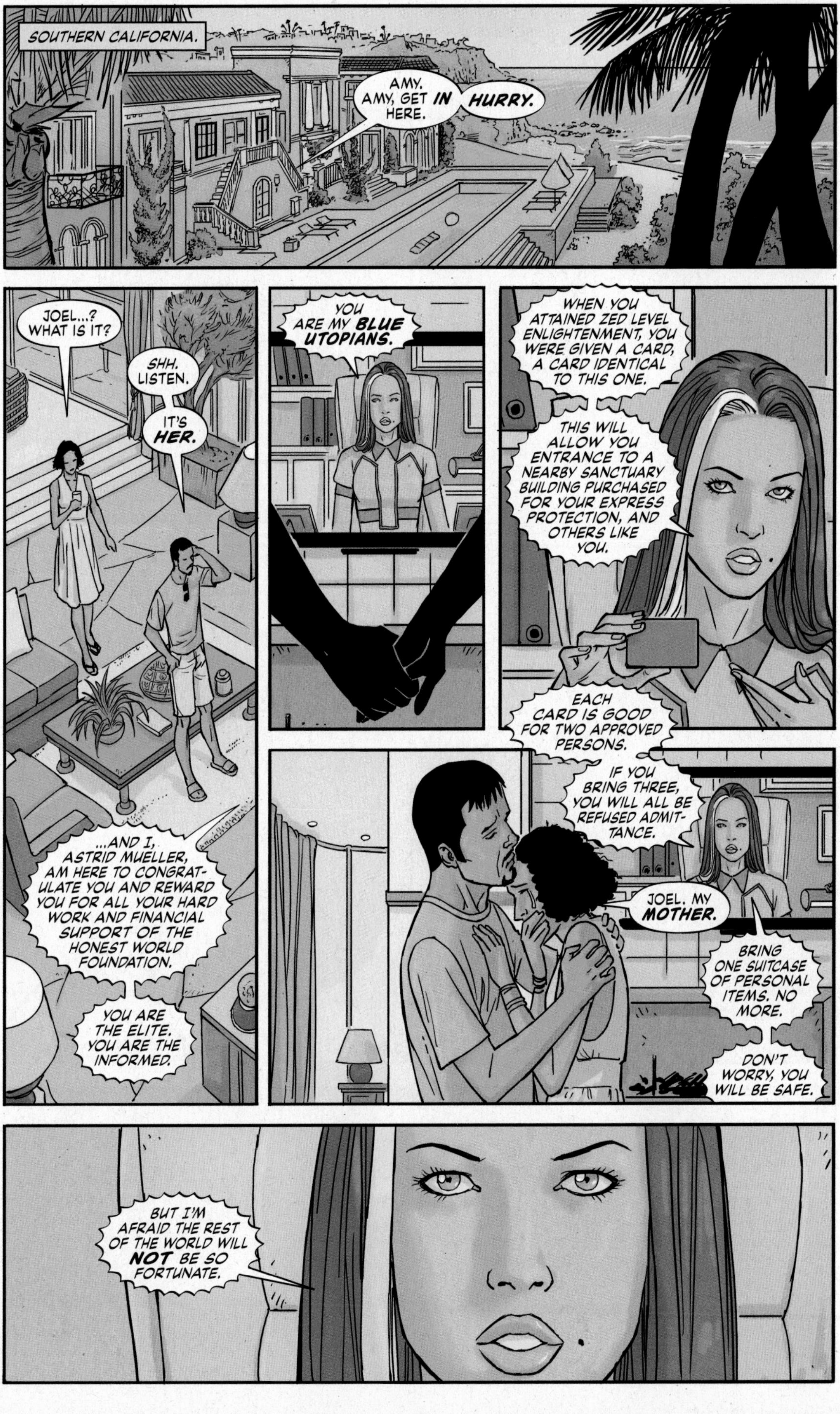
SOUTHERN CALIFORNIA.
AMY. AMY, GET IN HERE.
HURRY.
JOEL...? WHAT IS IT?
SHH. LISTEN.
IT'S HER.
...AND I, ASTRID MUELLER, AM HERE TO CONGRATULATE YOU AND REWARD YOU FOR ALL YOUR HARD WORK AND FINANCIAL SUPPORT OF THE HONEST WORLD FOUNDATION.
YOU ARE THE ELITE. YOU ARE THE INFORMED.
YOU ARE MY BLUE UTOPIANS.
WHEN YOU ATTAINED ZED LEVEL ENLIGHTENMENT, YOU WERE GIVEN A CARD, A CARD IDENTICAL TO THIS ONE.
THIS WILL ALLOW YOU ENTRANCE TO A NEARBY SANCTUARY BUILDING PURCHASED FOR YOUR EXPRESS PROTECTION, AND OTHERS LIKE YOU.
EACH CARD IS GOOD FOR TWO APPROVED PERSONS.
IF YOU BRING THREE, YOU WILL ALL BE REFUSED ADMITTANCE.
JOEL. MY MOTHER.
BRING ONE SUITCASE OF PERSONAL ITEMS. NO MORE.
DON'T WORRY, YOU WILL BE SAFE.
BUT I'M AFRAID THE REST OF THE WORLD WILL NOT BE SO FORTUNATE.

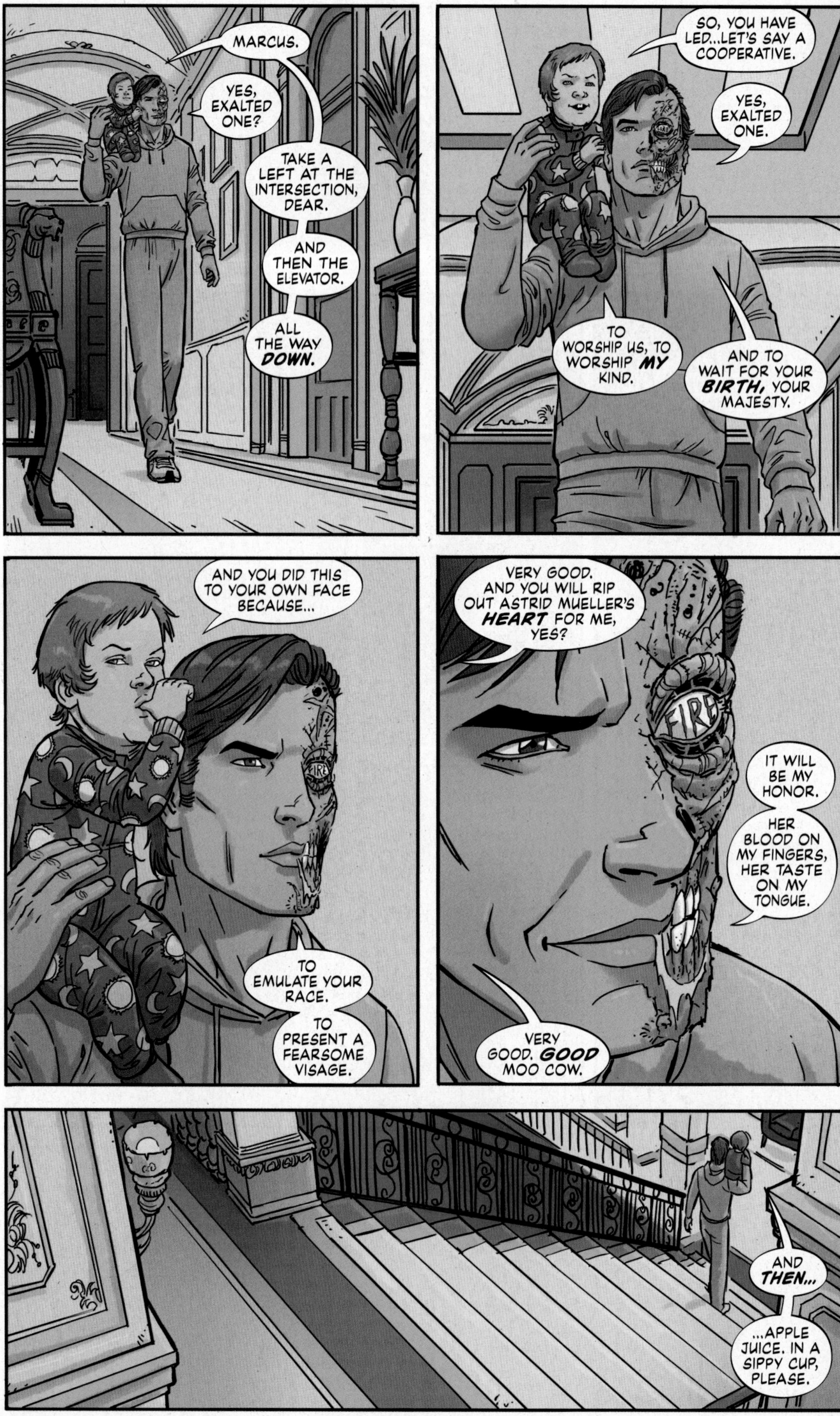
MARCUS.
YES, EXALTED ONE?
TAKE A LEFT AT THE INTERSECTION, DEAR.
AND THEN THE ELEVATOR.
ALL THE WAY **DOWN.**
SO, YOU HAVE LED...LET'S SAY A COOPERATIVE.
YES, EXALTED ONE.
TO WORSHIP US, TO WORSHIP **MY** KIND.
AND TO WAIT FOR YOUR **BIRTH,** YOUR MAJESTY.
AND YOU DID THIS TO YOUR OWN FACE BECAUSE...
TO EMULATE YOUR RACE.
TO PRESENT A FEARSOME VISAGE.
VERY GOOD. AND YOU WILL RIP OUT ASTRID MUELLER'S **HEART** FOR ME, YES?
IT WILL BE MY HONOR.
HER BLOOD ON MY FINGERS, HER TASTE ON MY TONGUE.
VERY GOOD. **GOOD** MOO COW.
AND **THEN...**
...APPLE JUICE. IN A SIPPY CUP, PLEASE.

AH. RAVEN. THANK YOU.

I THOUGHT I'D DIE.

WON'T YOU JOIN US?

NONE FOR ME, I HATE THAT SHIT.

ASTRID.

SHOULD WE NOT BE... YOU KNOW, EVACUATING? THE BUILDING IS ON *FIRE*.

I KNOW, DEAR. I *SET* THE FIRE.

I FELT IT BEST TO WORK IN ISOLATION.

WELL, WITH THE PEOPLE I...

THE PEOPLE THAT I MOST...

"TRUST"?

YES, TRUST. THANK YOU, CHLOE.

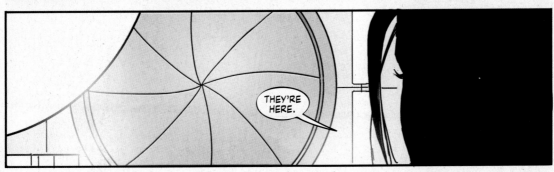

THEY'RE HERE.

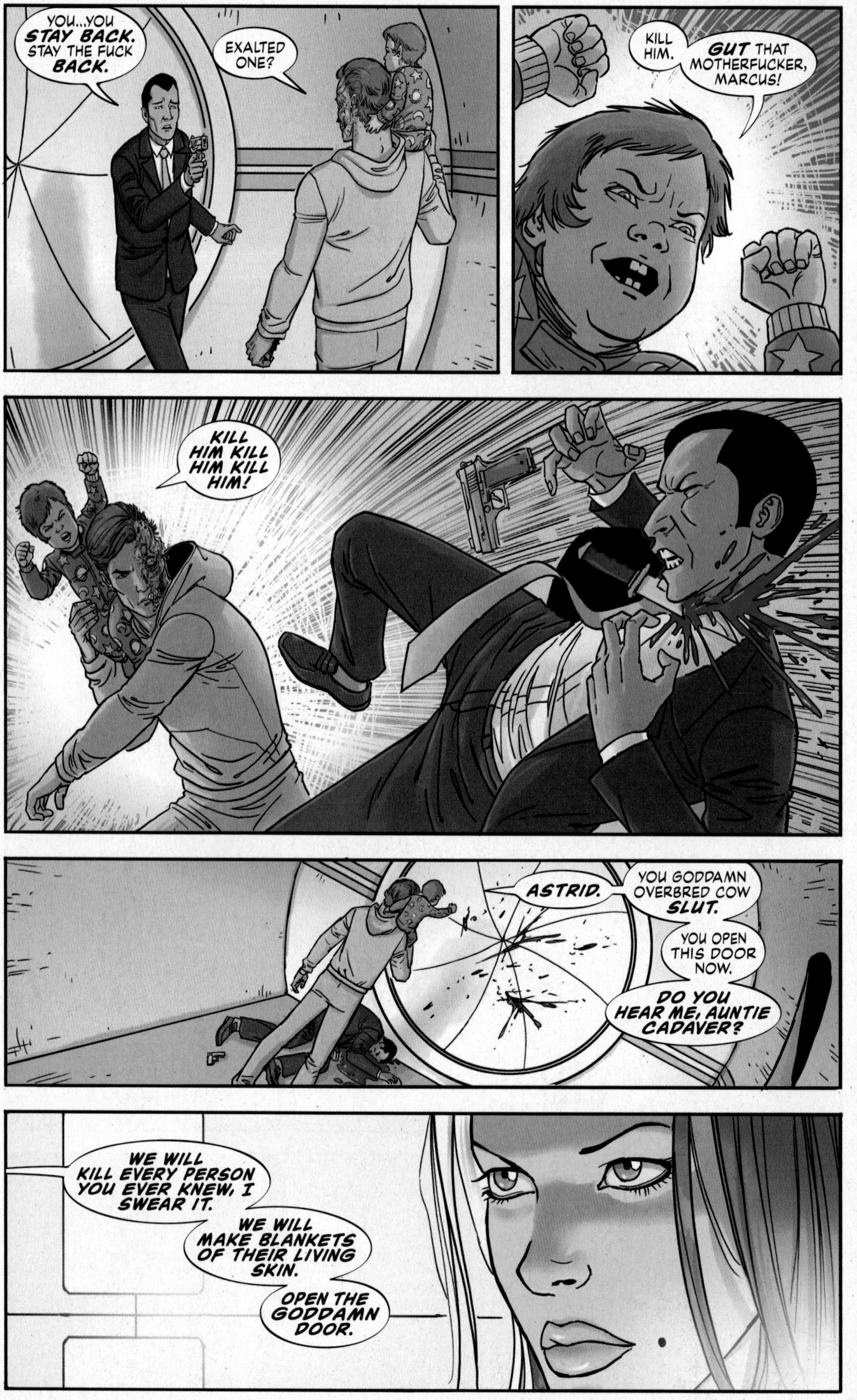
YOU...YOU STAY BACK. STAY THE FUCK BACK.
EXALTED ONE?
KILL HIM.
GUT THAT MOTHERFUCKER, MARCUS!
KILL HIM KILL HIM KILL HIM!
ASTRID.
YOU GODDAMN OVERBRED COW SLUT.
YOU OPEN THIS DOOR NOW.
DO YOU HEAR ME, AUNTIE CADAVER?
WE WILL KILL EVERY PERSON YOU EVER KNEW, I SWEAR IT.
WE WILL MAKE BLANKETS OF THEIR LIVING SKIN.
OPEN THE GODDAMN DOOR.

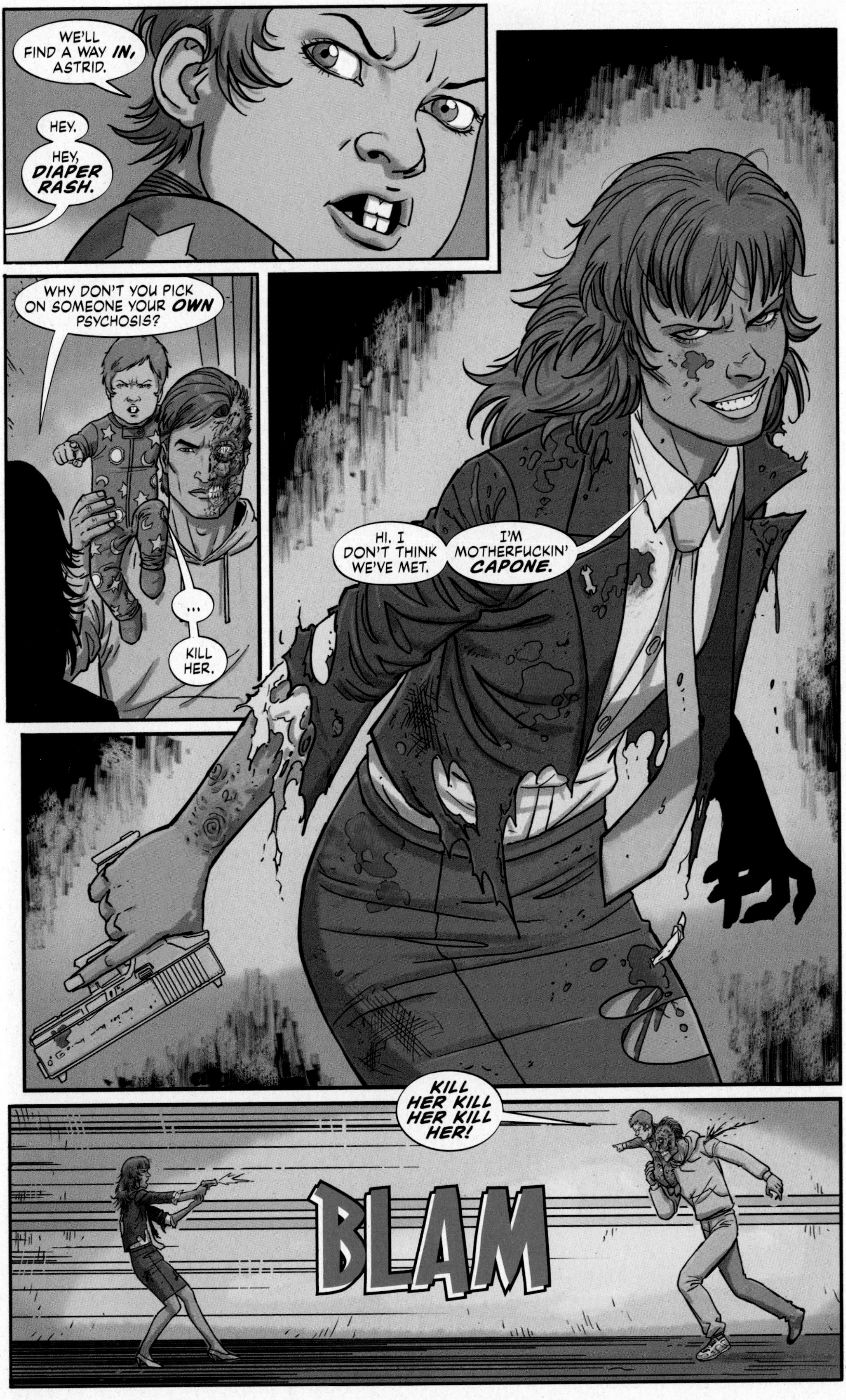
WE'LL FIND A WAY IN, ASTRID.
HEY.
HEY, DIAPER RASH.
WHY DON'T YOU PICK ON SOMEONE YOUR OWN PSYCHOSIS?
...
KILL HER.
HI. I DON'T THINK WE'VE MET.
I'M MOTHERFUCKIN' CAPONE.
KILL HER KILL HER KILL HER!
BLAM

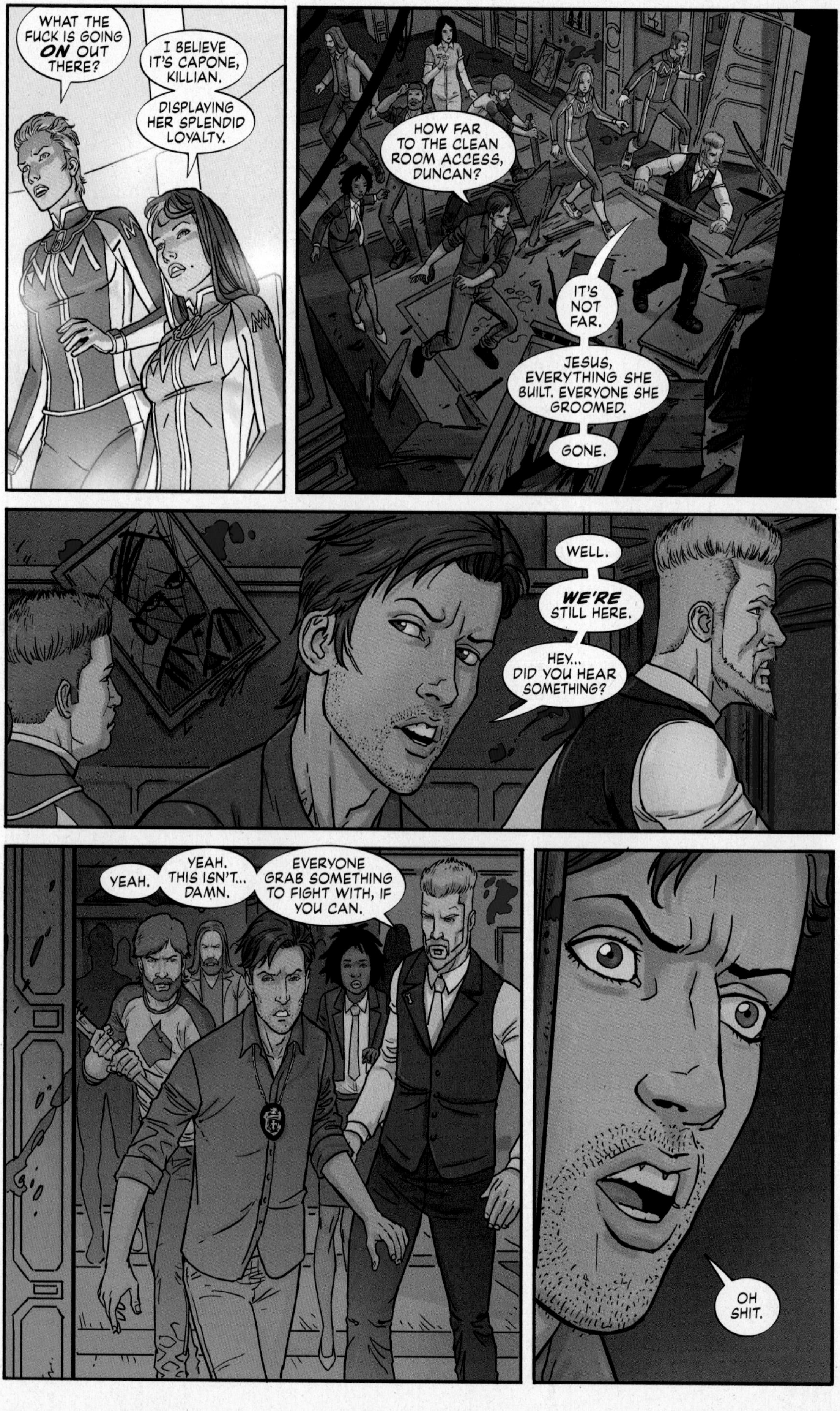
WHAT THE FUCK IS GOING ON OUT THERE?
I BELIEVE IT'S CAPONE, KILLIAN.
DISPLAYING HER SPLENDID LOYALTY.
HOW FAR TO THE CLEAN ROOM ACCESS, DUNCAN?
IT'S NOT FAR.
JESUS, EVERYTHING SHE BUILT. EVERYONE SHE GROOMED.
GONE.
WELL.
WE'RE STILL HERE.
HEY... DID YOU HEAR SOMETHING?
YEAH.
YEAH. THIS ISN'T... DAMN.
EVERYONE GRAB SOMETHING TO FIGHT WITH, IF YOU CAN.
OH SHIT.

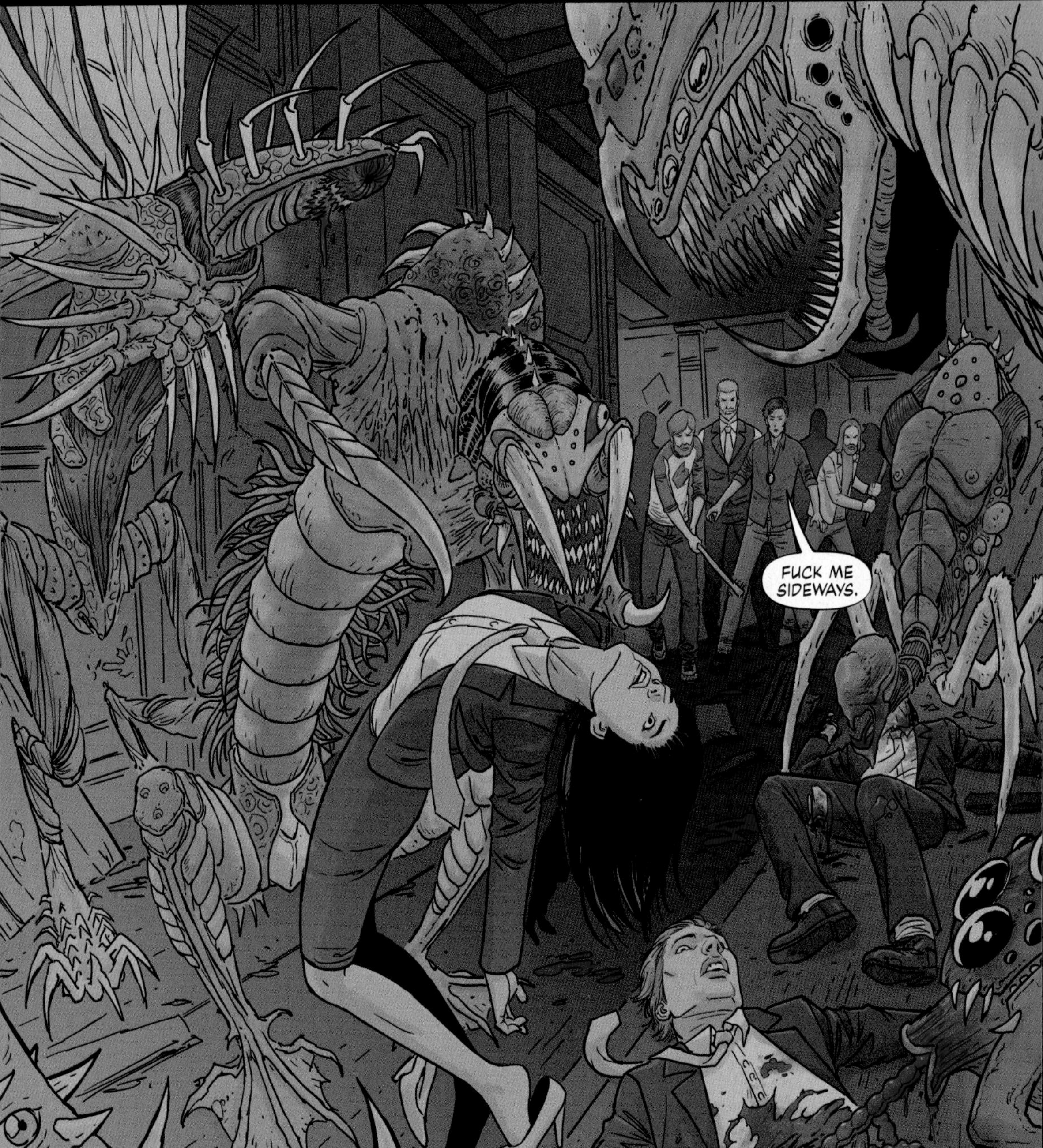
FUCK ME SIDEWAYS.

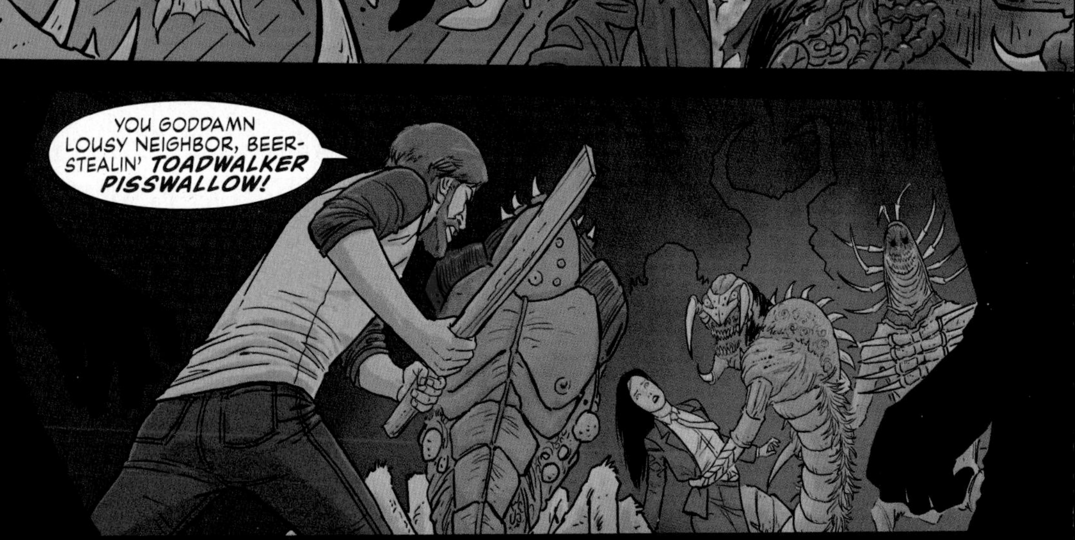
YOU GODDAMN LOUSY NEIGHBOR, BEER-STEALIN' *TOADWALKER PISSWALLOW!*

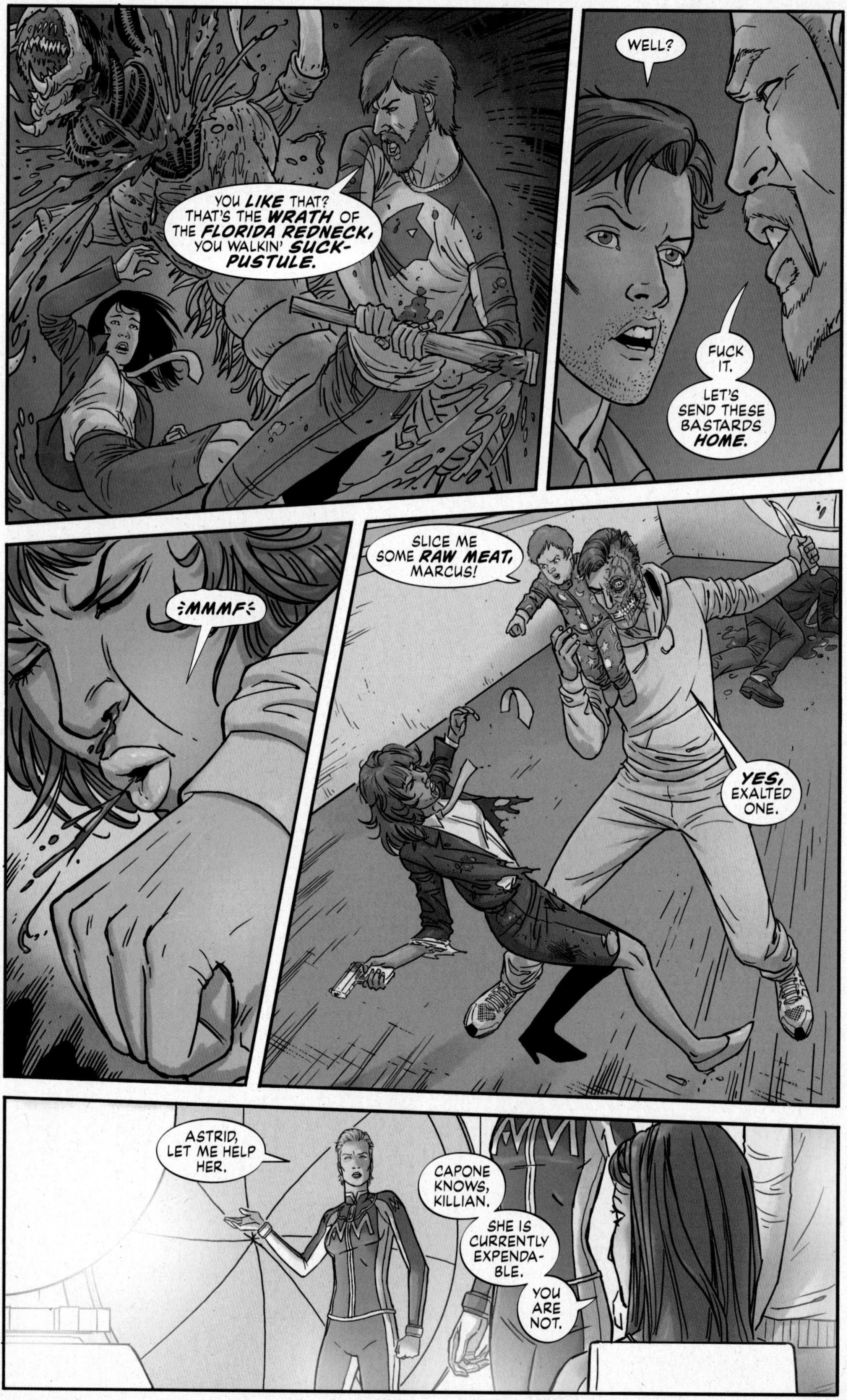
YOU LIKE THAT? THAT'S THE WRATH OF THE FLORIDA REDNECK, YOU WALKIN' SUCK-PUSTULE.
WELL?
FUCK IT.
LET'S SEND THESE BASTARDS HOME.
MMMF
SLICE ME SOME RAW MEAT, MARCUS!
YES, EXALTED ONE.
ASTRID, LET ME HELP HER.
CAPONE KNOWS, KILLIAN.
SHE IS CURRENTLY EXPENDA-BLE.
YOU ARE NOT.

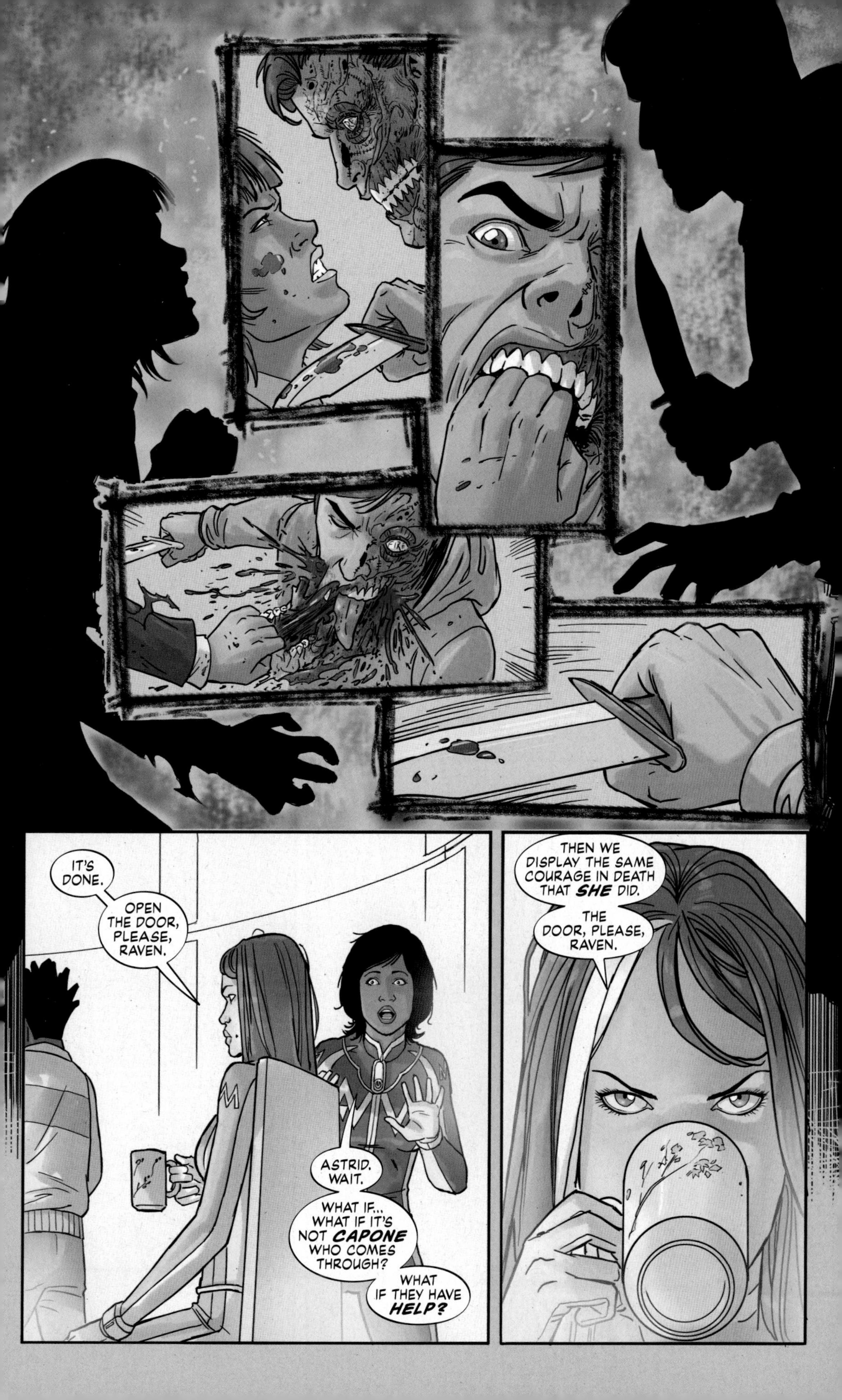
IT'S DONE.
OPEN THE DOOR, PLEASE, RAVEN.
ASTRID. WAIT.
WHAT IF... WHAT IF IT'S NOT CAPONE WHO COMES THROUGH?
WHAT IF THEY HAVE HELP?
THEN WE DISPLAY THE SAME COURAGE IN DEATH THAT SHE DID.
THE DOOR, PLEASE, RAVEN.

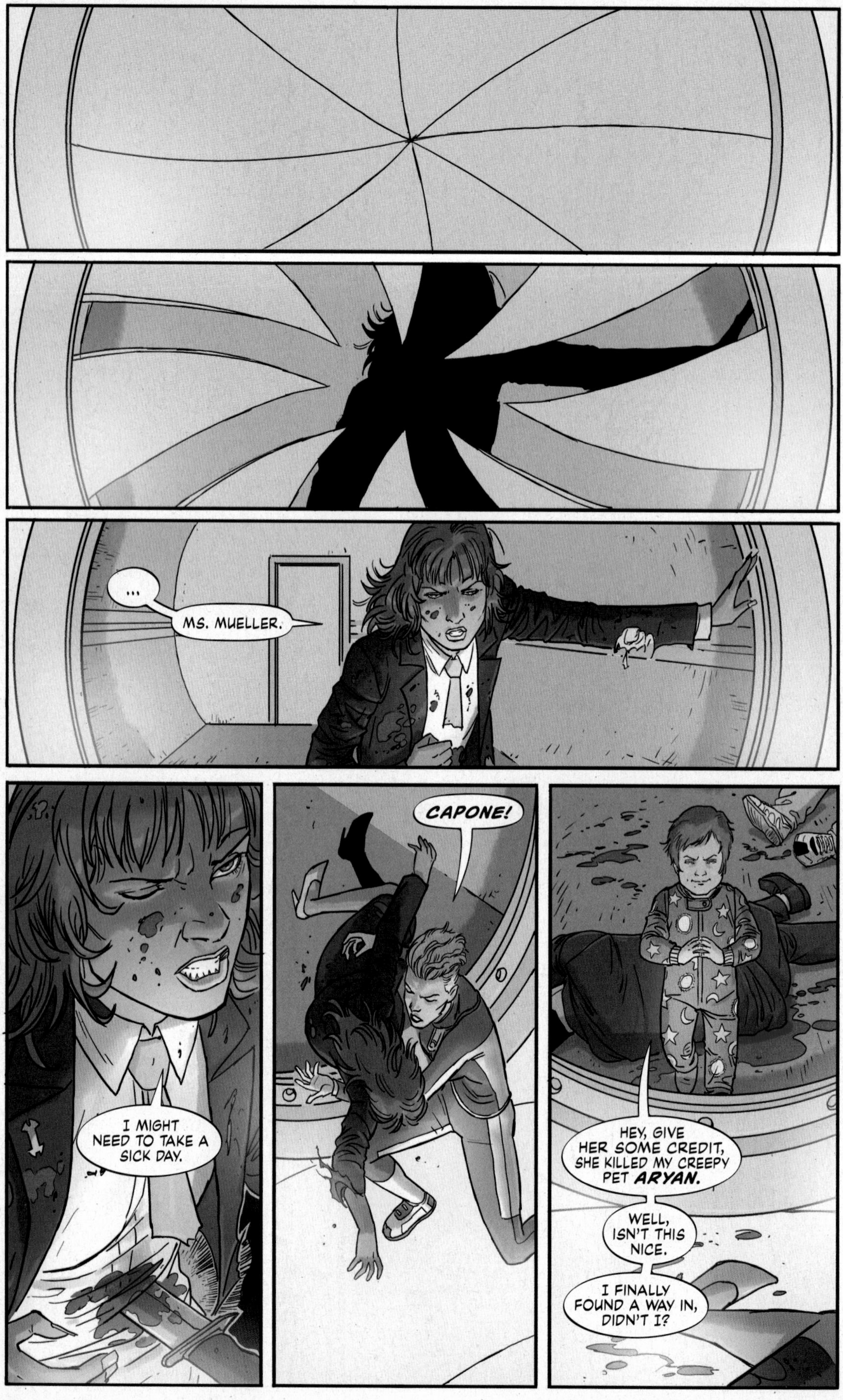
...
MS. MUELLER.
I MIGHT NEED TO TAKE A SICK DAY.
CAPONE!
HEY, GIVE HER SOME CREDIT, SHE KILLED MY CREEPY PET ARYAN.
WELL, ISN'T THIS NICE.
I FINALLY FOUND A WAY IN, DIDN'T I?

I'M AFRAID YOU HAVE IT WRONG, DERICA.

I *LET* YOU IN.

WAIT. WHAT?

DR. HAGEN, ARE YOU LISTENING?

I AM, MY BEAUTIFUL PINK SAUSAGE.

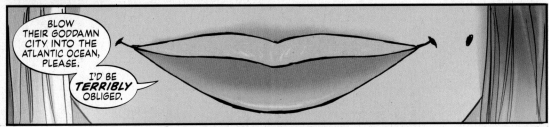

BLOW THEIR GODDAMN CITY INTO THE ATLANTIC OCEAN, PLEASE.

I'D BE *TERRIBLY* OBLIGED.

THE CLOUDBUSTER IS *AT YOUR SERVICE.*

AND MAY I SAY, MA'AM...

...I'VE NEVER HAD SUCH AN ERECTION IN MY *LIFE.*

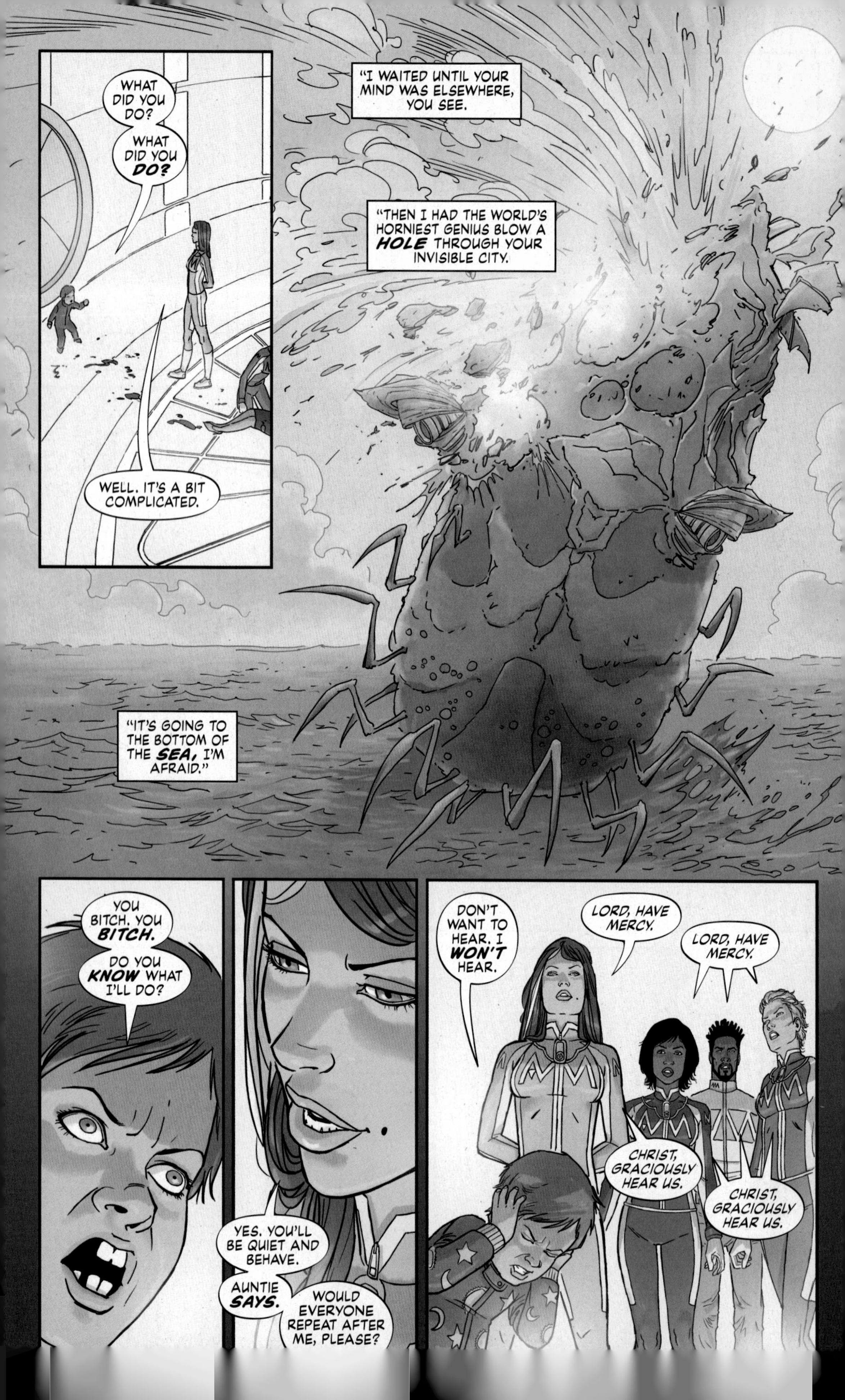
WHAT DID YOU DO?
WHAT DID YOU **DO?**
"I WAITED UNTIL YOUR MIND WAS ELSEWHERE, YOU SEE.
"THEN I HAD THE WORLD'S HORNIEST GENIUS BLOW A **HOLE** THROUGH YOUR INVISIBLE CITY.
WELL. IT'S A BIT COMPLICATED.
"IT'S GOING TO THE BOTTOM OF THE **SEA,** I'M AFRAID."
YOU BITCH. YOU **BITCH.**
DO YOU **KNOW** WHAT I'LL DO?
YES. YOU'LL BE QUIET AND BEHAVE.
AUNTIE **SAYS.**
WOULD EVERYONE REPEAT AFTER ME, PLEASE?
DON'T WANT TO HEAR. I **WON'T** HEAR.
LORD, HAVE MERCY.
LORD, HAVE MERCY.
CHRIST, GRACIOUSLY HEAR US.
CHRIST, GRACIOUSLY HEAR US.

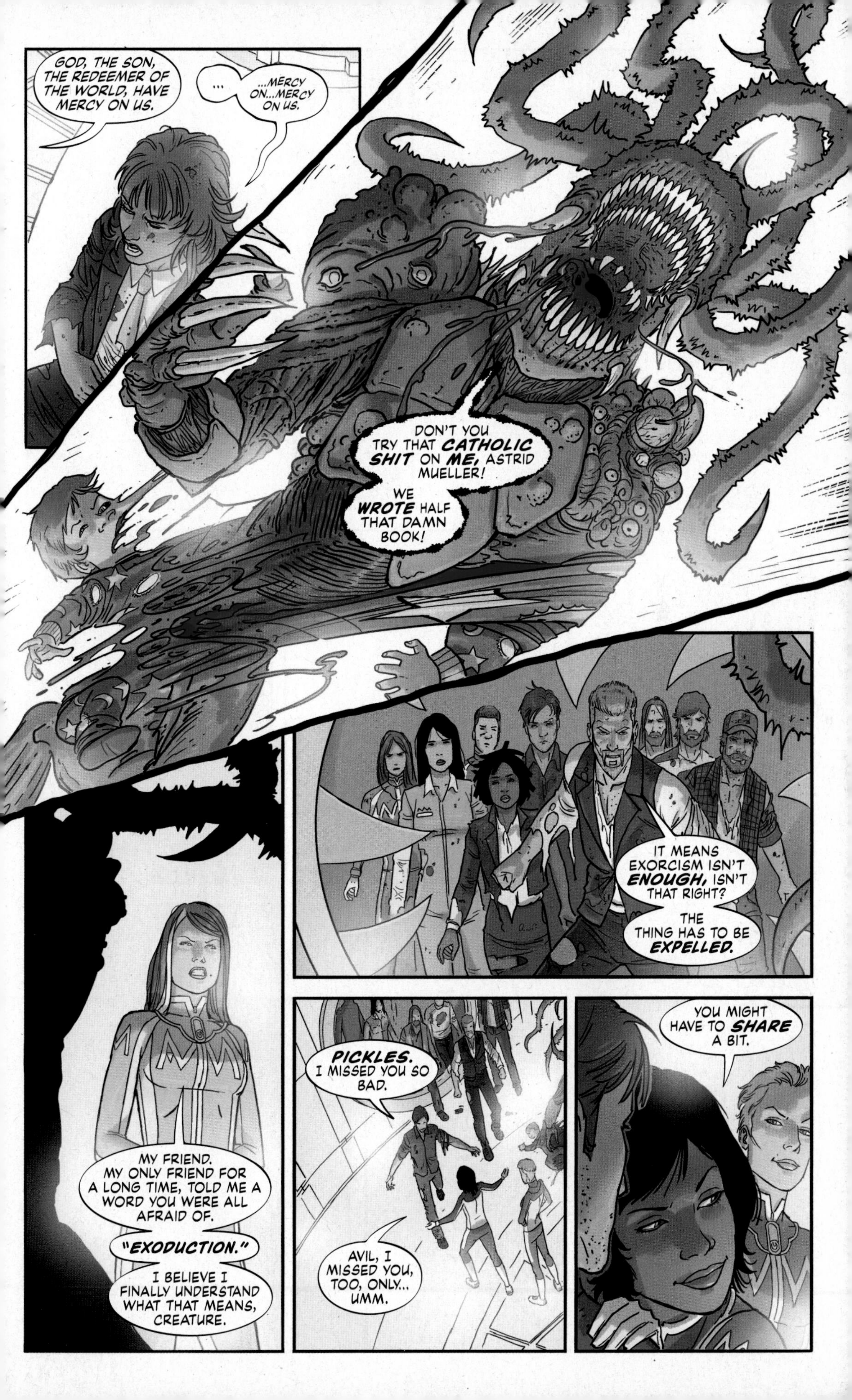
GOD, THE SON, THE REDEEMER OF THE WORLD, HAVE MERCY ON US.
...
...MERCY ON...MERCY ON US.
DON'T YOU TRY THAT **CATHOLIC SHIT** ON **ME,** ASTRID MUELLER!
WE **WROTE** HALF THAT DAMN BOOK!
IT MEANS EXORCISM ISN'T **ENOUGH,** ISN'T THAT RIGHT?
THE THING HAS TO BE **EXPELLED.**
MY FRIEND. MY ONLY FRIEND FOR A LONG TIME, TOLD ME A WORD YOU WERE ALL AFRAID OF.
"EXODUCTION."
I BELIEVE I FINALLY UNDERSTAND WHAT THAT MEANS, CREATURE.
PICKLES. I MISSED YOU SO BAD.
AVIL, I MISSED YOU, TOO, ONLY... UMM.
YOU MIGHT HAVE TO **SHARE** A BIT.

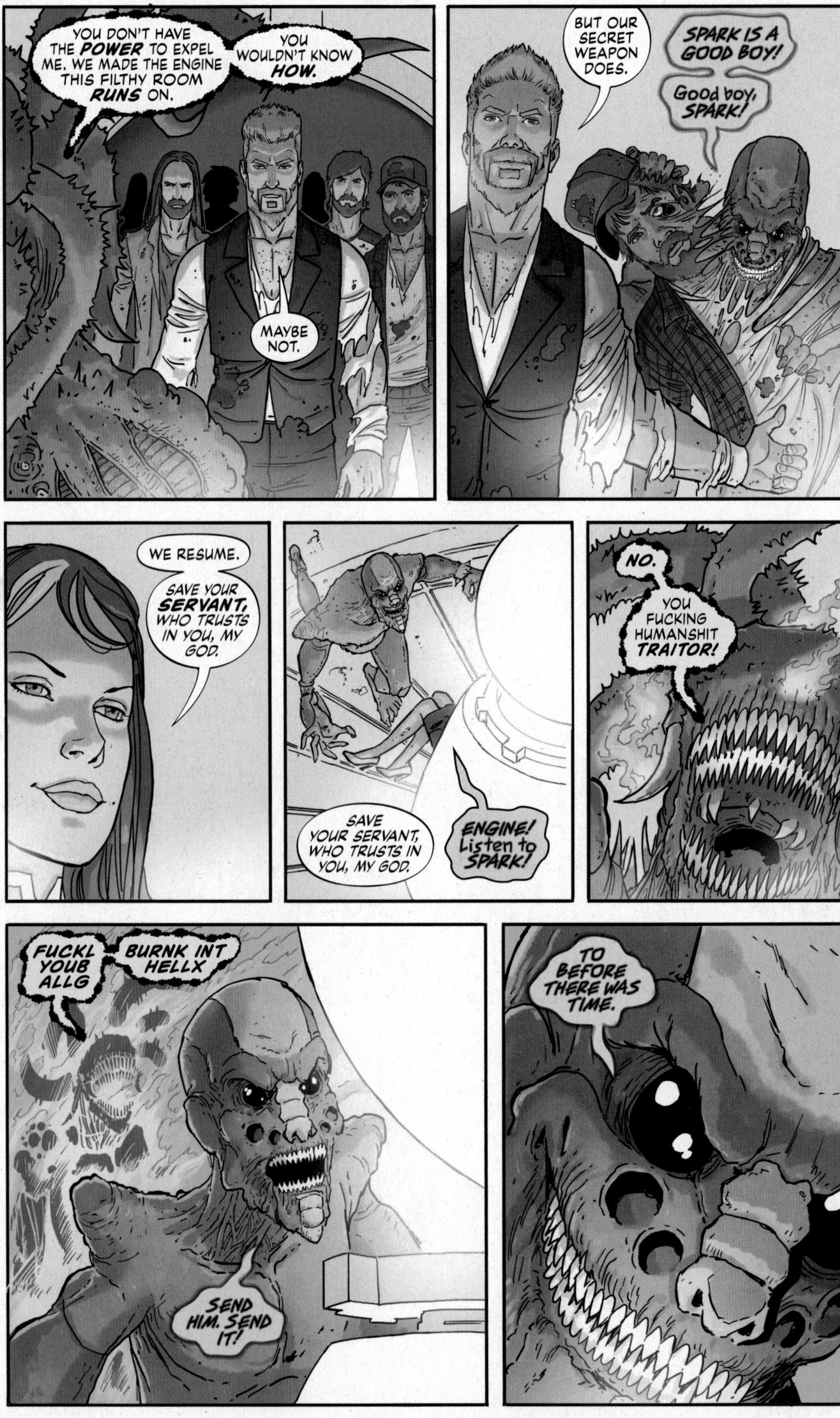
YOU DON'T HAVE THE POWER TO EXPEL ME. WE MADE THE ENGINE THIS FILTHY ROOM RUNS ON.
YOU WOULDN'T KNOW HOW.
MAYBE NOT.
BUT OUR SECRET WEAPON DOES.
SPARK IS A GOOD BOY!
Good boy, SPARK!
WE RESUME.
SAVE YOUR SERVANT, WHO TRUSTS IN YOU, MY GOD.
SAVE YOUR SERVANT, WHO TRUSTS IN YOU, MY GOD.
ENGINE! Listen to SPARK!
NO.
YOU FUCKING HUMANSHIT TRAITOR!
FUCKL YOUB ALLG
BURNK INT HELLX
SEND HIM. SEND IT!
TO BEFORE THERE WAS TIME.

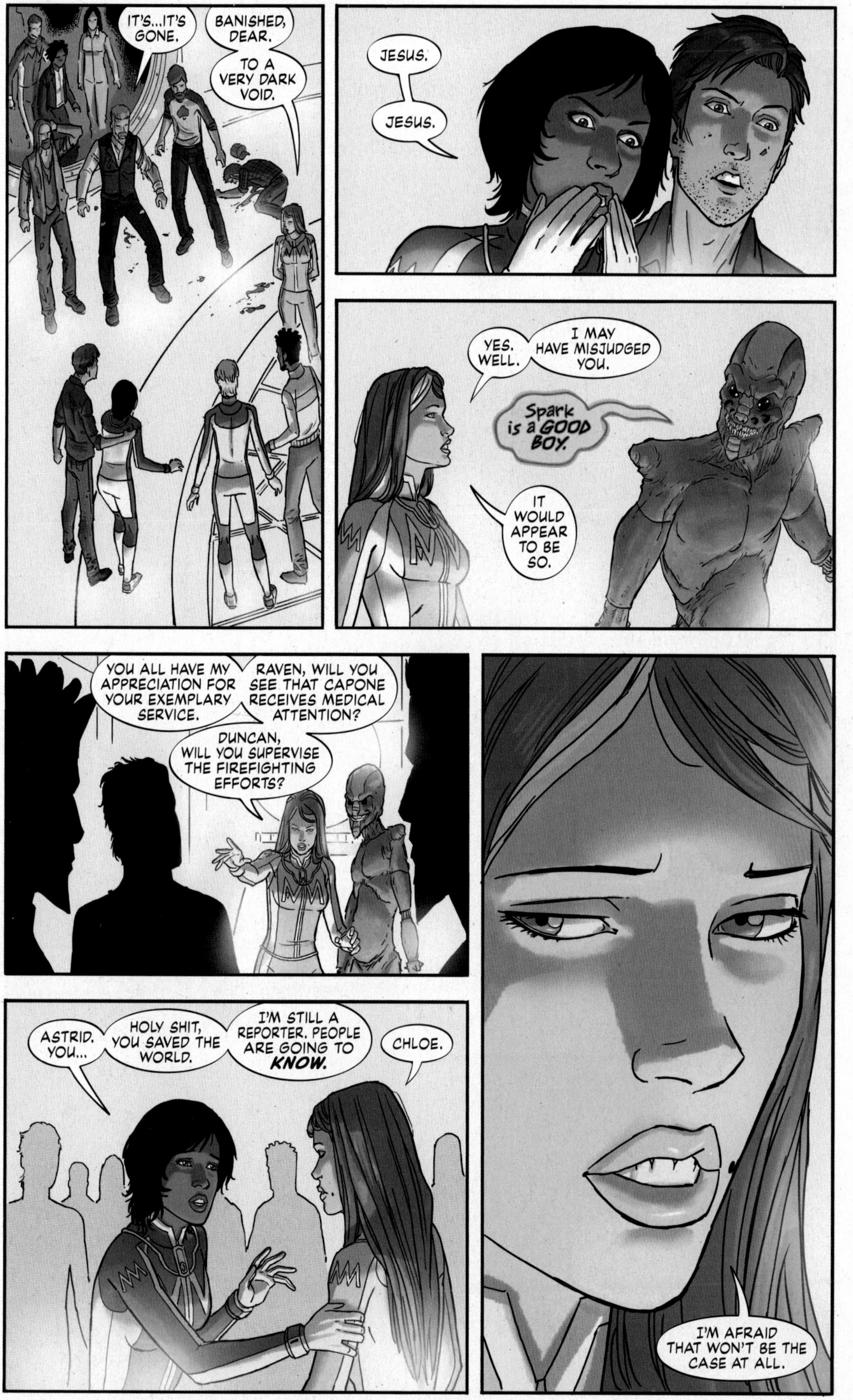
IT'S...IT'S GONE.
BANISHED, DEAR.
TO A VERY DARK VOID.
JESUS.
JESUS.
YES. WELL.
I MAY HAVE MISJUDGED YOU.
Spark is a GOOD BOY.
IT WOULD APPEAR TO BE SO.
YOU ALL HAVE MY APPRECIATION FOR YOUR EXEMPLARY SERVICE.
RAVEN, WILL YOU SEE THAT CAPONE RECEIVES MEDICAL ATTENTION?
DUNCAN, WILL YOU SUPERVISE THE FIREFIGHTING EFFORTS?
ASTRID. YOU...
HOLY SHIT, YOU SAVED THE WORLD.
I'M STILL A REPORTER. PEOPLE ARE GOING TO KNOW.
CHLOE.
I'M AFRAID THAT WON'T BE THE CASE AT ALL.

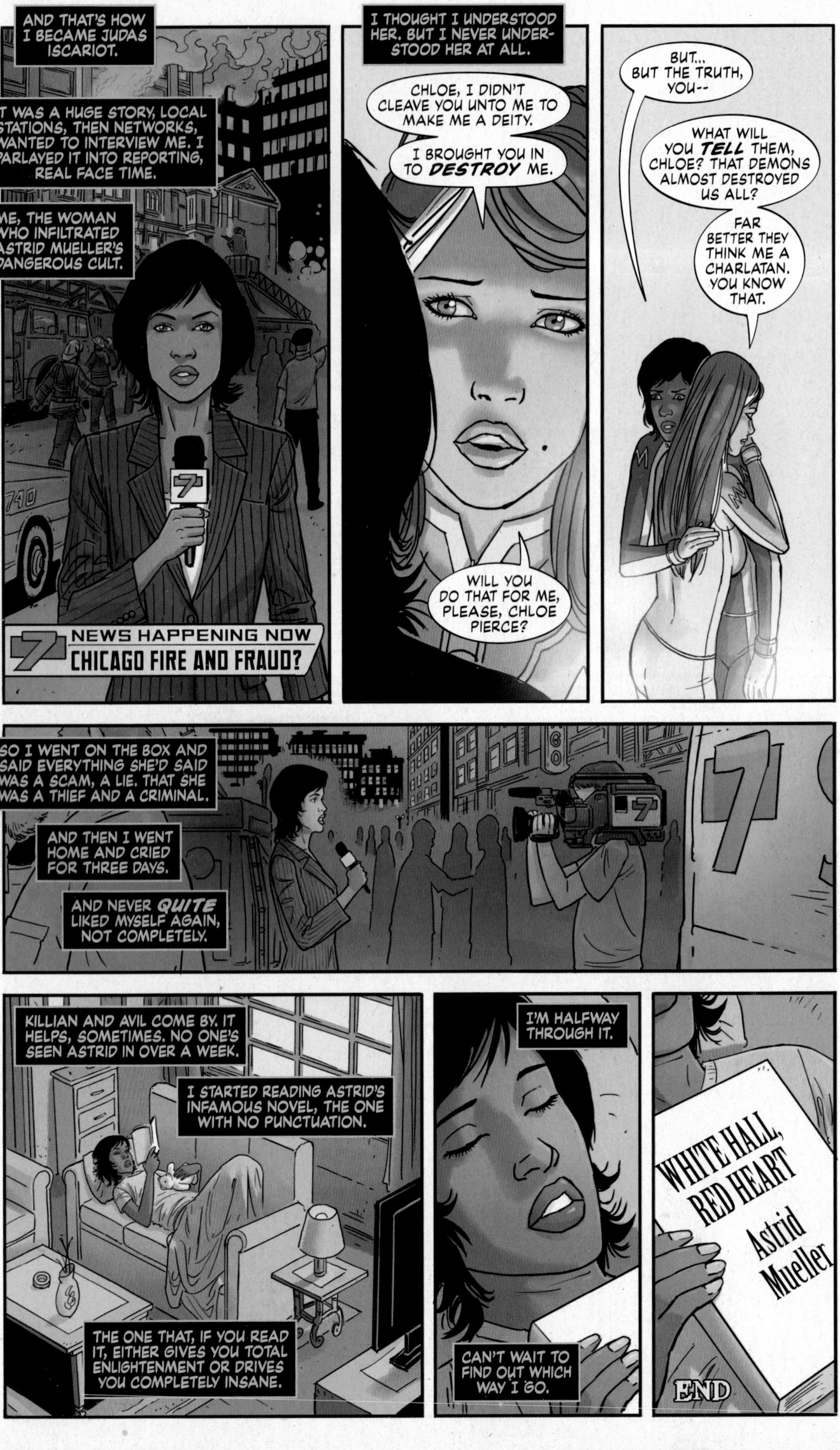
AND THAT'S HOW I BECAME JUDAS ISCARIOT.
IT WAS A HUGE STORY, LOCAL STATIONS, THEN NETWORKS, WANTED TO INTERVIEW ME. I PARLAYED IT INTO REPORTING, REAL FACE TIME.
ME, THE WOMAN WHO INFILTRATED ASTRID MUELLER'S DANGEROUS CULT.
740
7
7 NEWS HAPPENING NOW
CHICAGO FIRE AND FRAUD?
I THOUGHT I UNDERSTOOD HER. BUT I NEVER UNDERSTOOD HER AT ALL.
CHLOE, I DIDN'T CLEAVE YOU UNTO ME TO MAKE ME A DEITY.
I BROUGHT YOU IN TO DESTROY ME.
WILL YOU DO THAT FOR ME, PLEASE, CHLOE PIERCE?
BUT... BUT THE TRUTH, YOU--
WHAT WILL YOU TELL THEM, CHLOE? THAT DEMONS ALMOST DESTROYED US ALL?
FAR BETTER THEY THINK ME A CHARLATAN. YOU KNOW THAT.
SO I WENT ON THE BOX AND SAID EVERYTHING SHE'D SAID WAS A SCAM, A LIE. THAT SHE WAS A THIEF AND A CRIMINAL.
AND THEN I WENT HOME AND CRIED FOR THREE DAYS.
AND NEVER QUITE LIKED MYSELF AGAIN, NOT COMPLETELY.
7
7
KILLIAN AND AVIL COME BY. IT HELPS, SOMETIMES. NO ONE'S SEEN ASTRID IN OVER A WEEK.
I STARTED READING ASTRID'S INFAMOUS NOVEL, THE ONE WITH NO PUNCTUATION.
THE ONE THAT, IF YOU READ IT, EITHER GIVES YOU TOTAL ENLIGHTENMENT OR DRIVES YOU COMPLETELY INSANE.
I'M HALFWAY THROUGH IT.
CAN'T WAIT TO FIND OUT WHICH WAY I GO.
WHITE HALL, RED HEART
Astrid Mueller
END